EZ SOLUTIONS

TEST PREP SERIES

MATH REVIEW

ARITHMETIC

EZ SIMPLIFIED SOLUTIONS – THE BREAKTHROUGH IN TEST PREP!

LEADERS IN TEST PREP SOLUTIONS – WE MAKE IT EZ FOR YOU!

AUTHOR: PUNIT RAJA SURYACHANDRA

WWW.EZMETHODS.COM

EZ SOLUTIONS
USA

EZ SOLUTIONS
P.O. Box 10755
Silver Spring, MD 20914
USA

Conceived, conceptualized, written, and edited by:
Punit Raja SuryaChandra, EZ Solutions

PRINTED AND MANUFACTURED IN THE UNITED STATES OF AMERICA

TABLE OF CONTENTS

PREFACE

HIGHLIGHTS:
- About EZ Solutions
- About Our Author
- About EZ Books
- About This Book

▪ ABOUT EZ SOLUTIONS

EZ Solutions – *the breakthrough in test-preparation*!

EZ Solutions is an organization formed to provide **simplified solutions** for test-preparation and tutoring. Although EZ Solutions is a fairly new name in the publishing industry, it has quickly become a respected publisher of test-prep books, study guides, study aids, handbooks, and other reference works. EZ publications and educational materials are highly respected, and they continue to receive an unprecedented amount of praise from professionals, instructors, librarians, parents, and students.

OBJECTIVE: Our ultimate objective is to help you **achieve academic and scholastic excellence**. We possess the right blend and matrix of skills and expertise that are required to not only do justice to our programs and publications, but also to handle them most effectively and efficiently. We are confident that our state-of-the-art programs/publications will give you a completely **new dimension** by enhancing your skill set and improving your overall performance.

MISSION: Our mission is to foster continuous knowledge to develop and enhance each student's skills through innovative and methodical programs/publications coupled with our add-on services – leading to a **better career and life** for our students.

OUR PHILOSOPHY: We subscribe to the traditional philosophy that everyone is equally capable of learning and that the natural, though sometimes unfulfilled and unexplored impetus of people is towards growth and development. We know that the human brain is undoubtedly a very powerful and efficient problem-solving tool, and every individual is much more capable than they realize. We strive to implement this philosophy throughout our books by helping our students explore their **potential** so that they can **perform at their optimum level**.

OUR COMMITMENT TOWARDS YOUR SATISFACTION: Reinventing, Redesigning, and Redefining Success: We are committed to providing **total customer satisfaction** that exceeds your expectations! Your satisfaction is extremely important to us, and your approval is one of the most important indicators that we have done our job correctly.

Long-Term Alliance: We, at EZ, look forward to forming a **long-term alliance** with all our readers who buy our book(s), for the days, months, and years to come. Moreover, our commitment to client service is one of our most important and distinguished characteristics. We also encourage our readers to contact us for any further assistance, feedback, suggestions, or inquiries.

EZ Solutions publishing series include books for the following major standardized tests:
- GMAT
- SAT
- PSAT
- ASVAB
- PRAXIS Series
- GRE
- ACT
- CLEP
- TOEFL
- Other (national and state) Standardized Tests

EZ Solutions aims to provide good quality study aides in a wide variety of disciplines to the following:
- Students who have not yet completed high school
- High School students preparing to enter college
- College students preparing to enter graduate or post-graduate school
- Anyone else who is simply looking to improve their skills

Students from every walk of life, of any background, at any level, in any field, with any ambition, can find what they are looking for among EZ Solutions' publications.

FOREIGN STUDENTS: All of our books are designed, keeping in mind the unique needs of students from North and South America, U.K., Europe, Middle East, Far East, and Asia. Foreign students from countries around the world seeking to obtain education in the United States will find the assistance they need in EZ Solutions' publications.

CONTACT US: Feel free to contact us, and one of our friendly specialists will be more than happy to assist you with your queries, or feel free to browse through our website for lots of useful information.
E-Mail: info@EZmethods.com
Phone: (301) 622-9597
Mail: EZ Solutions, P.O. Box 10755, Silver Spring, MD 20914, USA
Website: www.EZmethods.com

FEEDBACK: The staff of EZ Solutions hopes that you find our books helpful and easy to use. If you have any specific suggestions, comments, or feedback, please email us at: feedback@EZmethods.com

BUSINESS DEVELOPMENT: If you are interested in exploring business development opportunities, including forming a partnership alliance with us, kindly email us at: partners@EZmethods.com.

PRODUCT REGISTRATION: In order to get the most up-to-date information about this and our other books, you must register your purchase with EZ solutions by emailing us at: products@EZmethods.com, or by visiting our website www.EZmethods.com.

ERRORS AND INACCURACIES: We are not responsible for any typographical errors or inaccuracies contained in this publication. The information, prices, and discounts given in this book are subject to change without prior notice. To report any kind of errors or inaccuracies in this publication, kindly email us at: errors@EZmethods.com.

▪ABOUT OUR AUTHOR

The name of the man behind EZ publication series is **Punit Raja SuryaChandra**, who is also the founder of our company. He holds a Bachelors in Business and an MBA. It took him many years to write and publish these unique books. He researched every single book available in the market for test-preparation, and actually realized there is not even one book that is truly complete with all the content and concepts. This was the single most important reason that prompted him to write these books, and hence our *EZ prep guidebooks were born*. He has made every effort to make these books as comprehensive and as complete as possible. His expertise and experience are as diverse as the subjects that are represented in our books. He has the breadth and depth of experience required to write books of this magnitude and intensity. Without his unparalleled and unmatched skills and determination, none of this would have been possible.

In developing these books, his primary goal has been to give everyone the same advantages as the students we tutor privately or students who take our classes. Our tutoring and classroom solutions are only available to a limited number of students; however, with these books, any student in any corner of the world can benefit the same level of service at a fraction of the cost. Therefore, you should take this book as your personal EZ tutor or instructor, because that's precisely how it has been designed.

ACKNOWLEDGEMENTS:
Our author would like to extend his vote of appreciation and gratitude to all his family members for their unconditional and continuous support, to all his close friends for their trust and confidence in him, and to all his colleagues for their helpful consultation and generous advice.

Our EZ books have benefited from dedicated efforts and labors of our author and other members of the editorial staff. Here at EZ, we all wish you the best as you get comfortable, and settle down with your EZ tutor to start working on preparing for your test. In pursuing an educational dream, you have a wonderful and an exciting opportunity ahead of you. All of us at EZ Solutions wish you the very best!

▪ABOUT EZ BOOKS

THE EZ NAME:
All our books have been written in a very easy to read manner, and in a very easy to understand fashion, so that students of any background, of any aptitude, of any capacity, of any skill-set, of any level, can benefit from them. These books are not specifically written for the **dummies** or for the **geniuses**; instead, they are written for students who fit into any category of intellectual acumen. This is how we acquired the name **"EZ Solutions"** for our publications – and as the name itself suggests, **we make everything EZ for you**!

THE EZ TUTOR:
Like any good tutor, EZ Tutor will work with you **individually and privately**, providing you with all the tools needed to improve your testing skills. It will assist you in recognizing your weaknesses, and enlighten you on how to improve upon them while transforming them into strengths. Of course, it will also point out your strengths as well, so that you can make them even stronger. By employing innovative techniques, EZ tutor will **stimulate, activate, and accelerate your learning process**. Soon after you start working with your EZ tutor, you will see **remarkable and noticeable improvement** in your performance by utilizing your newly acquired learning skills.

Whenever, Wherever, and However: EZ tutor also has the **flexibility** to work with you whenever you like – day or night, wherever you like – indoors or outdoors, and however you like – for as long or as short. While working with your EZ tutor, you can work at your own pace, you can go as fast or as slow as you like, repeat sections as many times as you need, and skip over sections you already know well. Your EZ tutor will also give you explanations, not just correct answers, and it will be **infinitely patient and adaptable**. Hence, our EZ Tutor will make you a more intelligent and smarter test-taker, and will help you maximize your score!

ADD-ON OPTIONS: *Turn your EZ Virtual Tutor into a Real Tutor!*

EZ TUTORING OVER THE PHONE:
Along with buying the entire series of our modules, students can also add on services like email/online support and/or telephone support. In fact, you can get the best preparation for your test by blending our professional 1-on-1 tutoring with our state-of-the-art books. The most important feature of our add-on features is our individualized and personalized approach that works toward building your self-confidence, and enhancing your ability to learn and perform better. This will also invigorate your motivational, organizational, as well as your learning skills. Our phone specialists are highly qualified, experienced, innovative, and well trained. You can do all this in the exclusivity and comfort of your home. Students can get in touch with one of our specialists anytime they need help – we'll be there for you, whenever you need us! We offer several packages with different levels, features, and customizations for tutoring over the phone to suit your individualized needs. Contact us for more details.

EZ 1-ON-1 TEST-TAKING & ADMISSION CONSULTATION:
We understand that standardized tests and school/college admissions can sometimes become very stressful. Our 1-on-1 Test-Taking & Admission Consulting Program can dramatically reduce your stress and anxiety. One of our consultants can personally guide you through the entire process, starting from familiarizing you with a test to getting you successfully admitted into a school/college of your choice. Again, you can do all this in the exclusivity and comfort of your home. We offer several packages with different levels, features, and customizations for test-taking and admission consultation over the phone to suit your individualized needs. Contact us for more details.
The following are some of the features of our EZ 1-on-1 Test-Taking & Admission Consulting Program:
* Familiarize you with a particular test
* Equip you with test-taking skills for each section of your test
* Reduce test-taking anxiety, stress, nervousness, and test-fever with personal counseling
* Draft and edit your essays
* Re-design your resume
* Prepare you for a telephone or personal interview
* Select the right school/college & help with admission application procedures
* Presentation Skills – how to present and market yourself

EZ UNIQUE FEATURES:

Your EZ Tutor offers you the following unique features that will highlight important information, and will let you find them quickly as and when you need to review them.

EZ STRATEGIES: It provides you with many powerful, effective, proven, and time tested strategies for various concepts, and shows you exactly how to use them to attack different question types. Many of these test-taking strategies cannot be found in any other books!

EZ SHORTCUTS: It gives you many time-saving shortcuts you can apply to save yourself some very valuable testing-time while solving a question on your actual test.

EZ TACTICS: It shows you several important tactics to use so that you can solve problems in the smartest way.

EZ DEFINITIONS: It defines all the key definitions in an easy to understand manner so that you get a clear description and concise understanding of all the key terms.

EZ RULES: It presents all the important rules in an orderly manner so that you can learn the basic rules of all the concepts.

EZ STEPS: It walks you through hundreds of concepts, showing you how to tackle every question type in an organized user-friendly step-by-step easy-to-understand methodology that adapts to your understanding and needs so that you get the best procedural knowledge.

EZ MULTIPLE/ALTERNATE METHODS: It gives you a choice of multiple methods of answering the same question so that you can choose the method that seems easiest to you.

EZ SUMMARIES: It lists a complete summary of all the important concepts in an ordered and organized manner so that you will never have to hunt for them.

EZ FACTS: It provides you with numerous key facts about various principles so that you know all the facts-and-figures of the material you are reviewing.

EZ HINTS: It supplies you with innumerable hints and clues so that you can use them to become a smarter and wiser test-taker.

EZ TIPS: It also presents you with many tips and pointers that will prevent you from making any careless mistakes or falling into traps.

EZ NOTES: It reminds you to make notes of some important points that will come handy while answering a question.

EZ WARNINGS/CAUTIONS: It warns you of some obvious mistakes that will prevent you from making them while answering a question.

EZ EXCEPTIONS: It makes you aware of the exceptions and exclusions that apply to any particular rule.

EZ REFERENCES: It gives you references of related materials that you may want to refer to in other parts of the same or different modules, while learning a specific concept.

EZ SPOTS: It lists buzzwords and phrases that will help you easily spot some specific question types.

EZ PROBLEM SET-UP: It converts even some of the most complex problems into an easy to understand mathematical statement so that you understand accurately how to interpret the problems.

EZ PROBLEM EXPLANATIONS: It provides easy to understand explanations within square brackets for each step of the problem so that you know exactly what you need to do in each step.

EZ SOLVED EXAMPLES: It also throws several realistic solved examples with easy to understand detailed explanations for each and every question type explained so that you can understand and learn how to apply the concepts.

EZ PRACTICE EXERCISES: Last but not the least; it also includes intensive realistic practice exercises with easy to understand detailed explanations for each and every question type explained so that you can put to practice what you learned in an actual test question – solved examples will help you understand the concepts & practice will make you perfect!

GUESS WHAT!! No other book offers you so much. Your EZ tutor strives to provide you with the *best possible training* for your test, and *best value for your time and money*; and it is infinitely committed to providing you with *state-of-the-art* material.

Advantages: Amazing results in the first few days of the program!

Disadvantages: Only if you don't make use of our programs and publications!

THE EZ ADVANTAGE:

EZ TEST-PREP PROGRAM BROKEN INTO MODULES:
Instead of having a *big fat ugly scary all-in-one gigantic book*, we have broken our entire test-prep program into *small easy-to-use modules*.
- **Exclusivity:** Each module is exclusively dedicated to covering one major content area in extensive depth and breadth, allowing you to master each topic by getting an in-depth review.
- **More Content:** You will find many more topics and many more pages per topic than what you can find in all other books combined.
- **Tailored and Customized:** Separated modules offer test-takers of all levels with a more tailored and customized approach towards building specific foundational and advanced skills, and successfully preparing for the test.

EZ TO READ, CARRY, AND MANAGE:
EZ Modules are convenient – they are *easier to read, carry, and manage*.
- **EZ to Read:** EZ Modules are easier to read with text in spacious pages with a bigger font size than those other books with overcrowded pages with a small print.
- **EZ to Carry:** EZ Modules are easier to carry and hold than those other big fat bulky gigantic books.
- **EZ to Manage:** EZ Modules are overall easier to manage than those other all-in-one books.

BUY ONE MODULE OR THE ENTIRE SERIES:
The individually separated modules give you the flexibility to buy only those modules that cover the areas you think you need to work on; nevertheless, we strongly suggest you buy our entire series of modules. In fact, the most efficient and effective way to get the most out of our publications is to use our entire set of modules in conjunction with each other, and not just a few. Each module can be independently bought and studied; however, the modules are somehow connected with and complement the other modules. Therefore, if you are serious about getting a good score on your test, we sincerely recommend you purchase our entire series of modules. Contact us to order, or go to www.EZmethods.com, or check your local bookstore (look at the EZ Book Store on the last page for more information).

NO NEED TO REFER TO ANY OTHER BOOK:
Almost all other test-prep books contain a small disclaimer in some corner. They themselves spell it out very loud and clear, and admit that their book is only a brief review of some important topics; hence, it should not be considered to be an overall review of all the concepts. Most other test-preparation guides only include information for you to get familiar with the kind of topics that may appear on the test, and they suggest that you refer to additional textbooks, or consult other reference books if you want more detailed information and to get an in-depth knowledge of all the concepts. These books are not designed to be a one-stop book to learn everything you must know; instead, they are more like a

summary of some important points. Moreover, they assume that you already know everything, or at least most of the concepts.

However, if you are using our EZ modules to prepare for your test, it's the opposite case, you don't need to refer or consult any other book or text or any other source for assistance. On the contrary, we, in fact, discourage you from referring to any other book, just because there is absolutely no reason to. Our EZ modules contain everything that you need to know in order to do well on your test. We haven't left anything out, and we don't assume anything. Even if you don't know anything, you will find everything in our modules from topics that are frequently tested to topics that are rarely tested, and everything in between. The only topics that you won't find in our books are the topics that will probably never appear on your test!

Frequently Tested: Included in our review – topics that are repeatedly tested on your test, on a regularly basis
Occasionally Tested: Included in our review – topics that are sometimes tested on your test, every now and then
Rarely Tested: Included in our review – topics that are seldom tested on your test, very infrequently
Never Tested: Not included in our review – since these topics are never tested on your test, we don't even mention them anywhere in our review

The bottom line is, if something can be on your test, you'll find it in our modules; and if something is not going to be on your test, it's not going to be in our modules. Each and every math concept that even has the slightest possibility to be on the test can be found in our modules.

THE OFFICIAL REAL PRACTICE TESTS:
Although we don't suggest you refer to any other book, the only time we recommend using other books is for practicing previously administered tests to exercise your skills. The best resources for actual practice tests are the official guides published by the test makers that have several actual previously administered tests. One can *replicate* these tests as closely as one can, but no one other than the test administrators can *duplicate* them, and have the ability to reproduce or publish them. Therefore, to get the maximum effect of our approach, you must practice the actual tests from the official guide. You can also take a free online practice test by going to their website. EZ's practice tests are also based upon the most recently administered tests, and include every type of question that can be expected on the actual exam.

HOW OUR BOOKS CAN HELP YOU:
Our books are designed to help you identify your strengths and the areas which you need to work on. If you study all our modules, you will be fully equipped with all the tools needed to take your test head-on. Moreover, you'll also have the satisfaction that you did all you possibly could do to prepare yourself for the test, and you didn't leave any stone unturned. The amount of content covered in our books is far more than what you would learn by studying all the other test-prep books that are out there, put together, or by even taking an online or an actual prep course, and of course, spending thousands of dollars in the process. This will give you an idea of how material we have covered in our books.

STRUCTURE OF OUR MODULES:
All our modules are *structured in a highly organized and systematic manner*. The review is divided into different modules. Each module is divided into units. Each unit is further subdivided into chapters. Each chapter covers various topics, and in each specific topic, you are given all that you need to solve questions on that topic in detail – explaining key concepts, rules, and other EZ unique features. Also included in some topics are test-taking strategies specific to the topics discussed. Following each topic are solved sample examples with comprehensive explanations, which are exclusively based on that topic, and utilizing the concepts covered in that topic and section. Finally, there are practice exercises with thorough explanations containing real test-like questions for each topic and section, which are very similar to actual test questions. All units, chapters, and topics are chronologically numbered for easy reference.

Moreover, the modules, units, chapters, and topics are all arranged in sequence so that later modules, units, chapters, and topics assume familiarity with the material covered in earlier modules, units, chapters, and topics. Therefore, the best way to review is to work through from the beginning to the end.

SERIES > MODULES > UNITS > CHAPTERS > TOPICS > SUB-TOPICS > SOLVED EXAMPLES > PRACTICE EXERCISES

THE EZ DIFFERENCE:

DIFFERENCE BETWEEN EZ SOLUTIONS' PUBLICATIONS AND OTHER BOOKS:

Most of the other test-prep books suggest that your exam only tests your ability to take the test, and it does not test any actual content knowledge. In other words, they claim that your test is all about knowing the test-taking strategies, and it has very little to do with the actual knowledge of content; others claim that your test is all about knowing a few most commonly tested topics. While we have great respect for these books and the people who write or publish them, all these books have one thing in common: they all want to give their readers a quick shortcut to success. They actually want their readers to believe that just by learning a few strategies and memorizing some key formulas, they'll be able to ace their test. We are not sure if it's the fault of the people who write these books or the people who use them; but someone is definitely trying to fool someone – either those test-prep books for making the readers believe it, or the readers for actually believing it (no pun intended).

With a test as vast as this, it's simply not possible to cover the entire content in just a few pages. We all wish; however, in life, there really aren't any shortcuts to success, and your test is no exception to this rule. Nothing comes easy in life, and that is also precisely the case with your test. You have to do it the hard way by working your way through. Unfortunately, there is no magic potion, which we can give you to succeed in math! Therefore, if you want to do well on your test – be mentally, physically, and psychologically prepared to do some hard work. In this case, efforts and results are directly proportional, that is, greater the efforts you make, better your results are going to be.

While most test-preparation books present materials that stand very little resemblance to the actual tests, EZ's publication series present tests that accurately depict the official tests in both, degree of difficulty and types of questions.

Our EZ books are like no other books you have ever seen or even heard of. We have a completely different concept, and our books are structured using a totally different model. We have *re-defined the way test-prep books should be*.

STRATEGIES SEPARATED FROM CONTENT:
What we have done in our modules is, *separated the actual content-knowledge from the test-taking strategies*. We truly believe that a test-prep program should be more than just a *cheat-sheet of tricks, tips, and traps*. The test you are preparing for is not a simple game that you can master by learning these quick tactics. What you really need to do well on your test is a program that builds true understanding and knowledge of the content.

PERFECT EQUILIBRIUM BETWEEN STRATEGIES AND CONTENT:
In our modules, we've tried our best to present a *truly unique equilibrium* between two competing and challenging skills: test-taking strategies and comprehensive content-knowledge. We have *blended* the two most important ingredients that are essential for your success on your test. We have *enhanced* the old traditional approach to some of the most advanced forms of test-taking strategies. To top all this, we have *refined* our solved examples with detailed explanations to give you hands-on experience to real test-like questions before you take your actual test.

Other Books: Most of the other test-prep books primarily concentrate on teaching their readers how to *guess* and *use the process of elimination,* and they get so obsessed with the tactics that in the process they completely ignore the actual content. Majority of the content of these books consists of pages of guessing techniques.

EZ Books: With our EZ Content-Knowledge Modules, you'll find *100% pure content* that has a highly organized and structured approach to all the content areas, which actually teaches you the content you need to know to do well on your test. Therefore, if you are looking to learn more than just guessing by process of elimination, and if you are serious about developing your skills and confidence level for your exam, then our highly organized and structured test-prep modules is the solution. By studying our books, you'll learn a systematic approach to any question that you may see on your test, and acquire the tools that will help you get there.

EZ Solutions' publications are packed with important information, sophisticated strategies, useful tips, and extensive practice that the experts know will help you do your best on your test.

You should use whichever concept, fact, or tip from that section that you think is appropriate to answer the question correctly in the least possible time. If you've mastered the material in our review modules and strategy modules, you should be able to answer almost all (99.99%) of the questions.

LEARN BACKWARDS AND MOVE FORWARD: Smart students are the ones who make an honest attempt to learn what they read, and also learn from their mistakes, but at the same time, who moves ahead. Therefore, you should learn backwards, that is, learn from your past experiences, and move forward, that is, keep moving ahead without looking back!

ONE CONCEPT, EZ MULTIPLE METHODS:
Our books often give you a *choice of multiple methods* of answering the same question – you can pick the method that seems easiest to you. Our goal is not to *prescribe* any *hard-and-fast* method for taking the test, but instead, to give you the *flexibility and tools you can use to approach your test with confidence and optimism*.

STRATEGIES OR CONTENT?

In order to do well on your test, it is absolutely essential that you have a pretty good grasp of all the concepts laid out in our review modules. Our review modules contain everything you need to know, or must know to crack your test. They cover everything from basic arithmetic to logical reasoning, and everything in between. Nonetheless, that's not enough. You should be able to use these concepts in ways that may not be so familiar or well known to you. This is where our EZ Strategies kick in.

CONTENT VERSUS STRATEGIES:

There is a *succinct* difference between knowing the math content and knowing the math strategies.

Hypothetically speaking, let's assume there is a student named Alex, who learns only the test-taking strategies; and there is another student named Andria, who learns only the math-content. Now when the test time comes, Andria who learns only the math-content is extremely likely to do a lot better than Alex, who learns only the test-taking strategies.

The truth is that someone who has the knowledge of all the math content, but doesn't know anything about the strategies, will almost always do better on the test than someone who knows all the strategies but doesn't know the content properly.

Now let's assume there is another student named Alexandria, who learns both, the test-taking strategies and the math-content. Yes, now we are talking! This student, Alexandria, who knows both the strategies and the content, is guaranteed to do a lot better than Alex, who only knows the strategies, or Andria who only knows the content.

This brings us to our conclusion on this topic: don't just study the strategies, or just the content; you need to know both simultaneously – the strategies and the content, in order to do well on your test. How quickly and accurately you can answer the math questions will depend on your knowledge of the content and the strategies, and that will have an overall effect on your success on the test.

Hence, the equation to succeed on your test is: **Strategies + Content = Success!**

We are confident that if you study our books on test-taking strategies along with our books on content-knowledge, you'll have everything you possibly need to know in order to do well on your test, in fact, to ace your test, and come out with flying colors!

The good thing is that you made the smart decision to buy this book, or if you are reading this online, or in a bookstore, or in a library, you are going to buy one soon!

CONTENT-KNOWLEDGE REVIEW MODULES:

THOROUGH IN-DEPTH REVIEW:
Most other test-prep books briefly touch upon some of the concepts sporadically. On the other hand, our books start from the basics, but unlike other books, they do not end there – **we go deep inside, beyond just touching up the surface** – all the way from fundamental skills to some of the most advanced content that many other prep books choose to ignore. **Each concept is first explained in detail, and then analyzed for most effective understanding** – each and every concept is covered, and we haven't left any stone unturned. Overall, our program is more challenging – you simply get the **best-of-the-best**, and you get more of everything!

COMPREHENSIVE REVIEW:
Our Content-Knowledge Review Modules provide the **most comprehensive and complete review** of all the concepts, which you need to know to excel in your test. Each module is devoted to one of the main subject areas so that you can focus on the most relevant material. The ideal way to review our modules is to go through each topic thoroughly, understand all the solved examples, and work out all of the practice exercises. You must review each topic, understand every solved example, and work out all of the practice exercises. If you don't have enough time, just glimpse through a section. If you feel comfortable with it, move on to something else that may potentially give you more trouble. If you feel uncomfortable with it, review that topic more thoroughly.

Moreover, if you carefully work through our review, you will probably find some topics that you already know, but you may also find some topics that you need to review more closely. You should have a good sense of areas with which you are most comfortable, and in which areas you feel you have a deficiency. Work on any weaknesses you believe you have in those areas. This should help you organize your review more efficiently. Try to give yourself plenty of time and make sure to review the skills and master the concepts that you are required and expected to know to do well on your test. Of course, the more time you invest preparing for your test and more familiar you are with these fundamental principles, the better you will do on your test.

There is a lot of content reviewed in our modules. Although the amount of material presented in our books may appear to be overwhelming, it's the most complete review to get prepared for your test. To some of you, this may seem like a great deal of information to assimilate; however, when you start reviewing, you'll probably realize that you are already comfortable with many concepts discussed in our review modules. We also suggest that you spread your use of our modules over several weeks, and study different modules at your own pace. Even if you are sure you know the basic concepts, our review will help to warm you up so that you can go into your test with crisp and sharp skills. Hence, we strongly suggest that you at least touch up on each concept. However, depending on your strengths and weaknesses, you may be able to move quickly through some areas, and focus more on the others that seem to be troublesome to you. You should develop a plan of attack for your review of the wide range of content. Work on your weaknesses, and be ready to take advantage of your strengths.

Finally, our main objective in the content review modules is to refresh your knowledge of key concepts on the test and we attempt to keep things as concrete and concise as possible.

PRACTICE MODULES:

BASIC WORKBOOK:
Our math practice basic workbook contains a variety of questions on each and every topic that is covered in our review modules. The best way is to first learn all the concepts from our review modules and then apply your skills to test your knowledge on the actual test-like questions in our basic workbook.

ADVANCED WORKBOOK:
Our math practice advanced workbook also contains a variety of questions on each and every topic that is covered in our review modules. Once you become comfortable with the questions in our basic workbook, you should try your hands on our advanced workbook so that you can gain more experience with some of the most difficult questions. For students who are aiming for a very high score, practicing from our advanced workbook is very important. For students who are aiming for a mediocre score, practicing from our advanced workbook is not so important.

-ABOUT THIS BOOK

In order to excel on your test, it's important that you master each component of your test. That's why we have broken the entire test into different sections and each book focuses only on only one component. It's important to learn the art of tackling the questions you'll see on the test; nevertheless, it's equally important to get a strong hold of the mathematical fundamentals and principles. Apparently it's not enough to only know the test taking strategies, you also need to have a solid knowledge of the math content, and know how to solve the problems mathematically. This book is exclusively dedicated to the **Arithmetic** that apply to the math section of your test.

WHAT'S COVERED IN THIS BOOK:
In this book, you will learn everything related to **Arithmetic** content that can be used on different types of questions throughout the math section. Mastering the content of this book will not only improve your performance on the math section, but will also make you a smarter and wiser test-taker. In this book, you'll learn all the strategies and the content related to arithmetic, so that you can solve the arithmetic quickly, correctly, and more efficiently. In fact, being able to solve arithmetic is one of the most important factors to succeed on the math section.

WHAT'S NOT COVERED IN THIS BOOK:
This book does not cover any content other than Arithmetic – to learn about other content areas, you must refer to the other books in the series.

PRE-REQUISITES FOR THIS BOOK:
The pre-requisite for this book is your thorough familiarity with basic math principles and concepts. Hence, when you go through this book, you are already expected to know the content covered in some of the other books in the series.

RELATED MODULES FOR THIS BOOK: You will get the best out of this book if you use it in conjunction with some of the other related books in the series that are listed below.

List of related modules for this book:
- EZ Solutions – Test Prep Series – General – Test Taker's Manual
- EZ Solutions – Test Prep Series – Math Review – Arithmetic
- EZ Solutions – Test Prep Series – Math Review – Algebra
- EZ Solutions – Test Prep Series – Math Review – Applications
- EZ Solutions – Test Prep Series – Math Review – Geometry
- EZ Solutions – Test Prep Series – Math Review – Word Problems
- EZ Solutions – Test Prep Series – Math Review – Logic & Stats
- EZ Solutions – Test Prep Series – Math Practice – Basic Workbook
- EZ Solutions – Test Prep Series – Math Practice – Advanced Workbook
- EZ Solutions – Test Prep Series – Math Strategies – Math Test Taking Strategies

Note: Look at the back of the book for a complete list of EZ books

PART 0.0: INTRODUCTION TO ARITHMETIC:

Arithmetic is the branch of pure mathematics dealing with the theory of numerical calculations relating to or involving arithmetic computations.

Arithmetic also involves many rules, and you must absolutely know most of the basic definitions, such as, difference between a number and an integer, even and odd numbers, etc.

You will find a few problems on your test that involve pure arithmetic, but most of the rest of the problems are likely to involve arithmetic to some degree, whether they are percent or ratio problems, average problems, geometry, word problems, or even some arithmetic problems. This is why a clear understanding of arithmetic is very important before moving onto any of the other topics in math.

Moreover, the arithmetic concepts covered in this book are not only directly tested on your test, but they are also essential for understanding some of the more advanced concepts that are covered in our other books. Without a clear knowledge about arithmetic, it would be impossible for you to understand any of our other books, such as algebra, geometry, etc.

Therefore, arithmetic is the first step in math, and it is important that you have a good and clear understanding of these concepts in order to proceed to the more advanced topics.

All this makes arithmetic inevitable; it is a necessary skill – you must acquire basic arithmetic skills in order to solve most of your test questions.

You should be able to simplify and evaluate arithmetic operations, solve fractions and decimals, and use arithmetic concepts in problem-solving situations.

THIS PAGE HAS BEEN INTENTIONALLY LEFT BLANK

PART 1.0: INTEGERS:

TABLE OF CONTENTS:

EZ REFERENCE: -To practice easy-to-medium level questions, please refer to our EZ Practice Basic Workbook.
                       -To practice medium-to-difficult level questions, please refer to our EZ Practice Advanced Workbook.

1.1: BASICS ABOUT INTEGERS:

1.1.1: TYPES OF NUMBERS:

NUMBER TREE: The following number tree is a visual representation of the different types of real numbers and their relationships:

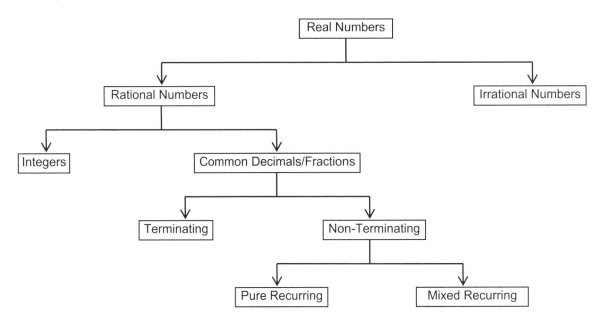

REAL NUMBERS:
All the numbers that can be expressed on the number line are real numbers. The types and properties of real numbers form the basis of the number properties problem type, so it's important that you understand it thoroughly.

(A) RATIONAL NUMBERS:
Rational numbers are numbers that can be expressed as the quotient of two integers (excluding division by 0); a number that can be represented by a fraction whose numerator and denominator are both integers (denominator must be nonzero). Rational numbers include integers, fractions, terminating decimals, and repeating decimals.
Rational Numbers: The set of numbers that can be expressed as the quotient or ratio of two integers, that is, any number that can be expressed in the form a/b, where a and b are integers (all integers and some fractions & decimals).

INTEGERS:
Integers are the set of all numbers that are whole, without a fractional or decimal part attached to it.

For Example: $\frac{5}{1} = 5$

TERMINATING NUMBER:

When a rational number "$\frac{a}{b}$" is simplified, meaning when the numerator "a" is divided by the denominator "b", the result is a decimal. If "b" divides "a" with a remainder of "0" after reaching a certain point, the result is a **terminating** decimal number.

For Example: $\frac{1}{2} = 0.5$

NON-TERMINATING OR REPEATING NUMBER:

When a rational number " $\frac{a}{b}$ " is simplified, meaning when the numerator "a" is divided by the denominator "b", the result is a decimal. If "b" continues to divide "a" indefinitely so that the decimal forms a repeating pattern of integers, the result is a **non-terminating** or **repeating** or **recurring** or **periodic** or **circulating** decimal number. In other words, the division does not terminate after one, two, three, four, or five decimal places; rather it goes on forever with a digit or set of digits repeating continually. The repeated figures or set of figures is called the Period of the decimal. Repeating decimals are represented by dots (.......)

PURE RECURRING NUMBER:
Decimals in which all the figures after the decimal point recur is called a **pure recurring decimal number**.

For Example: $\frac{7}{9}$ = 0.77777.......

MIXED RECURRING NUMBER:
Decimals in which some but not all the figures after the decimal point recur, is called a **mixed recurring decimal number**.

For Example: $\frac{11}{12}$ = 0.91666666.......

(B) IRRATIONAL NUMBERS: NON-TERMINATING & NON-REPEATING:
Irrational number is the set of all numbers that cannot be expressed as the quotient or ratio of two integers or functions (such as π and $\sqrt{2}$). When an irrational number " $\frac{a}{b}$ " is simplified, meaning when the numerator "a" is divided by the denominator "b", the result is a decimal. If "b" continues to divide "a" indefinitely so that the decimal form is **non-terminating** and **non-repeating**, the result is an **irrational number**. In other words, the division does not terminate after one, two, three, four, or five decimal places; rather it goes on forever. The irrational number cannot be expressed as the quotient of two integers but can be written as non-terminating and non-repeating decimals. In other words, an irrational number is a number that can't be represented by a fraction whose numerator and denominator are both integers. All real numbers that are not rational, both positive and negative are irrational numbers.

For Example: $\sqrt{2}$ = 1.4142135623730950548801.......

EZ NOTE: A number must be either rational or irrational; but it can't be both. All real numbers, rational or irrational correspond to points on the number line, and all points on the number line correspond to real numbers. For instance, π, which is approximately 3.14, would fit somewhere between 3 and 3.5 on the number line above. Similarly, $\sqrt{2}$, which is approximately 1.4, would fit somewhere between 1 and 1.5.

DIGITS:
- Each and every number, positive or negative, whole number or decimal, is composed or made-up of digits.
- Altogether, there are only ten digits in our number system: which are 0, 1, 2, 3, 4, 5, 6, 7, 8, and 9.
- The term "digit" refers to one element or building-block of a number; it does not refer to a number itself.
  For example: 1256 is a number composed of four digits: 1, 2, 5, and 6.
- Numbers are often classified by the number of digits they contain.

For example: 1; 7; and –9 $\Rightarrow$ are all one-digit numbers (they are all composed of one-digit)
              12; 69, and –87 $\Rightarrow$ are all two-digit numbers (they are all composed of two-digits)
              112; 169; and –807 $\Rightarrow$ are all three-digit numbers (they are all composed of three-digits)
              1257; 1569; and –9187 $\Rightarrow$ are all four-digit numbers (they are all composed of four-digits)
              12,579; 15,689; and –91,827 $\Rightarrow$ are all five-digit numbers (they are all composed of five-digits)
              1257908; and –9182790 $\Rightarrow$ are all seven-digit numbers (they are all composed of seven-digits)

The Sign of Equality: The sign of equality is indicated by the symbol (=) is read as *"equals"* or *"is equal to"*, and when placed between two quantities indicates that they are equal to one another.
For Example: 2 + 5 = 7 is read as 2 plus 5 equals 7, and means that 2 plus 5 is equal to 7.

1.1.2: NUMBER LINE:

All the numbers used in mathematics belong to a set called the real numbers. All real numbers can be represented graphically as points on a real number line. In other words, all numbers, including whole numbers, fractions, decimals, etc., that correspond to points on the number line are real numbers.

BASICS ABOUT NUMBER LINE:

A number line is used to graphically represent the relationships between numbers: integers, fractions, and/or decimals. A number line is a straight line that extends infinitely in both directions, on which real numbers are represented as points. Number line is useful in the determination of relative values. Every real number corresponds to a point on the real number line. Consider numbers as points on a number line. The real number line is infinitely long in both directions.

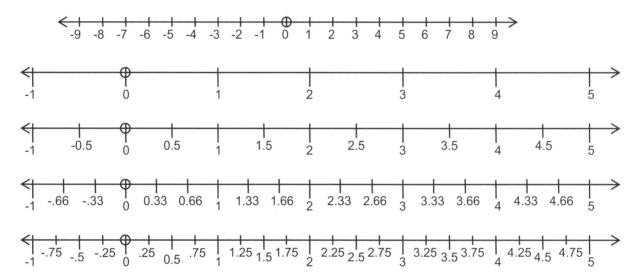

CONSTRUCTING NUMBER LINE:

To construct a number line, simply follow the method explained below:
- Draw a straight line that extends indefinitely in both directions.
- Arbitrarily fix a point and label it with the number 0, which is known as the origin.
- Make the right side of the number line:
  - Pick another point, on the line to the right of 0 and name it 1.
  - The point to the right of 1 which is exactly as far from 1 as 1 is from 0 is called 2.
  - The point to the right of 2 just as far from 2 as 1 is from 0 is called 3, and so on.
  - The point halfway between 0 and 1 is called ½.
  - The point half way between 0 and ½ is called ¼.
- Make the left side of the number line:
  - Pick a point, on the line to the left of 0 which is exactly the same distance as 0 is from 1, and label it as −1.
  - The point to the left of −1 which is exactly as far from −1 as −1 is from 0 is called −2.
  - The point to the left of −2 just as from −2 as −1 is from 0 is called −3, and so on.
  - The point halfway between 0 and −1 is called −½.
  - The point halfway between 0 and −½ is called −¼.

In a similar manner, you can label and identify any real number with a point on the line, depending on its position relative to 0.

Number line is divided into equal incremental units or segments, these points are labeled with real numbers.

For example, the point 5 units to the left of 0 is –5, while the point 5 units to the right of 0 is +5, and both are equidistant from 0.

TICK MARKS: The plotted boundary points or tick marks on the number line are always equally spaced. However, the distance between tick marks on a number line do not have to be measured in whole units. These tick marks actually represent the subset of the real numbers, which can be integers or decimals/fractions. As mentioned above, the distance between any two tick-marks can be in decimals or fractions.

SIGNED NUMBERS ON NUMBER LINE:

Signed Numbers: Numbers can be either positive or negative (except the number 0, which is neither). A number preceded by either a plus or a minus sign is called a signed number. All numbers can be signed numbers.
For example, +1, +1.5, –1, –1.5 are all signed numbers.
Note: If no sign is given with a number, a plus sign is assumed; thus, 5 is interpreted as +5.

The Number Line and Signed Numbers: A number line illustrates this idea. A signed number provides two important facts. The sign indicates the direction from zero on a number line, and the number indicates the distance from zero. For example, –5 lies five spaces to the left of zero, and +7 lies seven spaces to the right of zero. Signed numbers are sometimes also referred to as directed numbers.

For any number "a", exactly one and only one of the following is true:
(A) "a" is < 0 or negative
(B) "a" is = 0
(C) "a" is > 0 or positive

USES OF SIGNED NUMBERS:
Signed numbers can often be used to distinguish different concepts. For example, a profit of $10 can be denoted by +$10 and a loss of $10 by –$10. A temperature of 20 degrees above zero can be denoted by +20°F and below zero can be denoted by –20°F.

POSITIVE NUMBERS ON NUMBER LINE:
* Numbers with the plus (+) sign prefixed are called positive numbers.
* Positive numbers are the numbers that correspond to points to the right of "0" on a number line. So each point to the right of 0 is positive (such points are called positive signed numbers).
* Positive numbers on a number line can be shown with a positive or plus (+) sign, but are usually written without any sign. Unless otherwise noted, any number without any sign is assumed to be positive, so +2 is written simply as 2.
* Positive numbers are signed numbers whose sign is (+)
* A number is positive if it is greater than 0
For Example: 1, 1.5, 2 are all positive numbers.

NEGATIVE NUMBERS ON NUMBER LINE:
* Numbers with the minus (–) sign prefixed are called negative numbers.
* Negative numbers are the numbers that correspond to points to the left of "0" on a number line. So each point to the left of 0 is negative (such points are called negative signed numbers).
* Negative numbers on a number line are always preceded by a negative or minus (–) sign.
* Negative numbers are signed numbers whose sign is (–)
* A number is negative if it is less than 0.
For Example: –1, –1.5, –2 are all negative numbers.

ZERO ON NUMBER LINE:
Zero separates the positive numbers (to the right of zero) and the negative numbers (to the left of zero) along the number line. Zero is the only number that is neither positive nor negative. Any nonzero number can be either positive or negative, but not both.

MORE ABOUT NUMBER LINE:

VALUE OF A NUMBER ON A NUMBER LINE WITH MOVEMENT:
Numbers on the number line get progressively greater with movement to the right and progressively smaller with movement to the left.
Left to Right: The numbers on a number line always progressively increase in value as we move from left to right.
Right to Left: The numbers on a number line always progressively decrease in value as we move from right to left.
EZ RULE: If "*a*" is to the right of "*b*", it is said to be greater than "*b*" and if "*a*" is to the left of "*b*", it is said to be less than "*b*".
⇒ A number is greater than any number appearing to its left on the number line.
Positive numbers get bigger and bigger as they move further away from 0. (2 is greater than 1)
⇒ A number is less than any number appearing to its right on the number line.
Negative numbers get smaller and smaller as they move further away from 0. (–2 is smaller than –1)

NUMBER LINE EXTENDS INDEFINITELY IN BOTH DIRECTIONS:
The number line always has an arrow at each end – which means that the number line goes on infinitely in both positive and negative directions.

NUMBER LINES ARE DRAWN TO SCALE:
Numbers on number lines are usually drawn to scale, unless otherwise stated. You will be expected to make reasonable approximations of positions between labeled points on the number line.

USES OF NUMBER LINE:
- Number line can be used to represent whole numbers, fractions, or decimals.
- Number lines can be drawn to aid in basic arithmetical calculations.
- Number lines are also used to represent equation and inequalities.

THINGS YOU SHOULD BE ABLE TO FIGURE OUT FROM A NUMBER LINE:
Number line questions generally involve figuring out the relationships among different numbers placed on the number line. Number line questions may ask for one of the following:
- Relationship among different numbers placed on the number line.
- Where any given number should be placed in relation to other numbers.
- The sum or difference of any two given numbers.
- The product or quotient of any two given numbers.
- The lengths and the ratios/percents of the lengths of line segments represented on the number line.

UNDERSTANDING NEGATIVE NUMBERS:
- Negative numbers are the opposite of positive numbers and vice versa.
- Negative numbers are written with a negative (–) sign.

NEGATIVE NUMBERS CAN BE USED TO REPRESENT THE FOLLOWING:
- Temperatures lower than 0 (also known as negative temperatures or below zero temperatures)
- Bank balances lower than 0 (also known as negative balances)
- Net profits less than 0 (also known as losses)
- Stock market losses
- Negative growth
- Altitudes below sea level

NEGATIVE NUMBERS CANNOT BE USED TO REPRESENT THE FOLLOWING:
None of the following quantities can ever be negative:

▪ Age	▪ Weight	▪ Distance	▪ Speed	▪ Time	▪ Length	▪ Height
▪ Width	▪ Radius	▪ Perimeter	▪ Circumference	▪ Area	▪ Volume	

1.1.3: DIFFERENT TYPES OF INTEGERS:

PROPERTIES OF INTEGERS:
- Integers are the set of all numbers that are whole, without a fractional or decimal part attached to it.
- Integers are all multiples of 1.
- Integers include all whole numbers, their negatives, and zero.
- Integers extend infinitely in both positive and negative directions.

For Example: Set of Integers: {.......–5, –4, –3, –2, –1, 0, 1, 2, 3, 4, 5.......}

Difference between Integers and Numbers: Never get confused between a number and an integer, both are different things. So don't assume that numbers mean integers. All integers are numbers, but all numbers are not integers.
For instance: 7 is the only integer between 6 and 8; however, there are many other numbers between 6 and 8, such as, 6.01, 6.5, 7.5, 7.99, etc.......

The following are the different types of integers and their properties:

(A) WHOLE NUMBERS: (Also Known As: Counting Numbers)
- Whole numbers are the set of all positive numbers, zero and greater, which are whole, without a fractional or decimal value attached to it. It includes all positive integers including zero.

For Example: Set of Whole Numbers: {0, 1, 2, 3, 4, 5.......}

(B) POSITIVE INTEGERS: (Also Known As: Natural Numbers)
- Positive integers are the set of all integers greater than zero. It includes all positive integers except zero.

For Example: Set of Positive Integers: {1, 2, 3, 4, 5, 6, 7, 8, 9.......}

(C) NEGATIVE INTEGERS:
- Negative integers are the set of all integers less than zero.

For Example: Set of Negative Integers: {.......–9, –8, –7, –6, –5, –4, –3, –2, –1}

(D) EVEN & ODD INTEGERS:
The concept of even and odd applies only to integers. There are no even or odd non-integer numbers. Even and odd integers can be either positive or negative.

(I) EVEN INTEGERS:
- Even integers are the set of all positive or negative integers that are evenly or exactly divisible by 2.
- All even integers can be divided by 2 without leaving any remainder.
- All even numbers are multiples of 2.
- All integers that are not odd integers are even integers.
- The last digit of an even numbers is always 0, 2, 4, 6, or 8.

For Example: Set of Even Integers: {.......–8, –6, –4, –2, 0, 2, 4, 6, 8.......}
Note: The integer 0 is an even number.

(II) ODD INTEGERS:
- Odd integers are the set of all positive or negative integers that are not evenly or exactly divisible by 2.
- All odd integers leave a remainder of 1 when divided by 2.
- None of the odd numbers are multiples of 2.
- All integers that are not even integers are odd integers.
- The last digit of an odd number is always 1, 3, 5, 7, or 9.

For Example: Set of Odd Integers: {.......–7, –5, –3, –1, 1, 3, 5, 7.......}
Note: The integer 0 is not an odd number.

(E) PRIME NUMBERS: (Also Known As: Primes)
- Prime numbers are the set of all positive integers greater than 1 that are only divisible by 1 and themselves, i.e., the have exactly two distinct positive integer factors/divisors, which is itself and the number 1.
- Any positive integer n that has exactly two distinct positive divisors, 1 and n, is said to be a prime number.

Note: All Prime numbers are positive because every negative number has –1 as a factor in addition to 1 and itself.
For Example: Set of first ten Prime Numbers: {2, 3, 5, 7, 11, 13, 17, 19, 23, 29.......}
⇒ Number 7 is a prime number because its only factors are 1 & 7; or it's only divisible by 1 & 7.
⇒ Number 8 is not a prime number because its factors are 1, 2, 4 & 8; or it's divisible by 1, 2, 4, & 8.

EZ NOTE: ⇒ 0 is not a prime number.
⇒ 1 is not a prime number because it has only one factor, which is itself.
⇒ 2 is the first prime number and the only even prime number. The reason being that any other even number has 2 as a factor, and it will have at least 3 factors: 1, itself, and 2, therefore they cannot be prime.

(F) COMPOSITE NUMBERS:
- Composite number is any number (except 1) that is not a prime number.
- Composite number is any number that has more than two divisors or factors.
- Composite number is a number which has other factors, at least one more factor besides itself and 1.
- Composite number is composed of its prime factors.

For Example: Set of Composite Numbers: {4, 6, 8, 9, 10, 12, 14, 15, 16, 18, 20.......}
⇒ The number 20 is a composite number composed of the prime factors 2, 4, 5 and 10.

(G) CONSECUTIVE NUMBERS:
- Consecutive numbers are the set of numbers that occurs at either a fixed interval, or exhibit a fixed pattern.
- Consecutive numbers follow immediately, one after another, without skipping, from a given fixed starting point.

(I) CONSECUTIVE INTEGERS:
- Consecutive integers are the set of two or more integers that follow in consecutive sequence, each of which is 1 more than the preceding integer, and where the positive difference between any two successive integers is 1.
- Consecutive integers differ by 1 in consecutive or regular increasing order at an increment of 1, without any integers missing in between. They follow one another in the counting order; that is, each number is the successor of the number that precedes it.

For instance, –2, –1, 0, 1, and 2 are consecutive integers. On the other hand, 1, 5, 7, 8, 11 are not consecutive integers.
General mathematical notation for representing set of consecutive integers: {$n, n + 1, n + 2$.......} Where n = any integer
For Example: Set of Consecutive Integers: {–2, –1, 0, 1, 2, 3, 4, 5.......}

(II) CONSECUTIVE EVEN/ODD INTEGERS:
- Consecutive even or odd integers are the set of two or more integers that follow in sequence, each of which is 2 more than the preceding integer, and where the positive difference between any two successive integers is 2. Consecutive even or odd integers are two apart.
- Consecutive even or odd integers differ by 2 in consecutive or increasing order at an increment of 2.

General mathematical notation for representing set of consecutive even or odd Integers:
⇒ {$n, n + 2, n + 4, n + 6, n + 8$.......} Where n = any even/odd integer.
For Example: Set of Consecutive Even Integers: {–2, 0, 2, 4, 6, 8, 10, 12.......}
For Example: Set of Consecutive Odd Integers: {–3, –1, 1, 3, 5, 7, 9, 11.......}
Note: The mathematical notation for representing consecutive even or odd integers is the same because, any two consecutive even or odd integers are placed with a difference of 2 in between them.

(III) CONSECUTIVE PRIME NUMBERS:
- Consecutive prime numbers are the set of two or more prime numbers that follow in sequence, each of which is the next prime number in sequence.
- There is no fixed difference between any two consecutive prime numbers and there is no fixed increment.

For Example: Set of Consecutive Prime Numbers: {2, 3, 5, 7, 11, 13, 17, 19.......}

(H) DISTINCT NUMBERS:
- Distinct numbers are numbers that have different values and are different from one another.
- If two numbers are distinct, they can't be equal. For instance: if m & n are distinct, they must've different values.

For Example: 2 and 5 are distinct numbers.

1.1.4: PROPERTIES OF ZERO AND ONE:

PROPERTIES OF ZERO:

Identity Property of Zero: When 0 is added to any number n, the value of that number does not change; hence, it is said that 0 is the identity element for addition $\Rightarrow n + 0 = n$

#1:   Zero has absolutely no value if placed at the extreme left of any digit or number
$\Rightarrow$ For any number *"n"*, $0n = n$ **For Example:**   00000007 = 7

#2:   Zero is the only number that is neither positive nor negative $\Rightarrow 0 \neq$ positive or negative

#3:   Zero is smaller than every positive number and greater than every negative number.
$\Rightarrow$ For any number *"n"*: $0 < n$ and $0 > -n$ **For Example:** $0 < 7$ and $0 > -7$

#4:   Zero is an even integer and it is not an odd integer $\Rightarrow 0 =$ Even Number.

#5:   Zero is a multiple of every integer.

#6:   Zero is not a factor of any integer.

#7:   Zero is the only number that is equal to its opposite $\Rightarrow 0 = -0$

#8:   Adding zero to any number results in that same number.
$\Rightarrow$ For any number *"n"*: $n + 0 = n$ **For Example:** $7 + 0 = 7$ and $-7 + 0 = -7$

#9:   Subtracting zero from any number results in that same number.
$\Rightarrow$ For any number *"n"*: $n - 0 = n$ **For Example:** $7 - 0 = 7$ and $-7 - 0 = -7$

#10:   Multiplying any number by zero results in zero itself.
$\Rightarrow$ For every number *"n"*: $n \times 0 = 0$ **For Example:** $7 \times 0 = 0$ and $-7 \times 0 = 0$

#11:   Dividing zero by any number (other than 0) results in zero.
$\Rightarrow$ For every number *"n"*: $0 \div n = 0$ **For Example:** $0 \div 7 = 0$ and $0 \div -7 = 0$

#12:   Dividing any number (including 0) by zero is undefined.
$\Rightarrow$ For any number *"n"*: $n \div 0 = undefined$ **For Example:** $7 \div 0 = undefined$ $0 \div 0 = undefined$

#13:   Zero raised to the power of any integer results in zero.
$\Rightarrow$ For any integer *"n"*: $0^n = 0$ **For Example:** $0^7 = 0$

#14:   If the product of two or more numbers is zero, at least one of the numbers is zero.
$\Rightarrow$ If $m \times n = 0$; then at least one of the two numbers *"m"* or *"n"* is zero.

#15:   Adding zeros at the extreme right after a decimal point does not change the value of that number.
$\Rightarrow$ For every integer *"n"*: $n.00 = n$ **For Example:** $7.00 = 7$ or $7.50 = 7.5$

PROPERTIES OF ONE:

Identity Property of One: When any number n, is multiplies by 1, the value of that number does not change; hence, it is said that one is the identity element for multiplication $\Rightarrow n \times 1 = n$

#1:   1 is the smallest positive integer $\Rightarrow 1 < 2, 3, 4, 5, 6, 7.......$

#2:   1 is the smallest positive odd integer $\Rightarrow 1 < 3, 5, 7, 9, 11.......$

#3:   Multiplying 1 by any number results in that same number
$\Rightarrow$ For any number *"n"*: $n \times 1 = n$ **For Example:** $7 \times 1 = 7$ or $-7 \times 1 = -7$

#4:   Dividing any number by 1 results in that same number
$\Rightarrow$ For any number *"n"*: $n \div 1 = n$ **For Example:** $7 \div 1 = 7$ and $-7 \div 1 = -7$

#5:   1 is a divisor of every integer
$\Rightarrow$ For any integer *"n"*: $n \div 1 = n$ **For Example:** $7 \div 1 = 7$ and $-7 \div 1 = -7$

#6:   1 is the only integer with only one divisor $\Rightarrow 1$ can only be divided by 1.

#7:   1 to the power of any number is 1
$\Rightarrow$ For any integer *"n"*: $1^n = 1$ **For Example:** $1^7 = 1$

#8:   1 is not a prime number since it only has one factor, which is 1 itself $\Rightarrow 1 \neq$ Prime Number

#9:   1 is not a composite number $\Rightarrow 1 \neq$ Composite Number

1.2: ABSOLUTE VALUE OR MAGNITUDE:

1.2.1: ABOUT ABSOLUTE VALUE:

Definition of Absolute Value (also known as "magnitude"): The Absolute Value of a number can be expressed on the real number line, and referred as its distance from the origin or zero on the number line, regardless of its direction.

Absolute Value is Absolutely Positive: Since distance can never be negative, hence the absolute value of any given number can never be negative, it's always positive. Absolute value disregards the direction (positive or negative) from which the number approaches 0 on the number line. The absolute value of any number is just that number without its sign. The absolute value of any nonzero number, positive or negative, is always expressed as a positive number. In other words, you can think of the absolute value of a number as the "size" of the number, disregarding whether it is positive or negative.

If you want to take the absolute value of the numbers represented on the number line discussed earlier, you can simply extract each number from its sign. The absolute value of the point furthest left would therefore be the same as the absolute value of point furthest right. This reflects the fact that –5 and +5 are equidistant from 0, the origin. Absolute value is denoted via the placement of a vertical line on either side of a number: $|-7| = 7$ and $|7| = 7$.

You can also determine the absolute value of a number by finding how far away the number is from 0 on the number line. For instance, the number 7 is exactly 7 units away from 0, so the absolute value of 7 equals 7. Similarly, the number –7 is also exactly 7 units away from 0, so the absolute value of –7 also equals 7.
Therefore, every positive number is the absolute value of two numbers – itself and its negative counterpart.
For instance, both +7 and –7 are 7 units from zero, so their absolute values are both 7.

HOW TO WRITE ABSOLUTE VALUE: The Absolute Value of a number is represented by placing two vertical bars on both sides of the number, and its value is equal to the given number, regardless of its sign.
Symbol of Absolute Value: $|\ |$

1.2.2: FINDING ABSOLUTE VALUE:

The Absolute Value can also be found by extracting the number from its sign (or simply by dropping its sign).
Note: The only number whose absolute value is zero is zero $\Rightarrow |0| = 0$

EZ RULE: The absolute value of a number *"n"*, denoted by $|n|$, is the distance between 0 and *"n"* on the number line.

The number line extends on both sides of zero. Each positive number on the right of zero has a negative counterpart to the left of zero. Since each number of a pair is located the same distance from zero (though in different directions), each has the same absolute value.

For Example: The absolute value of +7 equals the absolute value of –7 $\Rightarrow$ both are equivalent to 7.
Since 7 is 7 units to the right of 0 on the number line, and –7 is 7 units to the left of 0 on the number line $\Rightarrow$ both have an absolute value of 7.
This means that –7 and 7 have the same absolute value or magnitude.
Note: –7 is less than 7, however, both numbers are at the same distance from 0.

Opposites: Two unequal numbers that have the same absolute value are called *"opposites"*
For example: 7 is the opposite of –7 and –7 is the opposite of 7.

EZ RULE: The absolute value of a number *n*, denoted by $|n|$, is defined as *"n"* if $n \geq 0$ and $-n$ if $n < 0$.
For Example: $|-7| = 7$ $\Rightarrow$ If $|n| = 7$, then *"n"* could be 7 or –7
Absolute value of the sum of two numbers is always less than or equal to the sum of the absolute value of each of the two numbers $\Rightarrow |a + b| \leq |a| + |b|$

For Example: If a = 8 and b = 2, then $\Rightarrow |a + b| = |a| + |b|$
                                                $\Rightarrow |8 + 2| = |8| + |2|$
                                                $\Rightarrow 10 = 10$
                    If a = 8 and b = –2, then $\Rightarrow |a + b| < |a| + |b|$
                                                $\Rightarrow |8 - 2| < |8| + |-2|$
                                                $\Rightarrow 6 < 10$

EZ CAUTION: If you have an operation within the absolute value, you can't take the absolute value without doing the operation. In other words, you first have to do the operation and then find the absolute value.
For Example: $|5 - 7| = |-2| = 2$
            $\Rightarrow$ In this case, you cant take the absolute value of –7 as 7 and add it to 5 and get 12, this would be wrong.

ABSOLUTE VALUE IS ALWAYS "EQUAL TO" OR "GREATER THAN" ZERO:
$\Rightarrow |n| \geq 0$ $\Rightarrow$ For $n > 0$, $|n| = n$
                $\Rightarrow$ For $n = 0$, $|n| = 0$
                $\Rightarrow$ For $n < 0$, $|n| = n$

Example #1: $|0| = 0$

Example #2: $|5| = 5$

Example #3: $|-5| = 5$

Example #4: $-|-5| = -(5) = -5$

Example #5: $||2 - 5| + 6 - 14|| = ||-3| + 6 - 14|| = |3 + 6 - 14| = |9 - 14| = |-5| = 5$

Example #6: $|-5| \times |4| + |-12| \div 2 = (5 \times 4) + (12 \div 2) = 20 + 6 = 26$

1.3: BASIC ARITHMETIC OPERATIONS:

1.3.1: ADDITION OF NUMBERS:

Addition is the operation that finds the sum of two or more numbers, including the sum of signed numbers. It is the process of finding a single number, which is equal to two or more given numbers added together. The single number obtained by adding two or more numbers is called their **sum** or **total**.

TERMS USED IN ADDITION:

(A) Addends: the numbers that are being added are called the **addends**.
(B) Sum: the solution to an addition problem is called the **sum** or **total**.
Symbol for Addition: The symbol for addition is (+) and is read as **"plus"**; and when placed before a number denotes that the number is to be added.
For instance, $a + b$ which is read as "a" plus "b" means that "a" is to be added to "b".

EZ RULE: $a + b = c$ $\Rightarrow a$ & b = addends   **For Example:** $9 + 7 = 16$ $\Rightarrow 9$ & 7 = addends
                        $\Rightarrow c$ = sum or total $\Rightarrow 16$ = sum or total

EZ NOTE: The addends of a sum can be taken in any order, i.e., the addends are interchangeable.

1.3.1.1: ADDITION OF TWO NUMBERS WITH LIKE SIGNS:

EZ STEP-BY-STEP METHOD: Apply the following step(s) to find the sum of two numbers with like signs, i.e., either both positive or negative:

STEP 1: Add the absolute values of the two numbers.

STEP 2: Next, write the result preceded by the common sign, i.e., with a plus (+) or (−) sign.
Note: The sign of the sum is the same as the sign of the numbers being added.

EZ RULE: The addition of two *positive* numbers is *positive* $\Rightarrow$ **(+) + (+) = (+)**
                     The addition of two *negative* numbers is *negative* $\Rightarrow$ **(−) + (−) = (−)**

Example #1: $2 + 5 = 7$
                         $\Rightarrow$ On a number line begin at +2, move 5 units in the positive (right) direction; and you'll end up at +7
Example #2: $(−2) + (−5) = −7$
                         $\Rightarrow$ On a number line begin at −2, move 5 units in the negative (left) direction; and you will end up at −7

1.3.1.2: ADDITION OF TWO NUMBERS WITH UNLIKE SIGNS:

EZ STEP-BY-STEP METHOD: Apply the following step(s) to find the sum of two numbers with unlike signs, i.e., one positive and the other negative:

STEP 1: Find the difference between the absolute values of the two numbers, i.e., subtract the absolute value of the number with the smaller absolute value from the absolute value of the number with the larger absolute value.

STEP 2: Next, write the result preceded by the sign of the number with the larger absolute value.
Note: The sign of the sum is the same as the sign of the number that is larger in absolute value.

EZ RULE: Subtract the smaller number from the bigger number, and put the sign of the bigger number $\Rightarrow$ **(+) + (−) = ±**

Example #1: $(−2) + 7 = 5$
                         $\Rightarrow$ The difference between 2 and 7 is 5, and the sign of the bigger number is (+) positive.
                         $\Rightarrow$ On a number line begin at −2, move 7 units in the positive (right) direction; and you will end up at +5
Example #2: $2 + (−7) = −5$
                         $\Rightarrow$ The difference between 2 and 7 is 5, and the sign of the bigger number is (−) negative.
                         $\Rightarrow$ On a number line begin at +2, move 7 units in the negative (left) direction; and you will end up at −5

Addition of Two Opposite Signed Numbers with the Same Absolute Value: When two opposite signed numbers with the same absolute value are added, the sum is zero.

EZ RULE: $(+n) + (-n) = 0$
Example 1: $(7) + (-7) = 0$ **Example 2:** $(5) + (-5) = 0$

1.3.1.3: ADDITION OF MORE THAN TWO NUMBERS WITH DIFFERENT SIGNS:

EZ STEP-BY-STEP METHOD: Apply the following step(s) to add more than two numbers with different signs:

STEP 1: First, group and add all the positive numbers $\Rightarrow$ the result is positive – use rules in 1.3.1.

STEP 2: Next, group and add all the negative numbers $\Rightarrow$ the result is negative – use rules in 1.3.1.

STEP 3: Finally, add the result of step 1 to the result of step 2 by using the rules given above.

EZ RULE: $(+) + (-) + (+) + (-)$
  $\Rightarrow [(+) + (+)] + [(-) + (-)]$ [Group all the positive and negative numbers]
  $\Rightarrow (+) + (-)$ [Add all the positive numbers and negative numbers]
  $\Rightarrow \pm$ [Find the difference between the two numbers and put the sign of the bigger number]

Alternately, if you are adding more than two signed numbers, you can also do so by adding the numbers from left to right, by adding the first number to the second number, and then adding the result to the third number and so on until the final result is reached.

Example #1: $20 + (-10) + 65 + (-15) \Rightarrow (20 + 65) + (-10 - 15) = 85 + (-25) = 60$
Example #2: $27 + (-12) + 69 + (-17) \Rightarrow (27 + 69) + (-12 - 17) = 96 + (-29) = 67$

1.3.2: SUBTRACTION OF NUMBERS:

Subtraction is the operation that finds the difference between two numbers, including the difference between signed numbers. It is the process of finding a single number, which is left when a number is taken or subtracted from another number. The single number obtained by subtracting two numbers is called their **difference**.

TERMS USED IN SUBTRACTION:

(A) Minuend: the number from which something is subtracted is the **minuend**.
(B) Subtrahend: the number being subtracted is the **subtrahend**.
(C) Difference: the answer is the *difference*.
Symbol for Subtraction: The symbol for subtraction is (–) and is read as **"minus"**; and when placed before a number denotes that the number is to be subtracted.
For instance, $a - b$ which is read as "a" minus "b" means that "b" is to be taken or subtracted from "a".

EZ RULE: $a - b = c$ $\Rightarrow a$ = minuend   **For Example:** $9 - 7 = 2$ $\Rightarrow 9$ = minuend
                  $\Rightarrow b$ = subtrahend $\Rightarrow 7$ = subtrahend
                  $\Rightarrow c$ = difference $\Rightarrow 2$ = difference

EZ NOTE: The numbers of a subtraction cannot be taken in any order, i.e., the minuend and the subtrahend are not interchangeable.

1.3.2.1: SUBTRACTION OF TWO NUMBERS WITH LIKE OR UNLIKE SIGNS:

EZ STEP-BY-STEP METHOD: Apply the following step(s) to subtract number "b" from another number "a", where "a" and "b" can have like or unlike signs:

STEP 1: Change the sign of the number you are subtracting, the subtrahend $\Rightarrow$ i.e., Reverse the sign of "b".

STEP 2: Next, add the result to the number being subtracted from, the minuend $\Rightarrow$ i.e., Add the result to "a".
Note: To add in step 2, use the same rules explained in preceding section.

EZ RULE: $(a) - (b) = (a) + (-b)$ **For Example:** $(7) - (2) = (7) + (-2) = 5$
          $(a) - (-b) = (a) + (b)$ **For Example:** $(7) - (-2) = (7) + (+2) = 9$
          $(-a) - (b) = (-a) + (-b)$ **For Example:** $(-7) - (2) = (-7) + (-2) = -9$
          $(-a) - (-b) = (-a) + (b)$ **For Example:** $(-7) - (-2) = (-7) + (+2) = -5$

EZ TIP: Subtracting a negative number is the same as adding a positive number.

A quick way to subtract signed numbers accurately involves placing the numbers in columns, reversing the sign of the number being subtracted, and then adding the two. Subtraction is the inverse (opposite) operation of addition; subtracting a number is the same as adding its inverse. To subtract signed numbers, rewrite the subtraction problem as an addition problem, change the operation symbol to addition and change the sign on the number being subtracted. Then apply the rules for addition of signed numbers.

Double Negative = Positive: A double negative occurs when a negative sign is preceded by a negative number, which already has its own negative sign. Double minus yields a plus.

EZ HINT ⇒ We subtract a positive number by adding a negative number of the same absolute value.
⇒ We subtract a negative number by adding a positive number with the same absolute value.

USING THE NUMBER LINE TO SUBTRACT SIGNED NUMBERS:
When subtracting signed numbers, it may be helpful to refer to the number line. We give the sign to the difference that represents the direction we are moving along the number line, from the number being subtracted to the number from which you are subtracting.

WHEN SUBTRACTING SIGNED NUMBERS:
(A) The distance between the two numbers gives us the absolute value of the difference.
(B) The direction in which we have to move from the number being subtracted, to get the number from which we are subtracting, gives us the sign of the difference.
⇒ Movement in positive direction results in a (+) sign
⇒ Movement in negative direction results in (−) sign
For example, if we subtract +2 from +7, we can use the number line to see that the difference is +5. In this case, since we are subtracting +2 from +7, we count five units in a positive direction from +2 to +7 on the number line. Distance on number line between +2 and +7 is 5 units. Direction is from +2 to +7, which is a positive direction. Therefore, the answer is +5

1.3.3: MULTIPLICATION OF NUMBERS:
Multiplication is the operation that finds the product of two or more numbers, including the product of signed numbers. It is the short process of finding a single number, which is equal to the sum of a given number of repetitions of the same number. The single number obtained by multiplying two or more numbers is called their *product*.

TERMS USED IN MULTIPLICATION:
(A) Multiplicand: The number to be repeated or multiplied is called the *multiplicand*.
(B) Multiplier: The number which indicates how often the multiplicand is to be repeated is called the *multiplier*.
(C) Product: the answer is called the *product*. It's the sum of the repetitions.
Symbol for Multiplication: The symbol for multiplication is (×) and is read as *"times"*; and when placed between two numbers denotes that the numbers are to be multiplied together.
For instance, $a \times b$ which is read as "a" times "b" means that "a" is to be multiplied by "b".

EZ RULE: $a \times b = c$ ⇒ a = multiplicand   **For Example:** $5 \times 2 = 10$ ⇒ 5   = multiplicand
⇒ b = multiplier   ⇒ 2   = multiplier
⇒ c = product   ⇒ 10   = product

EZ NOTE: The factors of a product can be taken in any order, i.e., the multiplicand and the multiplier are interchangeable.

Multiplication can be indicated in any one of the following ways:
(A) By Multiplication symbol: ⇒ $a \times b = n$ ⇒ $5 \times 2 = 10$
(B) By Dot: ⇒ $a \bullet b = n$ ⇒ $5 \bullet 2 = 10$
(C) By Parentheses: ⇒ $a(b) = n$ ⇒ $5(2) = 10$
(D) By Juxtaposition of symbols without any sign: $10ab$ ⇒ $10 \times a \times b$

1.3.3.1: MULTIPLICATION OF TWO NUMBERS WITH LIKE SIGNS:
EZ STEP-BY-STEP METHOD: Apply the following step(s) to multiply two numbers with like signs:
STEP 1: Multiply the absolute values of the two numbers.
STEP 2: Next, write the result (product) preceded by a positive sign, i.e., with a plus (+) sign.

EZ HINT: Multiplication of any two numbers with Like Signs, i.e., any two positive numbers or any two negative numbers is always positive.

EZ RULE: The multiplication of two positive numbers is positive   ⇒ **(+) × (+) = (+) For Example:** (2) × (5) = 10
The multiplication of two negative numbers is positive   ⇒ **(−) × (−) = (+) For Example:** (−2) × (−5) = 10

1.3.3.2: MULTIPLICATION OF TWO NUMBERS WITH UNLIKE SIGNS:
EZ STEP-BY-STEP METHOD: Apply the following step(s) to multiply two numbers with unlike signs:
STEP 1: Multiply the absolute values of the two numbers.
STEP 2: Next, write the result (product) with a negative (−) sign.

EZ HINT: Multiplication of any two numbers with Unlike Signs, i.e., any positive number and any negative number is always negative.

EZ RULE: The multiplication of a +ve by a −ve numbers is −ve   ⇒ **(+) × (−) = (−) For Example:** (2) (−5) = −10
The multiplication of a −ve by a +ve numbers is −ve   ⇒ **(−) × (+) = (−) For Example:** (−2) (5) = −10

1.3.3.3: MULTIPLICATION OF MORE THAN TWO NUMBERS:
EZ STEP-BY-STEP METHOD: Apply the following step(s) to multiply more than two numbers:
STEP 1: Multiply the first two factors as mentioned above.
STEP 2: Multiply the result of Step-1 by the third factor.
STEP 3: Multiply the result of Step-2 by the fourth factor.
STEP 4: Continue this process until you have used each factor.

Example #1:   (1) (2) (−5) (−7) = (2) (−5) (−7) = (−10) (−7) = 70
Example #2:   (2) (5) (−8) (−9) = (10) (−8) (−9) = (−80) (−9) = 720

SIGN OF THE PRODUCT WHEN MORE THAN TWO NUMBERS ARE MULTIPLIED:
To determine whether a product of more than two numbers is positive or negative, count the number of negative terms and use the following two rules:
(A) The Sign of the Product is Positive (+) ⇒ if there are even numbers of negative terms or there are no negative terms.
EZ RULE: An even number of negative signs will produce a positive answer:
⇒ (−) × (−) × (−) × (−) × (−) × (−) = (+)   ⇒ Six negative numbers result in a positive answer
For Example: (−2) × (−5) × (−1) × (−8) × (−9) × (−1) = 720

(B) The Sign of the Product is Negative (−) ⇒ if there are odd number of negative terms.
EZ RULE: An odd number of negative signs will produce a negative answer:
⇒ (−) × (−) × (−) × (−) × (−) = (−)   ⇒ Five negative signs result in a negative answer.
For Example: (−2) × (−5) × (−1) × (−8) × (−9) = −720

WHEN THE PRODUCT OF TWO OR MORE NUMBERS IS ZERO:
If the product of two or more numbers is 0, then at least one of them must be 0. Conversely, if one of the factors is zero, the product must be zero.
EZ RULE: For any number "n": n × 0 = 0
⇒ If ab = 0, then either a = 0 or b = 0   ⇒ If xyz = 0, then either x = 0 or y = 0 or z = 0

1.3.3.4: SHORT-CUT METHODS IN MULTIPLICATION:

(A) TO MULTIPLY BY NUMBERS THAT HAS ZEROS AT THE END:
EZ RULE: When there is a zero at the end of the multiplier or multiplicand or both – we may neglect the zeros, multiply only the remaining numbers, and finally add as many zeros to the product as we have neglected.
Example #1: 150×750 $= 15 \times 75$ $= 1125$ $= 112,500$
Example #2: $1,200 \times 9,600$ $= 12 \times 96$ $= 1152$ $= 11,520,000$

(B) TO MULTIPLY BY 5, 25, 125, 625
(i)   To multiply by 5 $\Rightarrow 5 =$ half of 10 $\Rightarrow$ add 1 zero and divide by 2
      For Example: $110 \times 5 = 1100 \div 2 = 550$
(ii)   To multiply by 25 $\Rightarrow 25 =$ quarter of 100 $\Rightarrow$ add 2 zero and divide by 4
      For Example: $110 \times 25 = 11000 \div 4 = 2750$
(iii)   To multiply by 125 $\Rightarrow 125 =$ eighth of 1,000 $\Rightarrow$ add 3 zero and divide by 8
      For Example: $110 \times 125 = 110000 \div 8 = 13,750$
(iv)   To multiply by 625 $\Rightarrow 625 =$ sixteenth of 10,000 $\Rightarrow$ add 4 zero and divide by 16
      For Example: $110 \times 625 = 1100000 \div 16 = 68,750$

(C) TO MULTIPLY BY 9, 99, 999, 9999, 99999, ETC.
EZ RULE: Place as many zeros to the right of the multiplicand as there are nines in the multiplier, and then from the result subtract the multiplicand itself.
(i)   To multiply by 9: $\Rightarrow 9 = 10 - 1$ $\Rightarrow$ add 1 zero & subtract the multiplicand
      For Example: $18 \times 9 = 180 - 18 = 162$
(ii)   To multiply by 99: $\Rightarrow 99 = 100 - 1$ $\Rightarrow$ add 2 zeroes & subtract the multiplicand
      For Example: $18 \times 99 = 1800 - 18 = 1,782$
(iii)   To multiply by 999: $\Rightarrow 999 = 1,000 - 1$ $\Rightarrow$ add 3 zeroes & subtract the multiplicand
      For Example: $18 \times 999 = 18000 - 18 = 17,982$
(iv)   To multiply by 9999: $\Rightarrow 9999 = 10,000 - 1$ $\Rightarrow$ add 4 zeroes & subtract the multiplicand
      For Example: $18 \times 9999 = 180000 - 18 = 179,982$
(v)   To multiply by 99999: $\Rightarrow 99999 = 100,000 - 1$ $\Rightarrow$ add 5 zeroes & subtract the multiplicand
      For Example: $18 \times 99999 = 1800000 - 18 = 1,799,982$
(vi)   To multiply by 999999: $\Rightarrow 999999 = 1000,000 - 1$ $\Rightarrow$ add 6 zeroes & subtract the multiplicand
      For Example: $18 \times 999999 = 18000000 - 18 = 17,999,982$

1.3.4: DIVISION OF NUMBERS:
Division is the operation that finds the division of two numbers, including the division of signed numbers. It is the short process of finding a single number, which is equal to the number of times one given number, called the **divisor** is contained in another given number, called the **dividend**. The number expressing the number of times the divisor is contained in the dividend is called the **quotient**. The excess of the dividend over the divisor, taken the greatest number of times that the dividend contains it exactly, is called the **remainder**.

TERMS USED IN DIVISION:
(A) Dividend: the number being divided is the **dividend**.
(B) Divisor: the number the dividend is divided by is the **divisor**.
(C) Quotient: the answer is the *quotient*.
(D) Remainder: any number leftover in the division is the **remainder**.
Symbol for Division: The symbol for division is ($\div$) and is read as **"divided by"**; and when placed between two numbers denote that the first number is to be divided by the second number.
For instance, $a \div b$ which is read as "a" divided by "b" means that "a" is to be divided by "b".

EZ RULE: $a \div b = c$ $\Rightarrow a =$ dividend   **For Example:** $10 \div 2 = 5$ $\Rightarrow 10$ = dividend
                                     $\Rightarrow b =$ divisor $\Rightarrow 2$ = divisor
                                     $\Rightarrow c =$ quotient $\Rightarrow 5$ = quotient
                                     $\Rightarrow 0 =$ remainder
Since $10 \div 2 = 5$ has no remainder $\Rightarrow$ 2 is called the "*divisor*" of 10

⇒ 10 is said to be "*divisible*" by 2

EZ NOTE: The numbers of a quotient cannot be taken in any order, i.e., the dividend and the divisor are not interchangeable.

REMAINDERS: The remainder is what is left over in a division problem.
⇒ A remainder is always smaller than the number we are dividing by   ⇒ In $(n \div a = b)$, remainder < a
⇒ A remainder is always equal to or greater than "zero"   ⇒ remainder ≥ 0
For Example: 11 divided by 5 is 2, with a remainder of 1.
⇒ This means that you can divide 11 into 2 equal parts, all of which have 5 units, plus 1 leftover unit. This also means how often 5 is contained in 11 with how many leftovers. Simply subtract 5 from 11, subtract it again and again from the remainder, and continue the process till a remainder less than 5 is obtained. It is obvious that 5 is contained in 11 two times with a left over of 1.

```
                   Quotient
     Divisor  )    Dividend
                      |
                   ------------------------
                   Remainder
```

BASIC RELATIONSHIP OR CONNECTION AMONG DIFFERENT TERMS IN DIVISION:
(A) Dividend is equal to the product of Divisor and Quotient plus any Remainder
⇒ Dividend = (Divisor × Quotient) + Remainder
(B) Dividend minus the Remainder is equal to the product of Divisor and Quotient:
⇒ Dividend – Remainder = (Divisor × Quotient)
(C) When there is an exact division, the remainder is 0, and in such cases, the above relationship becomes:
⇒ Dividend = (Divisor × Quotient)

1.3.4.1: DIVISION OF TWO NUMBERS WITH LIKE SIGNS:

EZ STEP-BY-STEP METHOD: Apply the following step(s) to divide two numbers with like signs:
STEP 1: Divide the absolute values of the two numbers.
STEP 2: Next, write the result (quotient) preceded by a positive sign, i.e., with a "plus" (+) sign.

EZ HINT: Division of any two numbers with Like Signs, i.e., any two positive numbers or any two negative numbers is always positive.

EZ RULE: The division of two *positive* numbers is *positive*   ⇒ **(+) ÷ (+) = (+)**   **For Example:** (10) ÷ (5) = 2
The division of two *negative* numbers is *positive*   ⇒ **(−) ÷ (−) = (+)**   **For Example:** (−10) ÷ (−5) = 2

1.3.4.2: DIVISION OF TWO NUMBERS WITH UNLIKE SIGNS:

EZ STEP-BY-STEP METHOD: Apply the following step(s) to divide two numbers with unlike signs:
STEP 1: Divide the absolute values of the two numbers.
STEP 2: Next, write the result (quotient) preceded by a negative sign, i.e., with a (−) minus sign.

EZ HINT: Division of any two numbers with Unlike Signs, i.e., any positive number and any negative number is always negative.

EZ RULE: The division of a +ve by a −ve numbers is −ve   ⇒ **(+) ÷ (−) = (−)**   **For Example:** (10) ÷ (−5) = −2
The division of a −ve by a +ve numbers is −ve   ⇒ **(−) ÷ (+) = (−)**   **For Example:** (−10) ÷ (5) = −2

DIVISION OF ZERO:
(A) We can never divide any given number "n" by 0, as it is not defined and is meaningless.
Any number "n" divided by zero is not defined   ⇒ $n \div 0$ = *not defined*   For example: $7 \div 0$ = *not defined*.
(B) However, we can divide zero by any other nonzero number "n", and the result will always be zero.
Zero divided by any number "n" is defined as 0 ⇒ $0 \div n = 0$ For example: $0 \div 7 = 0$

1.3.4.3: SHORT-CUT METHODS IN DIVISION:

(A) TO DIVIDE BY 5, 25, 125, 625
(i) To divide by 5: $\Rightarrow$ 5 = half of 10 $\Rightarrow$ multiply by 2 & move the decimal point 1 place to left
  For Example: 550 × 2 = 1100 = 1100 ÷ 10 = 110.0
(ii) To divide by 25: $\Rightarrow$ 25 = quarter of 100 $\Rightarrow$ multiply by 4 & move the decimal point 2 places to left
  For Example: 2750 × 4 = 11000 = 11000 ÷ 100 = 110.00
(iii) To divide by 125: $\Rightarrow$ 125 = eighth of 1,000 $\Rightarrow$ multiply by 8 & move the decimal point 3 places to left
  For Example: 13,750 × 8 = 110000 = 110000 ÷ 1,000 = 110.000
(iv) To divide by 625: $\Rightarrow$ 625 = sixteenth of 10,000 $\Rightarrow$ multiply by 16 & move the decimal point 4 places to left
  For Example: 68,750 × 16 = 1100000 = 1100000 ÷ 10,000 = 110.0000

1.3.5: MAKING ARITHMETIC OPERATIONS EASIER:

ARITHMETIC OPERATION WITH A NUMBER AND ITSELF:
#1: Any number added to itself is doubled $\Rightarrow n + n = 2n$ **For Example:** $5 + 5 = 5 \times 2 = 10$
#2: Any number subtracted from itself is zero $\Rightarrow n - n = 0$ **For Example:** $5 - 5 = 0$
#3: Any number multiplied by itself is squared $\Rightarrow n \times n = n^2$ **For Example:** $5 \times 5 = 5^2 = 25$
#4: Any number divided by itself is 1 $\Rightarrow n \div n = 1$ **For Example:** $5 \div 5 = 1$

MAKING ARITHMETIC PROBLEMS EASIER:
Many properties of arithmetic depend on the relationship between subtraction and addition, and between division and multiplication. Many problems involving subtraction and division can be simplified by changing them to addition and multiplication problems, respectively, in the following way:

EZ RULE: Subtracting a number is the same as adding its opposite $\Rightarrow a - b = a + (-b)$
Example: $7 - 5 = 7 + (-5) = 2$

EZ RULE: Dividing by a number is the same as multiplying by its reciprocal $\Rightarrow a \div b = a \times (1/b)$
Example: $5 \div 5/7 = 5 \times 7/5 = 7$

EZ RULE: Multiplying or Dividing a number by 1 does not change the sign:
  $\Rightarrow n \times (1) = n$ or $\Rightarrow -n \times (1) = -n$
Example: $5 \times 1 = 5$ or $-5 \times 1 = -5$
  $\Rightarrow n \div (1) = n$ or $\Rightarrow -n \div (1) = -n$
Example: $5 \div 1 = 5$ or $-5 \div 1 = -5$

EZ RULE: Multiplying or Dividing a number by −1 change the sign:
  $\Rightarrow n \times (-1) = -n$ or $\Rightarrow -n \times (-1) = n$ or $(a - b) \times (-1) = (-a + b) = (b - a)$
Example: $5 \times (-1) = -5$ or $-5 \times (-1) = -(-5) = 5$
  $\Rightarrow n \div (-1) = -n$ or $-n \div (-1) = n$
Example: $5 \div (-1) = -5$ or $-5 \div (-1) = -(-5) = 5$
Note: $0 \times (-1) = 0$

1.4: ORDER OF OPERATION:

When mathematical expression consists of more than one operation, its final value may depend on the order in which the operations are performed. To avoid errors and confusion, when simplifying a mathematical expression requires performing multiple operations, it is important to carry the operation in the following correct and proper order of operations:

1.4.1: PEMDAS:

PEMDAS is an acronym for the order in which mathematical operations should be performed as you move from left to right through an arithmetic or algebraic expression.

PEMDAS ⇒ **P**arentheses **E**xponents **M**ultiplication **D**ivision **A**ddition **S**ubtraction

EZ TIP: The following mnemonic is a quick & easy way to remember order of operations:
PEMDAS ⇒ **P**lease **E**xcuse **M**y **D**ear **A**unt **S**ally

P	**P**arentheses	⇒ First, perform all the operations that appears within the parentheses. If necessary, follow PEMDAS within parentheses. Note that absolute value signs are considered as parentheses as well. (Parentheses within parentheses take priority, work from the innermost out, or first solve for the smaller parentheses then the bigger parentheses).
E	**E**xponents	⇒ Next, solve all terms with exponents in the given expression.
M	**M**ultiplication	⇒ Next, perform all Multiplication/Division in order, straight-across from left-to-right, do the operation that comes first. (Note: Multiplication does not necessarily come before Division. So do not multiply first and then divide, do the operation that comes first from left to right).
D	**D**ivision	⇒ Next, perform all Multiplication/Division in order, straight-across from left-to-right, do the operation that comes first. (Note: Multiplication does not necessarily come before Division. So do not multiply first and then divide, do the operation that comes first from left to right).
A	**A**ddition	⇒ Next, perform all Additions/Subtractions in order, straight across from left-to-right, do the operation that comes first. (Note: Addition does not necessarily come before Subtraction. So do not add first and then subtract, do the operation that comes first from left to right).
S	**S**ubtraction	⇒ Next, perform all Additions/Subtractions in order, straight across from left-to-right, do the operation that comes first. (Note: Addition does not necessarily come before Subtraction. So do not add first and then subtract, do the operation that comes first from left to right).

EXPRESSION AND TERM:

Any collection of numbers connected by the signs (+) or (−) is called an **expression**.
The different parts of an expression separated by the (+) or (−) signs are called **terms**.

EZ RULE: $a + b − c − d$ is an expression and a, b, c, d are its terms.
Example: $9 + 7 − 5 − 2$ is an expression and 9, 7, 5, 2 are its terms.

TWO GOLDEN RULES OF ORDER OF OPERATION:

GOLDEN RULE #1:   When an expression involves multiplication and division: The operations of multiplication and division must be preformed in order from left to right.

RULE #1A: $\Rightarrow a \times b \div c \Rightarrow$ First multiply a by b, and then divide the result by c.

Example #1: $10 \times 5 \div 2$
$\Rightarrow 50 \div 2$ [Perform the operation of multiplication]
$\Rightarrow 25$ [Perform the operation of division]

Example #2: $10 \times 5 \div 25$
$\Rightarrow 50 \div 25$ [Perform the operation of multiplication]
$\Rightarrow 2$ [Perform the operation of division]

RULE #1B: $\Rightarrow a \div b \times c \Rightarrow$ First divide a by b, and then multiply the result by c.

Example #1: $10 \div 5 \times 2$
$\Rightarrow 2 \times 2$ [Perform the operation of division]
$\Rightarrow 4$ [Perform the operation of multiplication]

Example #2: $10 \div 5 \times 25$
$\Rightarrow 2 \times 25$ [Perform the operation of division]
$\Rightarrow 50$ [Perform the operation of multiplication]

GOLDEN RULE #2:   When an expression involves all or some of the signs $(+, -, \times, \div)$: The operations of multiplication and division must be preformed before those of addition and subtraction.
$\Rightarrow a \div b \times c + d - e$
$\Rightarrow$ First divide a by b, and then multiply the result by c; thereafter, add the result with d and subtract the result by e.

Example #1: $10 \times 5 \div 2 + 70 - 20$
$\Rightarrow 50 \div 2 + 70 - 20$ [Perform the operation of multiplication]
$\Rightarrow 25 + 70 - 20$ [Perform the operation of division]
$\Rightarrow 95 - 20$ [Perform the operation of addition]
$\Rightarrow 75$ [Perform the operation of subtraction]

Example #2: $10 \times 5 \div 25 + 70 - 20$
$\Rightarrow 50 \div 25 + 70 - 20$ [Perform the operation of multiplication]
$\Rightarrow 2 + 70 - 20$ [Perform the operation of division]
$\Rightarrow 72 - 20$ [Perform the operation of addition]
$\Rightarrow 52$ [Perform the operation of subtraction]

Example #3: $10 \div 5 \times 2 + 70 - 20$
$\Rightarrow 2 \times 2 + 70 - 20$ [Perform the operation of division]
$\Rightarrow 4 + 70 - 20$ [Perform the operation of multiplication]
$\Rightarrow 74 - 20$ [Perform the operation of addition]
$\Rightarrow 54$ [Perform the operation of subtraction]

Example #4: $10 \div 5 \times 25 + 70 - 20$
$\Rightarrow 2 \times 25 + 70 - 20$ [Perform the operation of division]
$\Rightarrow 50 + 70 - 20$ [Perform the operation of multiplication]
$\Rightarrow 120 - 20$ [Perform the operation of addition]
$\Rightarrow 100$ [Perform the operation of subtraction]

EXCEPTIONS TO PEMDAS RULES:

According to PEMDAS, you should always start with solving for what's inside the parentheses. However, there are some situations when you shouldn't start with what's in the parentheses.

Example #1:   What is the value of 8(100 − 1)?
Solution A: **Using PEMDAS:** If you followed the rules of PEMDAS, first solve within the parentheses and then multiply:
$\Rightarrow$ 8(100 − 1) = 8(99) = 792
Solution B: **Without using PEMDAS:** you can do the arithmetic quickly and more easily if you do it this way:
$\Rightarrow$ 8(100 − 1) = (8 × 100) − (8 × 1) = 800 − 8 = 792

Example #2:   What is the value of (88 + 64) ÷ 8?
Solution A: **Using PEMDAS:** If you followed the rules of PEMDAS, first add what's within the parentheses and then divide:
$\Rightarrow$ (88 + 64) ÷ 8 = 152 ÷ 8 = 19
Solution B: **Without using PEMDAS:** you can do the arithmetic quickly and more easily if you do it this way:
$\Rightarrow$ (88 + 64) ÷ 8 = (88 ÷ 8) + (64 ÷ 8) = 11 + 8 = 19

EZ TIP: We can solve these problems either way, but by using the rules of PEMDAS in this case is definitely more difficult and time-consuming than doing it the other way.
Both of these examples demonstrate the use and importance of the distributive law explained in the next section.

Some other exceptions to PEMDAS:
- At times, you can get rid of the parentheses indirectly, by using the distributive law first.
- You might also perform a series of additions or subtractions within a set of parentheses in backward order (from right to left).

EZ NOTE: PEMDAS is to be used in conjunction with the laws explained in the next section.

1.4.2: PARENTHESES & BRACKETS:

Multiple parentheses or brackets can sometimes get confusing. Following is the explanation of all that you need to know about parentheses and brackets:

Parentheses or Brackets denote that the expression enclosed within them is to be treated as a single and separate quantity. The operation within the parentheses gets the first preference and must be carried out first. Ignoring the parentheses can completely change the value of an expression.

EZ RULE: $a \times (b + c) \neq a \times b + c$
$\Rightarrow$ First add b and c, and then multiply the result by a. Observe that multiplying a by b and then adding the result to c results in an entirely different and incorrect value.
For Example: 2 × (5 + 7)   ≠   2 × 5 + 7
2 × 12   ≠   10 + 7
24   ≠   17

TYPES OF BRACKETS:
(A) Circular Brackets or Parentheses: ( )
(B) Curly Brackets   { }
(C) Square Brackets   [ ]

Correct Hierarchy: [{   (   )   }   ]
$\Rightarrow$ Work your way from the innermost or the smallest to the outermost or the largest.

REMOVAL OF PARENTHESES OR BRACKETS:

The sign outside parentheses is distributed across the parentheses, so every number within the parentheses should be multiplied by that sign. Always remember that multiplication with a positive sign does not change the sign of the product but multiplication with a negative sign changes the sign of the product to its opposite sign.

(A) When a Parentheses is Preceded by the Positive (+) Sign: the parentheses may be removed without making any change in the expression.

EZ RULE: $a + (b + c) = a + b + c$ **For Example:** $5 + (9 + 2) \Rightarrow 5 + 9 + 2 = 16$
              $a + (b - c) = a + b - c$ $5 + (9 - 2) \Rightarrow 5 + 9 - 2 = 12$

(B) When a Parentheses is Preceded by the Negative (–) Sign: the parentheses may be removed, but then the sign of every term within the parentheses has to be changed to its opposite sign.

EZ RULE: $a - (b + c) = a - b - c$ **For Example:** $9 - (5 + 2) \Rightarrow 9 - 5 - 2 = 2$
              $a - (b - c) = a - b + c$ $9 - (5 - 2) \Rightarrow 9 - 5 + 2 = 6$

(C) Two Negatives Results in a Positive: Students often are not able to understand or comprehend the dilemma of how two negatives can result in a positive. The concept can be illustrated with two simple rules:

EZ RULE: $-(-a) = +a$ **For Example:** $-(-7) \Rightarrow +7$

Let's say we have $-(-7)$; think of this as a removal of a loss of 7; now obviously removal of loss is actually a profit; therefore, add 7.

EZ RULE: $a - (-b) = a + b$ **For Example:** $9 - (-2) \Rightarrow 9 + 2 = 11$

Let's say we have $9 - (-2)$; think of this as a profit of 9 and the removal of a loss of 2; now obviously removal of loss is in turn a profit; therefore, add 9 to 2.

(D) Parentheses within Parentheses: When there are parentheses within parentheses or smaller brackets within bigger brackets: it is best to remove the innermost parentheses first, then the next innermost, or remove the smallest bracket first, then the next smallest, and so on.

EZ RULE: $(e + (c + (a - b) + d) + f)$ OR $[e + \{c + (a - b) + d\} + f]$
              $\Rightarrow$ Add the difference of a and b to sum of c and d to sum of e and f

For Example: $(9 + (7 + (18 - 17) + 2) + 6)$ OR $[9 + \{7 + (18 - 17) + 2\} + 6]$
                  $\Rightarrow (9 + (7 + (1) + 2) + 6)$ $\Rightarrow [9 + \{7 + (1) + 2\} + 6]$
                  $\Rightarrow (9 + (10) + 6)$ $\Rightarrow [9 + \{10\} + 6]$
                  $\Rightarrow (9 + 10 + 6)$ $\Rightarrow [9 + 10 + 6]$
                  $\Rightarrow 25$ $\Rightarrow 25$

MISCELLANEOUS EXAMPLES:

The best way to understand how to apply Order of Operation is by carefully studying the following miscellaneous examples:

Example #1a: $8 + 2 \times 5$
                  $\Rightarrow 8 + 10$ [Perform the operation of multiplication]
                  $\Rightarrow 18$ [Perform the operation of addition]

Example #1b: $(8 + 2) \times 5$
                  $\Rightarrow 10 \times 5$ [Perform the operation of addition within parentheses]
                  $\Rightarrow 50$ [Perform the operation of multiplication]

Example #2a: $2 + 8 \div 2$
                  $\Rightarrow 2 + 4$ [Perform the operation of division]
                  $\Rightarrow 6$ [Perform the operation of addition]

Example #2b: $(2 + 8) \div 2$
                  $\Rightarrow 10 \div 2$ [Perform the operation of addition within parentheses]
                  $\Rightarrow 5$ [Perform the operation of division]

Example #3a: $50 \div 2 \times 5$
       $\Rightarrow 25 \times 5$ [Perform the operation of division]
       $\Rightarrow 125$ [Perform the operation of multiplication]

Example #3b: $50 \div (2 \times 5)$
       $\Rightarrow 50 \div 10$ [Perform the operation of multiplication within parentheses]
       $\Rightarrow 5$ [Perform the operation of division]

Example #4a: $5 \times 50 \div 2$
       $\Rightarrow 250 \div 2$ [Perform the operation of multiplication]
       $\Rightarrow 125$ [Perform the operation of division]

Example #4b: $5 \times (50 \div 2)$
       $\Rightarrow 5 \times 25$ [Perform the operation of division within parentheses]
       $\Rightarrow 125$ [Perform the operation of multiplication]

Example #5a: $5 + 5 \div 5 + 5$
       $\Rightarrow 5 + 1 + 5$ [Perform the operation of division]
       $\Rightarrow 11$ [Perform the operation of addition]

Example #5b: $(5 + 5) \div (5 + 5)$
       $\Rightarrow 10 \div 10$ [Perform the operation of addition within parentheses]
       $\Rightarrow 1$ [Perform the operation of division]

Example #6a: 5×2^3
       $\Rightarrow 5 \times 8$ [Perform the operation of exponent]
       $\Rightarrow 40$ [Perform the operation of multiplication]

Example #6b: $(5 \times 2)^3$
       $\Rightarrow 10^3$ [Perform the operation of multiplication within parentheses]
       $\Rightarrow 1000$ [Perform the operation of exponent]

Example #7: $20 \times 10 \div 2 + (25 \div 5 \times 2 + 60 - 20)$
       $\Rightarrow 20 \times 10 \div 2 + (5 \times 2 + 60 - 20)$ [Perform the operation of division within parentheses]
       $\Rightarrow 20 \times 10 \div 2 + (10 + 60 - 20)$ [Perform the operation of multiplication within parentheses]
       $\Rightarrow 20 \times 10 \div 2 + (70 - 20)$ [Perform the operation of addition within parentheses]
       $\Rightarrow 20 \times 10 \div 2 + (50)$ [Perform the operation of subtraction within parentheses]
       $\Rightarrow 200 \div 2 + (50)$ [Perform the operation of multiplication]
       $\Rightarrow 100 + 50$ [Perform the operation of division]
       $\Rightarrow 150$ [Perform the operation of addition]

Example #8: $10^2 \div 5 - 50 + 2(5^2 \div 5 \times 10 + 70)$
       $\Rightarrow 10^2 \div 5 - 50 + 2(25 \div 5 \times 10 + 70)$ [Perform the operation of exponent within parentheses]
       $\Rightarrow 10^2 \div 5 - 50 + 2(5 \times 10 + 70)$ [Perform the operation of division within parentheses]
       $\Rightarrow 10^2 \div 5 - 50 + 2(50 + 70)$ [Perform the operation of multiplication within parentheses]
       $\Rightarrow 10^2 \div 5 - 50 + 2(120)$ [Perform the operation of addition within parentheses]
       $\Rightarrow 100 \div 5 - 50 + 2(120)$ [Perform the operation of exponent]
       $\Rightarrow 20 - 50 + 2(120)$ [Perform the operation of division]
       $\Rightarrow 20 - 50 + 240$ [Perform the operation of multiplication]
       $\Rightarrow 260 - 50$ [Perform the operation of addition]
       $\Rightarrow 210$ [Perform the operation of subtraction]

1.5: LAWS OF OPERATIONS:

1.5.1: COMMUTATIVE LAW OF OPERATION:

Commutative Law of Operation states that addition or multiplication operations can be performed in any order without changing their result. In other words, addition and multiplication are both commutative, i.e., it doesn't matter in what order the operation is performed.

EZ RULE: $\Rightarrow (a + b) = (b + a)$ **For Example:** $(2 + 5) = (5 + 2)$ $\Rightarrow$ both results in the same answer 7

$\Rightarrow (a \times b) = (b \times a)$ **For Example:** $(2 \times 5) = (5 \times 2)$ $\Rightarrow$ both results in the same answer 10

EZ NOTE: Commutative Law of Operation does NOT apply for subtraction or division. Changing the order within a subtraction or division operation may affect the result. In other words, subtraction and division are not commutative, i.e., it does matter in what order the operation is performed.

$\Rightarrow (a - b) \neq (b - a)$ **For Example:** $7 - 2 \neq 2 - 7$ $\Rightarrow$ both results in different answers

$\Rightarrow (a \div b) \neq (b \div a)$ **For Example:** $10 \div 2 \neq 2 \div 10$ $\Rightarrow$ both results in different answers

1.5.2: ASSOCIATIVE LAW OF OPERATION:

Associative Law of Operation states that addition or multiplication operations can be regrouped in any order. In other words, if a problem involves only addition or only multiplication, the parentheses may be changed without affecting the result. Parentheses act like grouping symbols that indicate operations to be done first. Therefore, addition and multiplication are associative, i.e., the terms or the operations can be regrouped in any order without changing the results.

EZ RULE: $\Rightarrow (a + b) + c = a + (b + c)$ **For Example:** $(25 + 50) + 75 = 25 + (50 + 75)$

$\Rightarrow$ both results in 150

$\Rightarrow (a+b+c+d) = (a+b) + (c+d) = (a+c) + (b+d)$ **For Example:** $(25+20+75+80) = (25+75)+(20+80)$

$\Rightarrow$ both results in 200

$\Rightarrow (a \times b) \times c = a \times (b \times c)$ **For Example:** $(2 \times 5) \times 20 = 2 \times (5 \times 20)$

$\Rightarrow$ both results in 200

$\Rightarrow (a \times b \times c \times d) = (a \times b) \times (c \times d) = (a \times c) \times (b \times d)$ **For Example:** $(2 \times 5 \times 20 \times 25) = (5 \times 20) \times (2 \times 25)$

$\Rightarrow$ both results in 5,000

EZ NOTE: Associate Law of Operation does NOT apply for subtraction or division. Subtraction or Division operations cannot be regrouped in any order. In other words, if a problem involves subtraction or division, the parentheses may not be changed without affecting the result. Operations within parentheses must be performed first. Therefore, subtraction and multiplication are not associative, i.e., the terms cannot be regrouped without changing the results.

$\Rightarrow a - (b - c) \neq (a - b) - c$ **For Example:** $9 - (7 - 5) \neq (9 - 7) - 5$ $\Rightarrow$ both results in different answers

$\Rightarrow a \div (b \div c) \neq (a \div b) \div c$ **For Example:** $20 \div (10 \div 5) \neq (20 \div 10) \div 5$ $\Rightarrow$ both results in different answers

1.5.3: DISTRIBUTIVE LAW OF OPERATION:

Distributive Law of Operation states that factors can be distributed across the terms being added or subtracted. In other words, the distributive law allows us to "distribute" a factor among the terms being added or subtracted.

DISTRIBUTIVE LAW OVER ADDITION:

If a sum is to be multiplied/divided by a number, instead of adding first and then multiplying/dividing, each addend may be multiplied/divided by the number and the products can then be added. In other words, multiplication and division are distributive, i.e., factors and divisors can be distributed across terms being added.

EZ RULE #1: $a(b + c) = (a \times b) + (a \times c)$ **For Example:** $2(5 + 7) = (2 \times 5) + (2 \times 7)$ $\Rightarrow$ both results in 24

EZ RULE #2: $\dfrac{b+c}{a} = \dfrac{b}{a} + \dfrac{c}{a}$ **For Example:** $\dfrac{5+7}{2} = \dfrac{5}{2} + \dfrac{7}{2}$ $\Rightarrow$ both results in 6

For any real numbers a, b, and c, where $a \neq 0$

DISTRIBUTIVE LAW OVER SUBTRACTION:

If a difference is to be multiplied/divided by a number, instead of subtracting first and then multiplying/dividing, the minuend and the subtrahend may be multiplied/divided by the number and the products can then be subtracted. In other words, multiplication and division are distributive, i.e., factors and divisors can be distributed across terms being subtracted.

EZ RULE #1: $a(b - c) = (a \times b) - (a \times c)$ **For Example:** $2(5 - 7) = (2 \times 5) - (2 \times 7)$ $\Rightarrow$ both results in -4

EZ RULE #2: $\dfrac{b - c}{a} = \dfrac{b}{a} - \dfrac{c}{a}$ **For Example:** $\dfrac{5 - 7}{2} = \dfrac{5}{2} - \dfrac{7}{2}$ $\Rightarrow$ both results in -1

For any real numbers a, b, and c, where $a \neq 0$

DISTRIBUTIVE PROPERTY WORKS IN BOTH DIRECTIONS:

Distributive property also works in the other direction.

EZ RULE #1: $(a \times b) + (a \times c) = a(b + c) = (a \times b) + (a \times c)$

EZ RULE #2: $(a \times b) - (a \times c) = a(b - c) = (a \times b) - (a \times c)$

EZ TIP: We can use distributive law with multiplication as well as division.

EZ NOTE: Be careful, when the sum or difference is in the denominator, no distribution is applicable.

$\Rightarrow \dfrac{a}{b + c} \neq \dfrac{a}{b} + \dfrac{a}{c}$ **For Example:** $\dfrac{2}{5 + 7} \neq \dfrac{2}{5} + \dfrac{2}{7}$ $\Rightarrow$ both results in different answers

EZ NOTE: All of the above laws are not only applicable to integers, but they also apply to fractions and decimals as well.

1.6: DIVISIBILITY TESTS:

Some questions may test you to determine whether you know if one number is divisible by another, so it is important to understand and memorize these rules. To check divisibility, you can either take the long-way by doing the necessary division by hand to see if the result is a whole number, or you can give yourself a shortcut and memorize our easy divisibility rules. There are various divisibility tests that are important **"shortcuts"** for determining if one integer is divisible by another.

Meaning of the term "*divisible by*": The term "divisible by" means divisible by "without any remainder or left-over" or "with a remainder of zero."
⇒ When we say that an integer N is divisible by an integer x, we mean that N divided by x yields a zero remainder.
For instance: 12 is divisible by 2 because 12 divided by 2 is 6 with a remainder of 0.
12 is not divisible by 5 because 12 divided by 5 is 2 with a remainder of 2.
Alternately, we can also say that 2 is a divisor or a factor of 12.
Remainder: If a number cannot be divided evenly by another number, any remaining number that is left over at the end of division is called the remainder.

1.6.1: GENERAL DIVISIBILITY TESTS:

(A) DIVISIBILITY TEST FOR 1:

EZ RULE: Any integer, that is, any number without a fractional or decimal value attached to it, is evenly divisible by 1.
            Set of numbers divisible by 1: {−1, 0, 1, 2, 3, 4, 5, 79, 96, 101, 1769.......}
Example #1:   9 is divisible by 1 because it's a whole number.
Example #2:   9.5 is not divisible by 1 because it's not a whole number.

(B) DIVISIBILITY TEST FOR 2:

EZ RULE: A number is evenly divisible by 2 if its unit's digit (last digit) is divisible by 2 or is a multiple of 2. In fact, divisibility by 2 is the definition of an even number; hence all even numbers are divisible by 2.
EZ TIP: A number is divisible by 2 if its last digit is 0, 2, 4, 6, or 8.
Set of numbers divisible by 2: {2, 12, 54, 76, 98, 100, 1578, 25796, 579152.......}
Example #1:   1,578 is divisible by 2 because its last digit 8 is divisible by 2.
Example #2:   1,587 is not divisible by 2 because its last digit 7 is not divisible by 2.

(C) DIVISIBILITY TEST FOR 3:

EZ RULE: A number is evenly divisible by 3 if the sum of all its digits is divisible by 3 or is a multiple of 3.
Set of numbers divisible by 3: {3, 9, 12, 18, 27, 36, 45, 72, 576, 756, 1575.......}
Example #1:   1,575 is divisible by 3 because the sum of all its digits: 1 + 5 + 7 + 5 = 18, and 18 is divisible by 3.
Example #2:   572 is not divisible by 3 because the sum of all its digits: 5 + 7 + 2 = 14, and 14 is not divisible by 3.

(D) DIVISIBILITY TEST FOR 4:

EZ RULE: A number is evenly divisible by 4 if the number made by its ten's and unit's digit (last two digits) is divisible by 4 or is a multiple of 4.
Alternately, a number is evenly divisible by 4 if it's divisible by 2 TWICE, i.e., if it can be cut in half two times.
Set of number divisible by 4: {4, 16, 112, 284, 588, 792, 8596, 97528.......}
Example #1:   792 is divisible by 4 because its last two digits 92 is divisible by 4.
            ⇒ 792 is divisible by 2 twice: once – 396; twice – 198.
Example #2:   726 is not divisible by 4 because its last two digits 26 is not divisible by 4.
            ⇒ 726 is divisible by 2 once: once – 363; twice – not divisible.

(E) DIVISIBILITY TEST FOR 5:

EZ RULE: A number is evenly divisible by 5 if its last digit (unit's digit) is either 0 or 5.
Set of numbers divisible by 5: {5, 75, 195, 265, 5265, 72590, 957210.......}
Example #1:   5265 is divisible by 5 because its last digit is 5.
Example #2:   7519 is not divisible by 5 because its last digit is not either 0 or 5.

(F) DIVISIBILITY TEST FOR 6:

EZ RULE: A number is evenly divisible by 6 if it is divisible by both 2 as well as 3; i.e., if its last digit is divisible by 2 and if the sum of its digits is divisible by 3.

Set of numbers divisible by 6: {6, 72, 126, 246, 576, 75924.......}

Example #1:   576 is divisible by 6, because it's divisible by 2 (since its last digit 6 is divisible by 2) and by 3 (since the sum of its digits: 5 + 7 + 6 = 18 is divisible by 3).

Example #2:   796 is not divisible by 6, because although it's divisible by 2 (since its last digit 6 is divisible by 2) however, it's not divisible by 3 (since the sum of its digits: 7 + 9 + 6 = 22 is not divisible by 3).

EZ NOTE: There is no divisibility test for 7.

(G) DIVISIBILITY TEST FOR 8:

EZ RULE: A number is evenly divisible by 8 if the last three digits are divisible by 8 or if it's divisible by 2 THRICE, i.e., if it can be cut in half three times.

Set of number divisible by 8: {8, 16, 112, 288, 592, 792, 8568, 97528.......}

Example #1:   792 is divisible by 8 because it's divisible by 2 thrice: once – 396; twice – 198; thrice – 99.

Example #2:   724 is not divisible by 8 because it's divisible by 2 only twice: once – 362; twice - 181; thrice – not divisible.

(H) DIVISIBILITY TEST FOR 9:

EZ RULE: A number is evenly divisible by 9 if the sum of its digits is divisible by 9 or is a multiple of 9.

Set of numbers divisible by 9: {9, 18, 27, 36, 45, 54, 63, 72, 81, 126, 252, 765, 1125, 726291.......}

Example 1:   765 is divisible by 9 because the sum of its digits: 7 + 6 + 5 = 18, and 18 is divisible by 9.

Example 2:   929 is not divisible by 9 because the sum of its digits: 9 + 2 + 9 = 20, and 20 is not divisible by 9.

(I) DIVISIBILITY TEST FOR 10:

EZ RULE: A number is evenly divisible by 10 if its last digit (unit's digit) is a zero.

Set of numbers divisible by 10: {10, 250, 5720, 72590, 927510.......}

Example #1:   72,590 is divisible by 10 because its last digit is 0.

Example #2:   70,205 is not divisible by 10 because its last digit is not 0.

(J) DIVISIBILITY TEST FOR 12:

EZ RULE: A number is evenly divisible by 12 if the sum of its digits is divisible by 3 or is a multiple of 3 and its last two digits are divisible by 4 or is a multiple of 4.

Set of numbers divisible by 12: {12, 144, 180, 192, 216, 780.......}

Example #1:   192 is divisible by 12 because the sum of its digits 1 + 9 + 2 = 12 is divisible by 3, and its last two digits 92 is divisible by 4.

Example #2:   195 is not divisible by 12 because although the sum of its digits 1 + 9 + 5 = 15 is divisible by 3; however, its last two digits 95 is not divisible by 4.

THE LAST DIGIT SHORTCUT:

There is a shortcut to find the last digit of the product of a series of numbers without actually multiplying all the numbers. The key is to solve the problem step-by-step instead of actually multiplying all the numbers in a series.

⇒ First, pair easy-to-multiply numbers and find their products, these will be your intermediary products.
⇒ Next, keep the last digit of these intermediate products and drop all other digits.
⇒ Then, multiply the last digits of the intermediate products found, this will be your secondary product.
⇒ Finally, keep the last digit of the secondary product and drop all other digits.
⇒ This last digit of the secondary products is the last digit of the product of a series of numbers.

Example #1:   What is the units digit of 1 × 2 × 6 × 9 × 11?
First, pair easy-to-multiply numbers and find their products:
⇒ 1 × 2 × 6 = 12   ⇒ Drop all the digits and keep only the last digit   ⇒ 2
⇒ 9 × 11 = 99   ⇒ Drop all the digits and keep only the last digit   ⇒ 9
Next, multiply the last digits of the products above:

$\Rightarrow 2 \times 9 = 18$ $\Rightarrow$ Drop all the digits and keep only the last digit $\Rightarrow 8$
Therefore, the last digit of the product of the given expression is 8

Example #2:   What is the units digit of $(2)^6 (5)^2 (9)^2$?
First, multiply all the individual exponents:
$\Rightarrow (2)^6 = 2 \times 2 \times 2 \times 2 \times 2 \times 2 = 64$ $\Rightarrow$ Drop all the digits and keep only the last digit $\Rightarrow 4$
$\Rightarrow (5)^2 = 5 \times 5 = 25$ $\Rightarrow$ Drop all the digits and keep only the last digit $\Rightarrow 5$
$\Rightarrow (9)^2 = 9 \times 9 = 81$ $\Rightarrow$ Drop all the digits and keep only the last digit $\Rightarrow 1$
Next, multiply the last digits of the products above:
$\Rightarrow 4 \times 5 \times 1 = 20 \Rightarrow$ Drop all the digits and keep only the last digit $\Rightarrow 0$
Therefore, the last digit of the product of the given expression is 0

1.6.2: DIVISIBILITY RULES OF CONSECUTIVE INTEGERS:

PRODUCTS OF SET OF CONSECUTIVE INTEGERS:

EZ RULE: If there is any set of n number of consecutive integers, then the product of all those n integers is always divisible by n, or is always a multiple of n.
In other words, for any set of consecutive integers, the product of all the integers is always divisible by the number of terms, or is always a multiple of the number of terms.
For instance $\Rightarrow$ The product of any set of 3 consecutive integers will be divisible by 3
$\Rightarrow$ The product of any set of 4 consecutive integers will be divisible by 4
$\Rightarrow$ The product of any set of 5 consecutive integers will be divisible by 5
$\Rightarrow$ The product of any set of 6 consecutive integers will be divisible by 6
$\Rightarrow$ and so on....... This rule applies to any number of consecutive integers.

Let's analyze one of these sets and understand the logic behind this rule:
Let's consider a set of 3 consecutive integers: $\Rightarrow 1 \times 2 \times 3 = 6$ $\Rightarrow$ 6 is divisible by 3
$\Rightarrow 2 \times 3 \times 4 = 24$ $\Rightarrow$ 24 is divisible by 3
$\Rightarrow 3 \times 4 \times 5 = 60$ $\Rightarrow$ 60 is divisible by 3
$\Rightarrow 4 \times 5 \times 6 = 120$ $\Rightarrow$ 120 is divisible by 3
$\Rightarrow 5 \times 6 \times 7 = 210$ $\Rightarrow$ 210 is divisible by 3
$\Rightarrow 6 \times 7 \times 8 = 336$ $\Rightarrow$ 336 is divisible by 3
$\Rightarrow 7 \times 8 \times 9 = 504$ $\Rightarrow$ 504 is divisible by 3
$\Rightarrow 8 \times 9 \times 10 = 720$ $\Rightarrow$ 720 is divisible by 3

As you can see, it's not possible to come up with a series of 3 consecutive integers in which none of the integers is a multiple of 3. In fact, any set of 3 consecutive integers must contain one multiple of 3. As a result, the product of any set of 3 consecutive integers must be divisible by 3.

As we explained earlier in this chapter, according to the factor rule, every number is divisible by all the factors of its factors. Therefore, if there is always a multiple of 3 in a set of 3 consecutive integers, the product of the integers will always be divisible by 3.

Now let's consider some more sets of consecutive integers:
Set of 4 consecutive integers $\Rightarrow 1 \times 2 \times 3 \times 4 = 24$ $\Rightarrow$ 24 is divisible by 4
Set of 5 consecutive integers $\Rightarrow 1 \times 2 \times 3 \times 4 \times 5 = 120$ $\Rightarrow$ 120 is divisible by 5
Set of 6 consecutive integers $\Rightarrow 1 \times 2 \times 3 \times 4 \times 5 \times 6 = 720$ $\Rightarrow$ 720 is divisible by 6
Set of 7 consecutive integers $\Rightarrow 1 \times 2 \times 3 \times 4 \times 5 \times 6 \times 7 = 5040$ $\Rightarrow$ 5040 is divisible by 7

We can extend this same logic to see that the rule will apply only to any set of consecutive integers. So, the same logic explained above applies to a set of 4 consecutive integers, 5 consecutive integers, and so on.

SUM OF SET OF CONSECUTIVE INTEGERS:

EZ RULE: If there is any set of n number of consecutive integers, where n is an odd integer, then the sum of all those n integers is always divisible by n, or is always a multiple of n.

In other words, for any set of consecutive integers with an odd number of terms, the sum of all the integers is always divisible by the number of terms, or is always a multiple of the number of terms.

For instance: ⇒ The sum of any set of 3 consecutive integers will be divisible by 3

⇒ The sum of any set of 5 consecutive integers will be divisible by 5

⇒ The sum of any set of 7 consecutive integers will be divisible by 7

⇒ The sum of any set of 9 consecutive integers will be divisible by 9

⇒ and so on....... This rule applies to any number of consecutive integers.

Note: Be careful, this rule does not apply for the sum of a consecutive set with an even number of terms.

Let's analyze one of these sets and understand the logic behind this rule:
Consider any set of consecutive integers: n, $n + 1$, $n + 2$, $n + 3$, $n + 4$, $n + 5$, $n + 6$, $n + 7$, $n + 8$, etc.......

First, let's analyze some of the sets of odd number of consecutive terms:

Set of 3 consecutive integers	⇒ $(n) + (n + 1) + (n + 2)$	⇒ $3n + 3$ (divisible by 3)
Sum of first 3 integers	⇒ $1 + 2 + 3 = 6$	⇒ 6 is divisible by 3
Set of 5 consecutive integers	⇒ $(n) + (n + 1) + (n + 2) + (n + 3) + (n + 4)$	⇒ $5n + 10$ (divisible by 5)
Sum of first 5 integers	⇒ $1 + 2 + 3 + 4 + 5 = 15$	⇒ 15 is divisible by 5
Set of 7 consecutive integers	⇒ $(n) + (n+1) + (n+2) + (n+3) + (n+4) + (n+5) + (n+6)$	⇒ $7n + 21$ (divisible by 7)
Sum of first 7 integers	⇒ $1 + 2 + 3 + 4 + 5 + 6 + 7 = 28$	⇒ 28 is divisible by 7
Set of 9 consecutive integers	⇒ $(n)+(n+1)+(n+2)+(n+3)+(n+4)+(n+5)+(n+6)+(n+7)+(n+8)$	⇒ $9n + 36$ (divisible by 9)
Sum of first 9 integers	⇒ $1 + 2 + 3 + 4 + 5 + 6 + 7 + 8 + 9 = 45$	⇒ 45 is divisible by 9

Next, let's analyze some of the sets of even number of consecutive terms:

Set of 4 consecutive integers	⇒ $(n) + (n + 1) + (n + 2) + (n + 3)$	⇒ $4n + 6$ (not divisible by 4)
Sum of first 4 integers	⇒ $1 + 2 + 3 + 4 = 10$	⇒ 10 is not divisible by 4
Set of 6 consecutive integers	⇒ $(n) + (n + 1) + (n + 2) + (n + 3) + (n + 4) + (n + 5)$	⇒ $6n + 15$ (not divisible by 6)
Sum of first 6 integers	⇒ $1 + 2 + 3 + 4 + 5 + 6 = 21$	⇒ 21 is not divisible by 6

As you can see, this rule only applies to sets of consecutive integers with an odd number of terms, and it doesn't apply to sets of consecutive integers with an even number of terms.

CONSECUTIVE INTEGERS AND DIVISIBILITY BY 2 AND 4:

(A) If there is one even integer in a consecutive series, the product of the series is divisible by 2.
For instance: There are two consecutive numbers: n and $n + 1$, and if n is even, then it means that one of the numbers is even, which is n; and hence, the product of n and $(n + 1)$ is definitely divisible by 2, or 2 is a factor of the product of n and $(n + 1)$.

(B) If there are two even integers in a consecutive series, the product of the series is divisible by 4.
For instance: There are three consecutive numbers: n, $n + 1$, and $n + 2$; and if n is even, then it means that two of the numbers are even, which are n and $n + 2$; and hence the product of n, $n + 1$, and $n + 2$ is definitely divisible by 4, or 4 is a factor of the product of n, $n + 1$, and $n + 2$.

For Example: If $n^3 - n = m$, and if n is even or if n is odd, is m divisible by 2 and 4?

⇒ $n^3 - n = m$

⇒ $n(n^2 - 1) = m$

⇒ $n(n + 1)(n - 1) = m$

⇒ $(n - 1)\, n\, (n + 1) = m$ ⇒ Now this is a product of three consecutive integers.

If n is even   ⇒ this is a series of two odds and one even. This means that the product of these three consecutive integers, m, is definitely divisible by 2, but it is not necessarily divisible by 4.

If n is odd   ⇒ this is a series of one odd and two evens. This means that the product of these three consecutive integers, m, is definitely divisible by 2, and it is also divisible by 4.

1.7: FACTORS & MULTIPLES:

1.7.1: FACTORS:

The *"factors,"* also known as *divisors*, of an integer are the positive integers that evenly divide into that number. A number is a factor of another number if it can be divided evenly into that number. In other words, the factors of a number are positive integers that can evenly be divided into the number without leaving any leftover or remainder. Therefore, factors are integers that are multiplied to give a product. Every integer has a finite set of factors or divisors.

EZ RULE: If the integer k divides m evenly, then we can say that m is divisible by k or that k is a factor of m.
             If a/b is an integer, then b is a factor of a.

For instance: Factors of 24 = 24, 12, 8, 6, 4, 3, 2, and 1 $\Rightarrow$ Each of these numbers can be divided evenly into 24.
The term "divisible by" means divisible by "without any remainder" or "with a remainder of zero".
For instance, 24 is divisible by 2 because 24 divided by 2 is 12 with a remainder of 0. However, 24 is not divisible by 9, because 24 divided by 9 is 2 with a remainder of 6.

DIFFERENT TYPES OF FACTORS:

(A) FACTORS OF 1: The only positive factor (or divisor) of 1 is 1 itself.
Note that 1 is the only number that has only one factor, every other positive integer has at least two positive factors or divisors, i.e., 1 and itself, and possibly many more.
For Example: Factors of 1 $\Rightarrow$ 1

(B) FACTORS OF PRIME NUMBERS: Prime numbers have exactly two factors (or divisors): 1 and itself.
For Example: Factors of 7 $\Rightarrow$ 1 and 7

(C) FACTORS OF COMPOSITE NUMBERS: Composite numbers have more than two factors (or divisors):
For Example: Factors of 20 $\Rightarrow$ 1, 2, 4, 5, 10, 20

FACTOR PAIRS: Factor pairs are set of two factors, the product of which results in the original number. Factors of a number can be grouped into pairs of factors.
For Example: Factor Pairs of 20 $\Rightarrow$ 1 × 20, 2 × 10, 4 × 5

EZ NOTE: The number 1 is a non-prime factor of all integers. Since every number is divisible by 1 and itself, remember to include 1 and the number itself when counting the factors of any number.

FACTORS-OF-FACTOR RULE:

EZ RULE: If a is divisible by b, then a is also divisible by all the factors of b.
             In other words, if b is a factor of a, then all the factors of b are also factors of a.
For Instance: If 96 is divisible by 12, then 96 is also divisible by all the factors of 12 (1, 2, 3, 4, 6, and 12).
             In other words, if 12 is a factor of 96, then all the factors of 12 are also factors of 96.
             $\Rightarrow$ So, if 6 is a factor of 12, and 12 is a factor of 96; then 6 is also a factor of 96.
             $\Rightarrow$ 12 and 6 are factors of 72; because 12 × 6 makes 72.
             $\Rightarrow$ 12, in turn, is made from its own factors; for example, 4 × 3 makes 12.
             Therefore, if 72 is made partly by its factor 12, and 12 in turn is made by its prime factors 2, 2, and 3; then it implies that 2, 2, and 3 are also factors of 72.
This rule allows us to visualize factors as elements that are the basis upon which all numbers are fabricated.

PRIME FACTORIZATION:

A useful way to evaluate a number is to break it down into its prime factors. Prime factors are the factors of a number that are prime numbers, that is, the prime factors of a number cannot be further divided into factors. Every integer greater than 1 (composite numbers) that is not a prime can be written as a product of prime numbers. Prime factors of composite numbers can be easily determined by creating factor trees. Once you know the prime factors of a number, you can determine all the factors of that number. All the factors of a number can be found by combining all the products of the prime factors. The prime factorization of a number is the expression of the number as the product of its prime factors. No matter how you factor a number, its prime factors will always be the same. To find a given number's prime factorization, figure out a pair of factors of the number, and then determine their factors, continuing the process until you're left with only prime numbers. Those primes will then be the prime factorization of the given number. Any integer greater than 1 is a prime or can be written as a product of primes.

EZ STEP-BY-STEP METHOD: Apply the following step(s) to write any number as a "product of prime factors":

STEP 1: If possible, divide the given number by 2; continue to divide by 2 until the factor is no more divisible by 2.

STEP 2: If possible, divide the result from above by 3, continue to divide by 3 until the factor is no more divisible by 3.

STEP 3: If possible, divide the result from above by 5, continue to divide by 5 until the factor is no more divisible by 5.

STEP 4: If possible, divide the result from above by 7, continue to divide by 7 until the factor is no more divisible by 7.

STEP 5: Continue the procedure with 11, 13, 17, 19, and so on, until all the factors are primes.
Note: If the number is not at all divisible by a prime number, skip that step and go to the next step.

Example #1:	Prime Factors of 20	$\Rightarrow \underline{2 \times 10} = 2 \times \underline{2 \times 5} = 2^2 \times 5$
Example #2:	Prime Factors of 24	$\Rightarrow \underline{2 \times 12} = 2 \times \underline{2 \times 6} = 2 \times 2 \times \underline{2 \times 3} = 2^3 \times 3$
Example #3:	Prime Factors of 80	$\Rightarrow \underline{2 \times 40} = 2 \times 2 \times 20 = \underline{2 \times 2 \times 2 \times 10} = \underline{2 \times 2 \times 2 \times 2 \times 5} = 2^4 \times 5$
Example #4:	Prime Factors of 252	$\Rightarrow \underline{2 \times 126} = 2 \times \underline{2 \times 63} = 2 \times 2 \times \underline{3 \times 21} = 2 \times 2 \times 3 \times \underline{3 \times 7} = 2^2 \times 3^2 \times 7$
Example #5:	Prime Factors of 1020	$\Rightarrow \underline{2 \times 510} = 2 \times 2 \times 255 = \underline{2 \times 2 \times 3 \times 85} = \underline{2 \times 2 \times 3 \times 5 \times 17} = 2^2 \times 3 \times 5 \times 17$
Example #6:	Prime Factors of 1050	$\Rightarrow \underline{2 \times 525} = 2 \times 3 \times 175 = \underline{2 \times 3 \times 5 \times 35} = \underline{2 \times 3 \times 5 \times 5 \times 7} = 2 \times 3 \times 5^2 \times 7$

PRIME FACTORIZATION USING A FACTOR TREE:

Prime factorization is the common method of finding all the prime factors of an integer using a factor tree. Every integer can be factored into a unique set of prime factors.

EZ STEP-BY-STEP METHOD: Apply the following step(s) to find all the prime factors using a factor tree:

STEP 1: Place the given integer at the top of the tree.

STEP 2: Then add the first branch that consists of two factors whose product is the given integer on the top.

STEP 3: Then add sub-branches to those branches that consist of two numbers whose product is the number at the second level of the tree.

STEP 4: Continue the branching process until the factor at the end of each branch is a prime number. Circle the end of each branch that is a prime number. The factor tree is complete only after all branches reach a prime number.

STEP 5: After completing the factor tree, the collection of circled numbers, also known as prime branches under any one of the above numbers represents the prime factors of that number.

EZ CHECK: To check if the factor tree is correct, the product of these prime factors should be the given number.

EZ NOTES: **(A)** One branch may end with a prime number where as the other branch may still continue to branch out until it reaches a prime number.
(B) The distinct prime factors of a given number are the different prime factors of that number, which could be determined by looking at the prime branches.
(C) All the factors listed are primes, and no other number has this same set of prime factors.
(D) Since each positive integer that evenly divides into a number is a factor of that number, composite numbers can have factors other than their prime factors, and those numbers are expressed in the middle branches of the factor trees.

For Example: Factor tree of 80

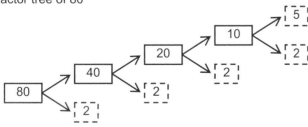

Factors of 80 $\Rightarrow$ 1, 2, 4, 5, 8, 10, 20, 40, 80
Prime Factors of 80 $\Rightarrow 2 \times 2 \times 2 \times 2 \times 5 = 2^4 \times 5$
Distinct Prime Factor $\Rightarrow$ 2 & 5

FINDING FACTORS FROM PRIME FACTORS:

All the factors of a number can also be generated by first finding the prime factors of that number and then creating all the possible prime products of those prime factors.

For Example: Prime Factors of 80 $\Rightarrow$ 1, 2, 2, 2, 2, 5 (from prime factorization)

                 Factors of 80 $\Rightarrow 1 \times 2 = 2$

                                $\Rightarrow 2 \times 2 = 4$

                                $\Rightarrow 1 \times 5 = 5$

                                $\Rightarrow 2 \times 2 \times 2 = 8$

                                $\Rightarrow 2 \times 5 = 10$

                                $\Rightarrow 2 \times 2 \times 2 \times 2 = 16$

                                $\Rightarrow 2 \times 2 \times 5 = 20$

                                $\Rightarrow 2 \times 2 \times 2 \times 5 = 40$

                                $\Rightarrow 2 \times 2 \times 2 \times 2 \times 5 = 80$

                 Factors of 80 $\Rightarrow$ 1, 2, 4, 5, 8, 10, 16, 20, 40, 80

USING PRIME FACTORS TO FIND FACTORS:

Prime factors can be used to determine whether a specific number is a factor or another number.

For Example: Is 8 a factor of 20?

                 Prime Factors of 20 $\Rightarrow$ 1, 2, 2, 5

                 Factor of 8 $\Rightarrow 2 \times 2 \times 2$

                 $\Rightarrow$ Since we cannot make 8 from the prime factors of 20, 8 is not a factor of 20.

COMMON FACTORS & GREATEST COMMON FACTOR:

COMMON FACTORS:

Common factors are factors that two numbers have in common.

EZ STEP-BY-STEP METHOD: Apply the following step(s) to find common factors:

STEP 1: First, find the prime factors of both the numbers using the factor tree.

STEP 2: Next, find the factors they share in common.

STEP 3: The common factors are those shared numbers plus any number found by multiplying those shared numbers in every possible combination.

Note: GCF is the number found by multiplying all those shared numbers.

EZ RULE: A number, k, is a common factor of two other numbers m & n if k is a factor of m & k is also a factor of n.

For Example: Find the common factors of 16 and 24.

                 Prime Factors of 16 $\Rightarrow 2 \times 2 \times 2 \times 2$

                 Prime Factors of 24 $\Rightarrow 2 \times 2 \times 2 \times 3$

                 Numbers they share in common $\Rightarrow 2 \times 2 \times 2$

                 Common Factors $\Rightarrow 2, 2 \times 2, 2 \times 2 \times 2 = 2, 4, 8$

                 Greatest Common Factor $\Rightarrow 2 \times 2 \times 2 = 8$

                 $\Rightarrow$ The primes that appear in both factorizations is 2. Since 2 appears 4 times in the factorization of 16 and 3 times in the factorization of 24, we take it just 3 times; 3 appears none in the factorization of 16 and once in the factorization of 24, so we can't take it.

GREATEST COMMON FACTOR (GCF):

The greatest common factor (GCF) or greatest common divisor (GCD) is the greatest factor that is common to all the given numbers. GCF of two or more integers is the largest integer that is a factor of each of them, or it is the largest number by which two integers can be divided. The GCF is the product of all the primes that appear in each of the factorizations, using each prime the smallest number of times it appears in any factorization.

METHOD #1: GCF of two or more numbers is the largest integer that is a factor of each of them.

EZ STEP-BY-STEP METHOD: Apply the following step(s) to find GCF:

STEP 1: List the factors of all the numbers.

STEP 2: The largest factor that is common with all the numbers is the GCF.

For Example: GCF of 16 & 24 can be found by forming the following table:

Factors of 16	1	2		4		8		16	
Factors of 24	1	2	3	4	6	8	12		24

GCF of 16 & 24 ⇒ 8

METHOD #2: By Using Prime Factorization:

To find the GCF, find the product of all the common prime factors of both numbers. If a number appears more than once, use the lower power of the repeated factor.

EZ STEP-BY-STEP METHOD: Apply the following step(s) to find GCF:

STEP 1: List all the prime factors of both the numbers using a factor tree.

STEP 2: Write all factors as exponents, especially if a number appears more than once.

STEP 3: Take all the common prime factors of both numbers, using the lowest power of repeated factors.

STEP 4: Multiply all these factors – the product of all these factors is the GCF.

Note: The GCF is the overlap or intersection of the two prime factorizations.

For Example: What is the GCF of 16 & 24?

Prime factors of 16   ⇒ $2 \times 2 \times 2 \times 2 = 2^4 \times 3^0$

Prime factors of 24   ⇒ $2 \times 2 \times 2 \times 3 = 2^3 \times 3^1$

GCF of 16 & 24   ⇒ $2^3 = 8$

DIFFERENCE BETWEEN COMMON FACTOR (CF) AND GREATEST COMMON FACTOR (GCF):

Common Factors (CF): Common factors are factors that two (or more) numbers have in common. For instance, 2 is a common factor of 12 and 18.

Greatest Common Factor (GCF): Greatest Common Factor (GCF) is the largest common factor of two (or more) numbers. For instance, 6 is the GCF of 12 and 18.

METHOD FOR DETERMINING PRIME NUMBERS:

Apply the following step(s) to determine if a number is prime:

STEP 1: First, find the approximate square root of the given number.

STEP 2: Next, test all the prime numbers that fall below your approximate number to see if they are factors of the number.

Note: There is need to test any prime number that is greater than the approximate square root of the given number

For Example: To determine if 151 is a prime number:

⇒ First find the approximate square root of 151: $\sqrt{151}$ = 12.5

⇒ List of prime numbers less than 12.5: 11, 7, 5, 3, 2

Since 151 is not divisible by any of these numbers, it's a prime number.

1.7.2: MULTIPLES:

An integer that is divisible by another integer is a **"multiple"** of that integer. In other words, the multiples of any given number are those numbers that can be divided by that given number without a remainder. Any integer is a multiple of each of its factors. All integers, both prime and composite have an infinite set of multiples.

EZ RULE: If k is a factor of m, then there is another integer n such that $m = k \times n$; in this case, m is called a multiple of k. In other words, a number m is considered to be a multiple of another number, k, if k times another integer, n, equals m. If a/b is an integer, then a is a multiple of b.

EZ TIP: Any integer, n, is a multiple of 1 and n, because $1 \times n = n$.

⇒ 15 is a multiple of 5 (5×3); 10 is also a multiple of 5 (5×2).

FINDING MULTIPLES OF A NUMBER:

To find the multiples of a given number, multiply that number by each of the natural numbers.

EZ RULE: The product of integer *n* and any integer is a multiple of *n*.

For Example: the product of 5 and any integer is a multiple of 5.

The multiples of a number can also be thought of as those numbers that you would get if you "*counted*" by that number. So, you can find the multiples of a number by multiplying it by 1, 2, 3, 4, 5, and so on.

For instance: If you counted by 5, you would get: 5, 10, 15, 20, 25, and so on.
⇒ All of these numbers are some of the multiples of 5.
⇒ 10 is a multiple of 5 because 10 is evenly divisible by 5: 10 = 5 × 2

Example #1:   Multiples of 2   ⇒ 2, 4, 6, 8, 10, 12, 14, 16, 18, 20.......
Example #2:   Multiples of 5   ⇒ 5, 10, 15, 20, 25, 30, 35, 40, 45, 50.......

COMMON MULTIPLE (CM) AND LOWEST COMMON MULTIPLE (LCM):

COMMON MULTIPLE (CM):

Any number that is a multiple of all the given numbers is called a common multiple.

A number, *m*, is a common multiple of two other numbers, *k* and *j*, if it is a multiple of each of them.

For example: ⇒ 12 is a common multiple of 4 and 6, since 3 × 4 = 12 and 2 × 6 = 12.
⇒ 12 is not a common multiple of 5 and 6, because 12 is not a multiple of 5.

LEAST/LOWEST COMMON MULTIPLE (LCM):

The smallest multiple of two (or more) numbers is called their least common multiple (LCM). The least common multiple (LCM) of two or more given integers is the smallest positive integer that is a common multiple of each of the given integers. LCM are commonly used to find Least/Lowest Common Denominator (LCD) in fractions. The following are the different methods of finding the Least/Lowest Common Multiple (LCM):

METHOD #1: LCM of two or more numbers is the smallest common multiple of all the given numbers.

EZ STEP-BY-STEP METHOD: Apply the following step(s) to find LCM:

STEP 1: List the multiples of all the numbers.

STEP 2: The lowest multiple that is common with all the numbers is the LCM.

For Example: LCM of 6 & 8 can also be found by forming the following table:

Multiples of 6	6		12		18	24	30		36
Multiples of 8		8		16		24		32	

LCM of 6 & 8 ⇒ 24

METHOD #2: By Using Prime Factorization:

The LCM of two or more numbers is the product of all the primes that appear in each of the factorizations, using each prime the largest number of times it appears in any factorization.

EZ STEP-BY-STEP METHOD: Apply the following step(s) to find LCM:

STEP 1: List the prime factors of both the numbers using a factor tree.

STEP 2: Circle all the prime factors of the first number.

STEP 3: Circle all the prime factors of the second number, except any factors which is already a factor of the first number, i.e., eliminate repeating factors.

STEP 4: Multiply all the circled numbers – the product of all these factors is the LCM.

Note: LCM is the multiplication of each factor by the maximum number of times it appears in either number.

For Example: What is the LCM of 12 & 18?
Prime factors of 12   ⇒ 2 × 2 × 3
Prime factors of 18   ⇒ 2 × 3 × 3
LCM of 12 & 18   ⇒ 2 × 2 × 3 × (3) = 36
⇒ We take the prime factors of 12 (2 × 2 × 3) and look at the prime factors of 18. There is one 2, but we already wrote that; there are two 3's, we already have one 3, so we need one more 3.

METHOD #3: By Using Prime Factorization and Exponents:

To find the LCM, find the product of all the prime factors of both numbers, if a number appears more than once, use the higher power of the repeated factor.

EZ STEP-BY-STEP METHOD: Apply the following step(s) to find LCM:

STEP 1: List the prime factors of both the numbers using a factor tree.

STEP 2: Write all factors as exponents, especially if a number appears more than once.

STEP 3: Take all the prime factors of both numbers, using the higher power of repeated factors.

STEP 4: Multiply all these numbers – the product of all these factors is the LCM.

For Example: What is the LCM of 12 & 18?

Prime factors of 12 $\Rightarrow 2 \times 2 \times 3 = 2^2 \times 3^1$

Prime factors of 18 $\Rightarrow 2 \times 3 \times 3 = 2^1 \times 3^2$

LCM of 12 & 18 $\Rightarrow 2^2 \times 3^2 = 4 \times 9 = 36$

METHOD #4: The LCM of two or more numbers is the product of all the numbers divided by their common factors.

EZ STEPS: Apply the following step(s) to find LCM:

STEP 1: Find the product of the two numbers by multiplying them – this is the common multiple, but not the LCM.

STEP 2: Divide that product by the common factors that those two numbers share – this will give the LCM.

Note: If there are no common factors, then the product above is the LCM.

For Example: What is the LCM of 12 & 18?

12 × 18 = 216 $\Rightarrow$ This is the common multiple, but not the least common multiple.

Prime factors of 12 $\Rightarrow 2 \times 2 \times 3$

Prime factors of 18 $\Rightarrow 2 \times 3 \times 3$

Common Factors (the factors they share) of 12 & 18 = 2 & 3

216 ÷ 2 = 108   [Divide the product by the first common factor: 2]

108 ÷ 3 = 36   [Divide the result above by the second common factor: 3]

Therefore, LCM of 12 & 18 = 36

DIFFERENCE BETWEEN COMMON MULTIPLE (CM) AND LEAST COMMON MULTIPLE (LCM):

Common Multiples: Common multiple is any number that is a multiple of two (or more) given numbers.
For instance, 24 and 96 are both common multiples of 6 and 8.

Least Common Multiple: LCM is a number that is the smallest multiple of two (or more) given numbers
For instance, 24 is the LCM of 6 and 8.

1.7.3: RELATIONSHIP BETWEEN FACTORS & MULTIPLES:

Sometimes it is easy to confuse factors and multiples. So let's now understand how factors and multiples are related to each other, and what are the similarities and differences between them. The multiplication of two integers yields a third integer. The first two integers are called factors, and the third integer is called the product. The product is said to be a multiple of both factors, and it is also divisible by both factors (provided the factors are nonzero).

If $a \times b = c$, then: Therefore, since (2) (9) = 18, we can say that:

$\Rightarrow a$ and b are factors and c is the product $\Rightarrow$ 2 and 9 are factors and 18 is the product

$\Rightarrow c$ is a multiple of both a and b $\Rightarrow$ 18 is a multiple of both 2 and 9

$\Rightarrow c$ is divisible by both a and b $\Rightarrow$ 18 is divisible by both 2 and 9

If a and b are integers, the following four terms are synonymous, i.e., they all mean the same thing:

For a and b Example: If $a = 2$ and $b = 10$

(A) a is a divisor of b $\Rightarrow$ 2 is a divisor of 10

(B) a is a factor of b $\Rightarrow$ 2 is factor of 10

(C) b is divisible by a $\Rightarrow$ 10 is divisible by 2

(D) b is a multiple of a $\Rightarrow$ 10 is a multiple of 2

Note: All the above statements mean that, when b is divided by a, there is no left over or remainder (remainder = 0).

RELATIONSHIP #1:   An integer is both a factor and a multiple of itself.

For Example: $\Rightarrow$ 10 is a factor of 10 and 10 is a multiple of 10.

RELATIONSHIP #2:   Factors and Multiples are Opposite of each other:
For Example: ⇒ 10 is a factor of 100 and 100 is a multiple of 10.

RELATIONSHIP #3:   Multiples of any number will always be multiples of all the factors of that number:
For Example: Multiples of 10   ⇒ 10, 20, 30, 40, 50, 60, 70, 80, 90, 100.......
                    And Factors of 10   ⇒ 2 and 5
                    This means that   ⇒ 10, 20, 30, 40, 50 are all also multiples of 2 and 5
Note: Notice that the multiples of 10 are also multiples of 2 and 5, which are factors of 10.

RELATIONSHIP #4:   Fewer Factors, Many Multiples: Every integer has a Finite Set of Factors (or divisors) and an Infinite Set of Multiples: "factors are few, multiple are many".
                    ⇒ Factors divide into an integer and are therefore less than or equal to that integer.
                    Hence, there are limited numbers of factors of a given integer.
                    ⇒ Multiples multiply out from an integer and are therefore greater than or equal to that integer
                    Hence, there are an unlimited number of multiples of an integer.
For Example: Factor of 12   ⇒ –12, –6, –4, –3, –2, –1, 1, 2, 3, 4, 6, 12
                    Multiple of 12   ⇒ ....–60, –48, –36, –24, –12, 0, 12, 24, 36, 48, 60.......

RELATIONSHIP #5:   The Sum and the Difference are also Divisible. If two numbers have a common divisor, then their sum and difference preserve that divisor as well.
                    If a number is a factor of two different numbers, then that number will also be a factor of the sum of those two numbers and the difference between those two numbers.
                    In other words: If two different numbers are divisible by a third number, then the sum of those two numbers and the difference between those two numbers is also divisible by that third number.
For Example: 8 is a factor of 72, and 8 is also factor of 16. In other words, 72 is divisible by 8, and 16 is also divisible by 8.
                    ⇒The sum of 72 & 16   ⇒ 72 + 16 = 88 ⇒ 88 is also divisible by 8; or 8 is also a factor of 88
                    ⇒ The difference bet 72 & 16 ⇒ 72 – 16 = 56 ⇒ 56 is also divisible by 8; or 8 is also a factor of 56

RELATIONSHIP #6:   The product of the GCF and LCM of any two given numbers is equal to the product of the two given numbers:

For any two real numbers "a" and "b" ⇒ GCF × LCM = $a \times b$ ⇒ GCF = $\dfrac{a \times b}{LCM}$ &   LCM = $\dfrac{a \times b}{GCF}$

For Example: GCF of 12 & 18 ⇒ 6
                    LCM of 12 & 18 ⇒ 36
                    Product of 12 & 18 = GCF × LCM
                    ⇒ 12 × 18 = 6 × 36
                    ⇒ 216 = 216

EZ Hint: It is sometimes easier to find the GCF than the LCM or vice versa.
For instance in example given above, you may immediately see that the GCF of 12 and 18 is 6; you can easily find the LCM by dividing the product of the two numbers (12 × 18 = 216) by the GCF (6) to get the LCM (216 ÷ 6 = 36).

For Example: What is the GCF and LCM of 6 and 8?
Solution: GCF of 6 & 8 = 2   [There is no number greater than 2 that divides evenly into both 6 & 8]

$$LCM = \frac{a \times b}{GCF} = \frac{6 \times 8}{2} = 24$$ [LCM is the product of the two numbers divided by the GCF]

1.8: RULES OF ODD AND EVEN NUMBERS:

Some questions may test your knowledge of how odd and even numbers combine through addition, subtraction, multiplication, and division. Use the following shortcut rules of odd and even numbers to easily predict the final result or outcome of operations with odd and even numbers.

ADDING/SUBTRACTING WITH ODD AND EVEN NUMBERS:

(A) If two integers are both even or both odd $\Rightarrow$ their sum and difference is even
(B) If one integer is even and the other odd $\Rightarrow$ their sum and difference is odd
(C) Sum/Difference of two Even Numbers $\Rightarrow$ Even
(D) Sum/Difference of two Odd Numbers $\Rightarrow$ Even
(E) Sum/Difference of an Even number and an Odd number $\Rightarrow$ Odd

Even	±	Even	=	Even		Odd	±	Odd	=	Even
2	+	6	=	8		5	+	7	=	12
8	−	2	=	6		7	−	5	=	2

Even	±	Odd	=	Odd		Odd	±	Even	=	Odd
6	+	5	=	11		5	+	6	=	11
6	−	5	=	1		7	−	6	=	1

MULTIPLYING/DIVIDING WITH ODD AND EVEN NUMBERS:

(A) Multiplication/Division of two Even numbers $\Rightarrow$ Even/Odd
(B) Multiplication/Division of two Odd numbers $\Rightarrow$ Odd
(C) Multiplication/Division of an Even Number and an Odd Number $\Rightarrow$ Even
(D) If there is a series of numbers being multiplied, and if there is just one Even number in the set, no matter what all the others are $\Rightarrow$ the product will always be Even. For Example: $1 \times 5 \times 7 \times 11 \times 15 \times 2 = 11,550$
(E) If there is a series of numbers getting multiplied, and if there is no Even number in the set, that is, all are odd numbers $\Rightarrow$ the product will always be Odd. For Example: $1 \times 5 \times 7 \times 11 \times 15 = 5,775$

Note: The product of two integers is even unless both of them are odd.

Even	×	Even	=	Even		Even	÷	Even	=	Even/Odd
2	×	2	=	4		10	÷	2	=	5

Odd	×	Odd	=	Odd		Odd	÷	Odd	=	Odd
5	×	5	=	25		25	÷	5	=	5

Even	×	Odd	=	Even		Even	÷	Odd	=	Even
2	×	5	=	10		10	÷	5	=	2

Odd	×	Even	=	Even		Odd	÷	Even	=	NA
5	×	2	=	10		5	÷	2	=	NA

EZ TIP: It isn't necessary to memorize these rules, but you must know that the relationships always hold true. The rules for odd and even numbers can be derived in seconds. You can easily establish the above rules by picking sample numbers and testing them. Pick simple number like 1 and 2, plug in and see what happens.
For instance: If m is even and n is odd, is the product "mn" even or odd?
$\Rightarrow$ Let, $m = 2$ and $n = 1 \Rightarrow$ Then, $mn = 2 \times 1 = 2 \Rightarrow$ Therefore, mn is even.
You can now generalize that whenever you multiply an even number with an odd number, you will get an even number. While the above tip is definitely a valid tip, it's always better to memorize the rules for operating with odds and evens. However, if you ever forget these rules, as a last resort, you can always figure them out by picking real numbers.

THE SUM OF TWO PRIMES:

All prime numbers are odd, except the number 2, that is, 2 is the only even prime number. All other even numbers are, by definition, divisible by 2, so none of them could be prime. The following can be concluded about sum of two primes:
(A) The sum of any two primes will be even (addition of two odds), unless one of those primes is the number 2.
(B) If the sum of two primes is odd (addition of even and odd), one of those primes must be the number 2.

PRACTICE EXERCISE – QUESTIONS AND ANSWERS WITH EXPLANATIONS: INTEGERS:

ADDITION: Add and simplify the following:

Question #1:	$7 + 8 + 1 + 5 + 6$	
Solution:	$\Rightarrow 27$	[Add all the numbers, and put the common sign]

Question #2:	$(-7) + (-5) + (-2) + (-6) + (-9)$	
Solution:	$\Rightarrow -29$	[Add all the numbers, and put the common sign]

Question #3:	$9 + (-2) + (5) + (-6) + (8)$	
Solution:	$\Rightarrow 22 + (-8)$	[Combine all the positive and negative numbers separately}
	$\Rightarrow 14$	[Find the difference and put the sign of the higher number]

Question #4:	$(-9) + (5) + (-8) + (1) + (-7)$	
Solution:	$\Rightarrow 6 + (-24)$	[Combine all the positive and negative numbers separately]
	$\Rightarrow -18$	[Find the difference and put the sign of the higher number]

Question #5:	$8 + (-1) + (6) + (-5) + (9)$	
Solution:	$\Rightarrow 23 + (-6)$	[Combine all the positive and negative numbers separately]
	$\Rightarrow 17$	[Find the difference and put the sign of the higher number]

Question #6:	$(-8) + (1) + (-9) + (5) + (-8)$	
Solution:	$\Rightarrow 6 + (-25)$	[Combine all the positive and negative numbers separately]
	$\Rightarrow -19$	[Find the difference and put the sign of the higher number]

Question #7:	$(17) + (-9) + (29) + (-19) + (71)$	
Solution:	$\Rightarrow 117 + (-28)$	[Combine all the positive and negative numbers separately]
	$\Rightarrow 89$	[Find the difference and put the sign of the higher number]

Question #8:	$(-11) + (18) + (-27) + (22) + (-78)$	
Solution:	$\Rightarrow 40 + (-116)$	[Combine all the positive and negative numbers separately]
	$\Rightarrow -76$	[Find the difference and put the sign of the higher number]

Question #9:	$|2 + (-9)| + |17 + (-76)|$	
Solution:	$\Rightarrow |-7| + |-59|$	[Add the numbers within the absolute value bars]
	$\Rightarrow 7 + 59$	[Take the absolute values]
	$\Rightarrow 66$	[Add the two numbers, and put the common sign]

Question #10:	$|7 + (-18)| + |59 + (-176)|$	
Solution:	$\Rightarrow |-11| + |-117|$	[Add the numbers within the absolute value bars]
	$\Rightarrow 11 + 117$	[Take the absolute values]
	$\Rightarrow 128$	[Add the two numbers, and put the common sign]

SUBTRACTION: Subtract and simplify the following:

Question #11:	$19 - 11$	
Solution:	$\Rightarrow 8$	[Find the difference and put the sign of the higher number]

Question #12:	$12 - 19$	
Solution:	$\Rightarrow -7$	[Find the difference and put the sign of the higher number]

Question #13:	$7 - (-9)$	
Solution:	$\Rightarrow 7 + 9$	[Eliminate the parentheses and put the appropriate sign]

	$\Rightarrow$ 16	[Add the two numbers, and put the common sign]

Question #14: 11 – (–16)
Solution: $\Rightarrow$ 11 + 16   [Eliminate the parentheses and put the appropriate sign]
$\Rightarrow$ 27   [Add the two numbers]

Question #15: –17 –8
Solution: $\Rightarrow$ –25   [Add the two numbers, and put the common sign]

Question #16: –12 –7
Solution: $\Rightarrow$ –19   [Add the two numbers, and put the common sign]

Question #17: (–2) – (–17)
Solution: $\Rightarrow$ –2 + 17   [Eliminate the parentheses and put the appropriate sign]
$\Rightarrow$ 15   [Find the difference and put the sign of the higher number]

Question #18: (–18) – (–1)
Solution: $\Rightarrow$ –18 + 1   [Eliminate the parentheses and put the appropriate sign]
$\Rightarrow$ –17   [Find the difference and put the sign of the higher number]

Question #19: |16 – 67| – |59 – 86|
Solution: $\Rightarrow$ |–51| – |–27| [Subtract the numbers within the absolute value bars]
$\Rightarrow$ 51 – 27   [Take the absolute values]
$\Rightarrow$ 24   [Find the difference and put the sign of the higher number]

Question #20: |11 – 87| – |19 – 116|
Solution: $\Rightarrow$ |–76| – |–97| [Subtract the numbers within the absolute value bars]
$\Rightarrow$ 76 – 97   [Take the absolute values]
$\Rightarrow$ –21   [Find the difference and put the sign of the higher number]

MULTIPLICATION: Multiply and simplify the following:

Question #21: 8 × 9
Solution: $\Rightarrow$ 72   [Multiply the numbers and put the appropriate sign]

Question #22: (–7) × (–27)
Solution: $\Rightarrow$ 189   [Multiply the numbers and put the appropriate sign]

Question #23: (–8) × 21
Solution: $\Rightarrow$ –168   [Multiply the numbers and put the appropriate sign]

Question #24: (–2) × 7 × (–8)
Solution: $\Rightarrow$ 112   [Multiply the numbers and put the appropriate sign]

Question #25: 6 × (–2) × 9
Solution: $\Rightarrow$ –108   [Multiply the numbers and put the appropriate sign]

Question #26: 2 × –5 × 7 × –8 × 9
Solution: $\Rightarrow$ 5,040   [Multiply the numbers and put the appropriate sign]

Question #27: (–1) × 2 × (–5) × 8 × (–9)
Solution: $\Rightarrow$ –720   [Multiply the numbers and put the appropriate sign]

Question #28: 11 × (–6) × 19 × (–7) × 0
Solution: $\Rightarrow$ 0   [Anything multiplied by 0 is 0]

Question #29: |–9| × |58|

Solution: ⇒ 9 × 58   [Take the absolute values]
                   ⇒ 522   [Multiply the numbers and put the appropriate sign]

Question #30: −|−7| × |−24|
Solution: ⇒ −7 × 24   [Take the absolute values]
                   ⇒ −168   [Multiply the numbers and put the appropriate sign]

DIVISION: Divide and simplify the following:

Question #31: 119 ÷ 7
Solution: ⇒ 17   [Divide the numbers and put the appropriate sign]

Question #32: (−108) ÷ (−9)
Solution: ⇒ 12   [Divide the numbers and put the appropriate sign]

Question #33: 126 ÷ (−6)
Solution: ⇒ −21   [Divide the numbers and put the appropriate sign]

Question #34: (−189) ÷ 7
Solution: ⇒ −27   [Divide the numbers and put the appropriate sign]

Question #35: 0 ÷ 172
Solution: ⇒ 0   [Divide the numbers and put the appropriate sign]

Question #36: 196 ÷ 0
Solution: ⇒ Not Defined   [Any number divided by zero is undefined]

Question #37: 171 ÷ (−1)
Solution: ⇒ −171   [Divide the numbers and put the appropriate sign]

Question #38: 1 ÷ (−1)
Solution: ⇒ −1   [Divide the numbers and put the appropriate sign]

Question #39: |128| ÷ |−16|
Solution: ⇒ 128 ÷ 16   [Take the absolute values]
                   ⇒ 8   [Divide the numbers and put the appropriate sign]

Question #40: |216| ÷ − |−12|
Solution: ⇒ 216 ÷ (−12)   [Take the absolute values]
                   ⇒ −18   [Divide the numbers and put the appropriate sign]

ORDER OF OPERATIONS: Simplify the following by using the Order of Operations:

Question #41: 7 + 2 × 9
Solution: ⇒ 7 + 18   [Perform the operation of multiplication]
                   ⇒ 25   [Perform the operation of addition]

Question #42: (9 + 2) × 7
Solution: ⇒ 11 × 7   [Perform the operation of addition within parentheses]
                   ⇒ 77   [Perform the operation of multiplication]

Question #43: 8 + 18 ÷ 2
Solution: ⇒ 8 + 9   [Perform the operation of division]
                   ⇒ 17   [Perform the operation of addition]

Question #44: (6 + 18) ÷ 2
Solution: ⇒ 24 ÷ 2   [Perform the operation of addition within parentheses]

| | $\Rightarrow 12$ | [Perform the operation of division] |

Question #45: $56 \div 2 \times 7$
Solution:
$\Rightarrow 28 \times 7$ [Perform the operation of division]
$\Rightarrow 196$ [Perform the operation of multiplication]

Question #46: $96 \div (8 \times 2)$
Solution:
$\Rightarrow 96 \div 16$ [Perform the operation of multiplication within parentheses]
$\Rightarrow 6$ [Perform the operation of division]

Question #47: $96 \div 2 \div 4 \div 3 \div 2$
Solution:
$\Rightarrow 48 \div 4 \div 3 \div 2$ [Perform the operation of first division]
$\Rightarrow 12 \div 3 \div 2$ [Perform the operation of next division]
$\Rightarrow 4 \div 2$ [Perform the operation of next division]
$\Rightarrow 2$ [Perform the operation of last division]

Question #48: $5040 \div 6 \div 5 \div 4 \div 3 \div 2 \div 1$
Solution:
$\Rightarrow 840 \div 5 \div 4 \div 3 \div 2 \div 1$ [Perform the operation of first division]
$\Rightarrow 168 \div 4 \div 3 \div 2 \div 1$ [Perform the operation of next division]
$\Rightarrow 42 \div 3 \div 2 \div 1$ [Perform the operation of next division]
$\Rightarrow 14 \div 2 \div 1$ [Perform the operation of next division]
$\Rightarrow 7 \div 1$ [Perform the operation of next division]
$\Rightarrow 7$ [Perform the operation of last division]

Question #49: $7 \times 8 \div 2 \times 8 \div 4$
Solution:
$\Rightarrow 56 \div 2 \times 8 \div 4$ [Perform the operation of first multiplication]
$\Rightarrow 28 \times 8 \div 4$ [Perform the operation of first division]
$\Rightarrow 224 \div 4$ [Perform the operation of next multiplication]
$\Rightarrow 56$ [Perform the operation of next division]

Question #50: $7 \times 8 \div 4 \times 9 \div 7$
Solution:
$\Rightarrow 56 \div 4 \times 9 \div 7$ [Perform the operation of first multiplication]
$\Rightarrow 14 \times 9 \div 7$ [Perform the operation of first division]
$\Rightarrow 126 \div 7$ [Perform the operation of next multiplication]
$\Rightarrow 18$ [Perform the operation of next division]

Question #51: 6×5^2
Solution:
$\Rightarrow 6 \times 25$ [Perform the operation of exponent]
$\Rightarrow 150$ [Perform the operation of multiplication]

Question #52: $(7 + 5)^2$
Solution:
$\Rightarrow 12^2$ [Perform the operation of addition within parentheses]
$\Rightarrow 144$ [Perform the operation of exponent]

Question #53: $[25 \div 5 \times 10 + (56 \div 7 \times 9)] \div 2$
Solution:
$\Rightarrow [25 \div 5 \times 10 + (8 \times 9)] \div 2$ [Perform the operation of division within parentheses]
$\Rightarrow [25 \div 5 \times 10 + (72)] \div 2$ [Perform the operation of multiplication within parentheses]
$\Rightarrow [5 \times 10 + (72)] \div 2$ [Perform the operation of division within brackets]
$\Rightarrow [50 + (72)] \div 2$ [Perform the operation of multiplication within brackets]
$\Rightarrow [122] \div 2$ [Perform the operation of addition within brackets]
$\Rightarrow 61$ [Perform the last operation of division]

Question #54: $[2 \times 28 \div 7 + (16 \times 7 \div 8)] \div 2$
Solution:
$\Rightarrow [2 \times 28 \div 7 + (112 \div 8)] \div 2$ [Perform the operation of multiplication within parentheses]
$\Rightarrow [2 \times 28 \div 7 + (14)] \div 2$ [Perform the operation of division within parentheses]
$\Rightarrow [56 \div 7 + (14)] \div 2$ [Perform the operation of multiplication within brackets]

$\Rightarrow$ [8 + (14)] ÷ 2   [Perform the operation of division within brackets]
$\Rightarrow$ [22] ÷ 2   [Perform the operation of addition within brackets]
$\Rightarrow$ 11   [Perform the last operation of division]

Question #55: [(24 − 5 − 7) × 8] ÷ [(28 − 5 − 7) ÷ 4]
Solution: $\Rightarrow$ [12 × 8] ÷ [16 ÷ 4]   [Perform the operation of subtraction within parentheses]
$\Rightarrow$ 96 ÷ 4   [Perform the operation within the two brackets]
$\Rightarrow$ 24   [Perform the operation of division]

Question #56: [(9 + 15) × 8] ÷ [(12 × 8) ÷ 6]
Solution: $\Rightarrow$ [24 × 8] ÷ [96 ÷ 6]   [Perform the operation within parentheses]
$\Rightarrow$ 192 ÷ 16   [Perform the operation within the two brackets]
$\Rightarrow$ 12   [Perform the operation of division]

Question #57: |−8| − |23 − 81| × 2
Solution: $\Rightarrow$ |−8| − |−58| × 2   [Perform the operation within the absolute value bars]
$\Rightarrow$ 8 − 58 × 2   [Take the absolute value of the numbers with the bars]
$\Rightarrow$ 8 − 116   [Perform the operation of multiplication]
$\Rightarrow$ −108   [Perform the operation of subtraction]

Question #58: |68 − 186| ÷ 2 + |−7|
Solution: $\Rightarrow$ |−118| ÷ 2 + |−7| [Perform the operation within the absolute value bars]
$\Rightarrow$ 118 ÷ 2 + 7   [Take the absolute value of the numbers with the bars]
$\Rightarrow$ 59 + 7   [Perform the operation of division]
$\Rightarrow$ 66   [Perform the operation of addition]

Question #59: |7 − 18| × 2 − |12 − 168| ÷ 2
Solution: $\Rightarrow$ |−11| × 2 − |−156| ÷ 2   [Perform the operation within the absolute value bars]
$\Rightarrow$ 11 × 2 − 156 ÷ 2   [Take the absolute value of the numbers with the bars]
$\Rightarrow$ 22 − 156 ÷ 2   [Perform the operation of multiplication]
$\Rightarrow$ 22 − 78   [Perform the operation of division]
$\Rightarrow$ −56   [Perform the operation of subtraction]

Question #60: |22 − 118| ÷ 6 + |8 − 59| × 2
Solution: $\Rightarrow$ |−96| ÷ 6 + |−51| × 2   [Perform the operation within the absolute value bars]
$\Rightarrow$ 96 ÷ 6 + 51 × 2   [Take the absolute value of the numbers with the bars]
$\Rightarrow$ 16 + 51 × 2   [Perform the operation of division]
$\Rightarrow$ 16 + 102   [Perform the operation of multiplication]
$\Rightarrow$ 118   [Perform the operation of addition]

LCM: Find the Least Common Multiple of the following numbers:

Question #61: 6 & 8
Solution: Multiples of 6 $\Rightarrow$ 6, 12, 18, 24
Multiples of 8 $\Rightarrow$ 8, 16, 24
LCM $\Rightarrow$ 24

Question #62: 15 & 20
Solution: Multiples of 15 $\Rightarrow$ 15, 30, 45, 60
Multiples of 20 $\Rightarrow$ 20, 40, 60
LCM $\Rightarrow$ 60

Question #63: 12 & 28
Solution: Multiples 12 $\Rightarrow$ 12, 24, 36, 48, 60, 72, 84
Multiples of 28 $\Rightarrow$ 28, 56, 84
LCM $\Rightarrow$ 84

Question #64: 12 & 16
Solution: Multiples of 12 $\Rightarrow$ 12, 24, 36, 48
              Multiples of 16 $\Rightarrow$ 16, 32, 48
              LCM $\Rightarrow$ 48

Question #65: 18 & 28
Solution: Multiples of 18 $\Rightarrow$ 18, 36, 54, 72, 90, 108, 126, 144, 162, 180, 198, 216, 234, 252
              Multiples of 28 $\Rightarrow$ 28, 56, 84, 112, 140, 168, 196, 224, 252
              LCM $\Rightarrow$ 252

Question #66: 12 & 26
Solution: Multiples of 12 $\Rightarrow$ 12, 24, 36, 48, 60, 72, 84, 96, 108, 120, 132, 144, 156
              Multiples of 26 $\Rightarrow$ 26, 52, 78, 104, 130, 156
              LCM $\Rightarrow$ 156

Question #67: 8 & 28
Solution: Multiples of 8 $\Rightarrow$ 8, 16, 24, 32, 40, 48, 56
              Multiples of 28 $\Rightarrow$ 28, 56
              LCM $\Rightarrow$ 56

Question #68: 6 & 22
Solution: Multiples of 6 $\Rightarrow$ 6, 12, 18, 24, 30, 36, 42, 48, 54, 60, 66
              Multiples of 22 $\Rightarrow$ 22, 44, 66
              LCM $\Rightarrow$ 66

Question #69: 15 & 25
Solution: Multiples of 15 $\Rightarrow$ 15, 30, 45, 60, 75
              Multiples of 25 $\Rightarrow$ 25, 50, 75
              LCM $\Rightarrow$ 75

Question #70: 8 & 96
Solution: Multiples of 8 $\Rightarrow$ 8, 16, 24, 32, 40, 48, 56, 64, 72, 80, 88, 96
              Multiples of 96 $\Rightarrow$ 96
              LCM $\Rightarrow$ 96

GCF: Find the Greatest Common Factor of the following numbers:

Question #71: 18 & 24
Solution: Factors of 18 $\Rightarrow$ 1, 2, 3, 6, 18
              Factors of 24 $\Rightarrow$ 1, 2, 3, 4, 6, 8, 12, 24
              GCF $\Rightarrow$ 6

Question #72: 20 & 50
Solution: Factors of 20 $\Rightarrow$ 1, 2, 4, 5, 10, 20
              Factors of 50 $\Rightarrow$ 1, 2, 5, 10, 25, 50
              GCF $\Rightarrow$ 10

Question #73: 12 & 28
Solution: Factors of 12 $\Rightarrow$ 1, 2, 3, 4, 6, 12
              Factors of 28 $\Rightarrow$ 1, 2, 4, 7, 14, 28
              GCF $\Rightarrow$ 4

Question #74: 18 & 27
Solution: Factors of 18 $\Rightarrow$ 1, 2, 3, 6, 9, 18
              Factors of 27 $\Rightarrow$ 1, 3, 9, 27

	GCF	$\Rightarrow 9$

Question #75: 8 & 26
Solution:

	Factors of 8	$\Rightarrow$ 1, 2, 4, 8
	Factors of 26	$\Rightarrow$ 1, 2, 13, 26
	GCF	$\Rightarrow$ 2

Question #76: 25 & 125
Solution:

	Factors of 25	$\Rightarrow$ 1, 5, 25
	Factors of 125	$\Rightarrow$ 1, 5, 25, 125
	GCF	$\Rightarrow$ 25

Question #77: 51 & 85
Solution:

	Factors of 51	$\Rightarrow$ 1, 3, 17, 51
	Factors of 85	$\Rightarrow$ 1, 5, 17, 85
	GCF	$\Rightarrow$ 17

Question #78: 75 & 90
Solution:

	Factors of 75	$\Rightarrow$ 1, 3, 5, 15, 25, 75
	Factors of 90	$\Rightarrow$ 1, 2, 3, 6, 9, 10, 15, 30, 45, 90
	GCF	$\Rightarrow$ 15

Question #79: 57 & 95
Solution:

	Factors of 57	$\Rightarrow$ 1, 19, 57
	Factors of 95	$\Rightarrow$ 1, 5, 19, 95
	GCF	$\Rightarrow$ 19

Question #80: 17 & 19
Solution:

	Factors of 17	$\Rightarrow$ 1, 17
	Factors of 19	$\Rightarrow$ 1, 19
	GCF	$\Rightarrow$ 1

PART 2.0: FRACTIONS:

TABLE OF CONTENTS:

EZ REFERENCE: -To practice easy-to-medium level questions, please refer to our EZ Practice Basic Workbook.
                -To practice medium-to-difficult level questions, please refer to our EZ Practice Advanced Workbook.

2.1: BASICS ABOUT FRACTIONS:

Numbers, in which one integer is written over another integer, are called **"fractions"**. Fractions are made up of two numbers written one above the other and separated by a horizontal central line known as a fraction bar. The number above the bar is known as the numerator, and the number below the bar is known as the denominator. Fractions (sometimes called rational numbers) include not only the integers but also the numbers between integers. In fact, fraction is a way of expressing the numbers that fall in between the whole numbers. For instance, the fraction 7½ falls between the integer 7 and 8.

PARTS OF FRACTIONS:
(A) Numerator: It's the number written above the bar.
(B) Denominator: It's the number written below the bar.
(C) Fraction Bar: It's the center-line that divides the numerator and the denominator.

The line in fraction means, *"divided by"*. A fraction in the form of $\frac{a}{b}$, where "a" and "b" are integers and $b \neq 0$; "a" is the numerator and "b" is the denominator $\Rightarrow$ it implies that "a" is being divided by "b".

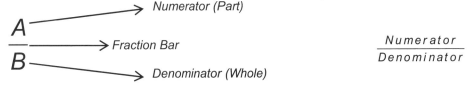

$$\frac{Numerator}{Denominator}$$

FRACTIONS ON NUMBER LINE:

We have already seen how integers are placed on a number line. A number line can also be used to show how fractions are ordered. In fact, a number line is the best way to understand how fractions are placed relative to integers.

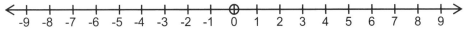

Each number represents a particular value that determines its place when numbers are ordered. When we count "1, 2, 3, 4, 5,.....," we follow the order of the counting numbers. You should be familiar with the order not only of the counting numbers, but also of integers and fractions. Number lines can be useful for showing both order and equivalence.

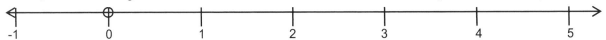

UNITS PARTITIONED INTO HALVES (2 EQUAL PARTS):

In this case, each unit has been partitioned into halves or two equal parts, and the midpoint of each unit has been given a fraction name with 2 as the denominator. On the number line, you can see that ½ is between 0 and 1; 3/2 is between 1 and 2; 5/2 is between 2 and 3; and so on. Likewise, –½ is between 0 and –1; –3/2 is between –1 and –2; –5/2 is between –2 and –3; and so on.
If each unit were partitioned into two equal parts, the number line would look like the following:

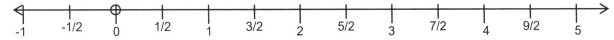

UNITS PARTITIONED INTO THIRDS (3 EQUAL PARTS):

In this case, each unit has been partitioned into thirds or three equal parts, and the 2 midpoints of each unit have been given a fraction name with 3 as the denominator. On the number line, you can see that 1/3 and 2/3 are between 0 and 1; 4/3 and 5/3 are between 1 and 2; 7/3 and 8/3 are between 2 and 3; and so on. Likewise, –1/3 and –2/3 are between 0 and –1; –4/3 and –5/3 are between –1 and –2; –7/3 and –8/3 are between –2 and –3; and so on.
If each unit were partitioned into three equal parts, the number line would look like the following:

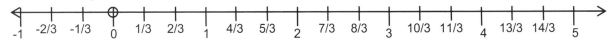

UNITS PARTITIONED INTO FOURTHS (4 EQUAL PARTS):

In this case, each unit has been partitioned into fourths or four equal parts, and the 3 midpoints of each unit have been given a fraction name with 4 as the denominator. On the number line, you can see that ¼, 2/4, and 3/4 are between 0 and 1; 5/4, 6/4, and 7/4 are between 1 and 2; 9/4, 10/4, and 11/4 are between 2 and 3; and so on. Likewise, –¼, –2/4, and –3/4 are between 0 and –1; –5/4, –6/4, and –7/4 are between –1 and –2; –9/4, –10/4, and –11/4 are between –2 and –3; and so on.
If each unit were partitioned into four equal parts, the number line would look like the following:

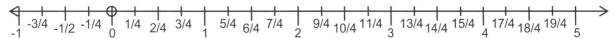

The units on the number line can have any number of subdivisions; we would simply continue the sequence. Here is another example that could come from other subdivisions:

UNITS PARTITIONED INTO TENTHS (10 EQUAL PARTS):

In this case, each unit has been partitioned into tenths or ten equal parts, and the 9 midpoints of each unit has been given a fraction name with 10 as the denominator. On the number line, you can see that 1/10 is between 0 and 1; 2/10 is between 1 and 2; and so on. Likewise, –1/10 is between 0 and –1; –2/10 is between –1 and –2; and so on.

UNDERSTANDING FRACTIONS: PART – WHOLE RELATIONSHIP:

If any given unit is divided into any number of equal parts, one or more of these parts is called a fraction of the unit.

When a whole is divided into "*n*" equal parts, each part is called *one-nth* of the whole, written as $\dfrac{1}{n}$.

For Instance:	$\Rightarrow$ If a pie is divided into 10 equal slices, each slice is one-tenth of the pie.
	$\Rightarrow$ If a cube is divided into 5 equal blocks, each block is one-fifth of the cube.
	$\Rightarrow$ A day is divided into 24 equal hours, so an hour is one-twenty-fourth of a day.
	$\Rightarrow$ An hour is divided into 60 equal minutes, so a minute is one-sixtieth of an hour.
	$\Rightarrow$ If a cube is divided into 5 equal blocks, and if 2 of those blocks are white, then it means that two-fifth of the blocks are white.
	$\Rightarrow$ If a pie is divided into 10 equal slices, and if John buys 7 of those slices, then it means that John bought seven-tenth of the pie.

For Example: There are 7 boys and 11 girls in a choir. What fractional part of the choir are boys?

Solution: Boys $\Rightarrow$ 7   Girls $\Rightarrow$ 11   Total $\Rightarrow$ 7 + 11 = 18

Fractional Part of Boys $\Rightarrow \dfrac{Number\ of\ Boys}{Total} = \dfrac{7}{18}$

TERMS OF FRACTION:

Fractions use the following two terms or numbers to represent part of a whole:

(A) Numerator represents the Parts: The top or the upper number, called the numerator, indicates the number of parts taken to form the fraction or how many parts we are working with.

(B) Denominator represents the Whole: The bottom or the lower number, called the denominator, indicates the number of equal parts into which something is divided or how many of these equal parts are contained in the whole.

For example in the fraction $\dfrac{5}{7}$, the whole is 7 and the part is 5; the whole of 7 is divided into 5 equal parts.

FRACTION AS QUOTIENT:

Fractions are nothing but the quotient of two numbers. Suppose $1 is the unit; and it is divided into 5 equal parts. Clearly, each part contains 20 cents; and two such parts contain 40 cents & three such parts contain 60 cents. $\Rightarrow \dfrac{2}{5}$ of a dollar = 40 cents. Similarly, suppose $9 is the unit; and it is divided into 15 equal parts. Clearly, each part contains 60 cents; and ten such parts contain $6. $\Rightarrow \dfrac{10}{15}$ of $9 = $6. Therefore, a fraction may also be defined as the quotient obtained on dividing one number (the numerator) by the other number (the denominator).

DIFFERENT WAYS OF READING FRACTIONS:

Fractions can be read in the following different ways:

(A) "Out of": Translate the fraction bar as "*out of*" to understand the meaning of a fraction.

For Example: The fraction $\dfrac{5}{7}$ means 5 out of 7.

(B) "Over": Translate the fraction bar as "*over*" to understand the meaning of a fraction.

For Example: The fraction $\dfrac{5}{7}$ means 5 over 7.

(C) "Divided by": Translate the fraction bar as "*divided by*" to understand the meaning of a fraction.

For Example: The fraction $\dfrac{5}{7}$ means 5 divided by 7 or $5 \div 7$.

EZ NOTE: The denominator of a fraction can never be zero since any number divided by zero is not defined.

INTEGERS AS FRACTIONS:
It needs to be noted that each integer can be written as a fraction.

Example 1: $\dfrac{25}{5} = \dfrac{5}{1} = 5$ **Example 2:** $-\dfrac{10}{5} = -\dfrac{2}{1} = -2$

FRACTION OF A NUMBER:
Fraction of a number is a part or portion of the number.

For Example: 5 is what fraction of 7? OR: What fraction of 7 is 5? $\Rightarrow \dfrac{5}{7}$

For Example: What fractional part of a week is 98 hours? $\Rightarrow \dfrac{98}{1\ week} = \dfrac{98}{24 \times 7} = \dfrac{98}{168} = \dfrac{7}{12}$

FRACTIONS ARE USED TO EXPRESS THE FOLLOWING:
(A) The relationship of a part to the whole – the numerator of the fraction represents the part and the denominator shows how many parts make a whole.
(B) Division of one number by another number – the fraction bar is the symbol for division, the number above the bar that is the numerator is divided by the number below the bar that is the denominator.
(C) The ratio of two quantities. (For example ½ in fraction is 1:2 in terms of ratio)
(D) Percentage. (For example, ½ in fraction is 50% in percentage)
(E) Probability of an event. (For example, ½ in fraction represent a probability of 1 out of 2)

CONVERSION BETWEEN FRACTIONS AND DECIMALS:

(A) CONVERTING FRACTIONS TO DECIMALS:
EZ STEP-BY-STEP METHOD: Apply the following step(s) to convert any type of Fraction into a Decimal:
STEP 1: First, reduce the given fraction to its lowest terms.
STEP 2: Next, divide the numerator by the denominator, and insert the decimal point at the appropriate place, adding zeros accordingly.

Example #1: $\dfrac{1}{10} \Rightarrow 0.10$ **Example #2:** $\dfrac{1}{2} \Rightarrow 0.50$

(B) CONVERTING DECIMALS TO FRACTIONS:
Any decimal number can be converted into fractions with a power of ten in the denominator and it can then be simplified.
EZ STEP-BY-STEP METHOD: Apply the following step(s) to convert any Decimal into a Fraction:
STEP 1: **(A)** First, eliminate the decimal point in the given number, and write that as the numerator of the resulting fraction.
         (B) Next, divide it by 1 followed by as many zeros as the number of places to the right of the decimal point of the given number, and write that as the denominator of the resulting fraction.
STEP 2: Finally, simplify the resulting fraction to its lowest form by dividing the numerator and the denominator by the greatest common factor.

Example #1: $0.10 \Rightarrow \dfrac{10}{100} = \dfrac{1}{10}$ **Example #2:** $0.50 \Rightarrow \dfrac{50}{100} = \dfrac{1}{2}$

For example: $\dfrac{5}{20} = 5 \div 20 = 0.25$ $\Rightarrow$ So, if five pies are divided equally among twenty people, each person gets $\dfrac{5}{20}$ of a pie. If you actually divide 5 by 20, you would get $\dfrac{5}{20} = ¼ = 0.25$

2.2: CLASSIFICATION OF FRACTIONS:

2.2.1: DIFFERENT TYPES OF FRACTION:

PROPER FRACTIONS:
A Proper or Common Fraction is a fraction in which the numerator is less (smaller) than its denominator.
$\Rightarrow$ Proper Fraction represents a value that is greater than 0 but less than 1.
Improper fractions are made up of a whole number and a proper fraction.

EZ RULE: Proper Fraction $\dfrac{a}{b}$, where $a < b$ $\Rightarrow$ Proper Fraction < 1   **Examples:** $\dfrac{5}{7}$ & $\dfrac{19}{25}$

IMPROPER FRACTIONS:
Improper Fraction is a fraction in which the numerator is greater than or equal to (equal or larger) its denominator.
$\Rightarrow$ Improper Fraction represents a value that is greater than or equal to 1.

EZ RULE: Improper Fraction $\dfrac{a}{b}$, where $a > b \Rightarrow$ Improper Fraction > 1   **Examples:** $\dfrac{7}{5}$ & $\dfrac{25}{19}$

Improper Fraction that represents ONE: A fraction in which the numerator and denominator are the same, is also known as improper fraction and it represents a value that is equal to 1.

EZ RULE: Improper Fraction $\dfrac{a}{b}$, where $a = b \Rightarrow$ Improper Fraction = 1   **Examples:** $\dfrac{7}{7}$ & $\dfrac{25}{25}$

MIXED NUMBER:
A mixed number is a number, such as $A\dfrac{B}{C}$, that consists of an integer A (whole number) part followed by a proper fraction part, where $B < C$.

A mixed number is an abbreviation for the sum of the integer and the fraction $\Rightarrow$ so the mixed number, $A\dfrac{B}{C}$ is an abbreviation for $A + \dfrac{B}{C}$

The value of the mixed number can be determined by finding the sum of the integer and the proper fractional part. Mixed Number must always represent a value that is greater than 1. Every mixed number can be written as an improper fraction, and every improper fraction can be written as a mixed number.

EZ NOTE: Mixed number cannot contain an improper fraction.

EZ RULE: Mixed Number: $A\dfrac{B}{C} = A + \dfrac{B}{C} = A$ is the whole number part and $\dfrac{B}{C}$ is the fractional part

Example #1: $1\dfrac{2}{7} = 1 + \dfrac{2}{7} = \dfrac{1}{1} + \dfrac{2}{7} = \dfrac{7}{7} + \dfrac{2}{7} = \dfrac{9}{7}$ and: $\dfrac{9}{7} = \dfrac{7}{7} + \dfrac{2}{7} = \dfrac{1}{1} + \dfrac{2}{7} = 1 + \dfrac{2}{7} = 1\dfrac{2}{7}$

Example #2: $2\dfrac{5}{7} = 2 + \dfrac{5}{7} = \dfrac{2}{1} + \dfrac{5}{7} = \dfrac{14}{7} + \dfrac{5}{7} = \dfrac{19}{7}$ and: $\dfrac{19}{7} = \dfrac{14}{7} + \dfrac{5}{7} = \dfrac{2}{1} + \dfrac{5}{7} = 2 + \dfrac{5}{7} = 2\dfrac{5}{7}$

SPECIAL TYPES OF FRACTIONS:

(A) FRACTIONS THAT REPRESENTS ITS "NUMERATOR":
A fraction that has 1 as the denominator is the same as the whole number which is its numerator.

EZ RULE: $\dfrac{n}{1} = n$ **For Example:** $\dfrac{7}{1} = 7$

(B) FRACTIONS THAT REPRESENTS "UNITY" OR "ONE":
If the numerator and denominator of a fraction are identical, the fraction actually represents 1.

EZ RULE: $\dfrac{n}{n} = 1$ **For Example:** $\dfrac{7}{7} = 1$

(C) FRACTIONS THAT REPRESENTS "ZERO":
If the numerator of any fraction is 0, the fraction actually represents 0.

EZ RULE: $\dfrac{0}{n} = 0$ **For Example:** $\dfrac{0}{7} = 0$

(D) FRACTIONS THAT ARE "NOT DEFINED":
Any fraction with 0 as the denominator has no meaning and is "*not defined*" since division by 0 is not defined.

EZ RULE: $\dfrac{n}{0} = not\ defined$ **For Example:** $\dfrac{7}{0} = not\ defined$

(E) FRACTIONS THAT REPRESENTS "WHOLE NUMBER":
Any whole number, k, is represented by a fraction with its numerator equal to k times its denominator.

EZ RULE: $\dfrac{m}{n} = k$ $\Rightarrow$ where $m = k \times n$ **For Example:** $\dfrac{10}{2} = 5 \Rightarrow$ where $10 = 5 \times 2$

(F) WRITING WHOLE NUMBERS AS FRACTIONS:
Whole numbers can also be written in the form of fractions by putting the whole number over a denominator of 1.

EZ RULE: $n = \dfrac{n}{1}$ $\Rightarrow$ where n is a whole number   **For Example:** $5 = \dfrac{5}{1}$

2.2.2: CONVERSIONS BETWEEN DIFFERENT TYPES OF FRACTION:
To convert a mixed number to an improper fraction, or an improper fraction to a mixed number, apply the following rules:

CONVERSION OF MIXED NUMBERS INTO IMPROPER FRACTIONS:
EZ STEP-BY-STEP METHOD: Apply the following step(s) to change a mixed number into an improper fraction:

STEP 1: Multiply the whole number by the denominator of the fractional part and add it to the numerator of the fractional part $\Rightarrow$ the result becomes the numerator of the required fraction.

STEP 2: Write the above result over the denominator, which remains the same as that of the original mixed number.

EZ RULE: $A\dfrac{B}{C} = \dfrac{(C \times A) + B}{C}$

Example #1: $1\dfrac{2}{7} = \dfrac{(7 \times 1) + 2}{7} = \dfrac{7 + 2}{7} = \dfrac{9}{7}$ **Example #2:** $2\dfrac{5}{7} = \dfrac{(7 \times 2) + 5}{7} = \dfrac{14 + 5}{7} = \dfrac{19}{7}$

CONVERSION OF IMPROPER FRACTIONS INTO MIXED NUMBERS:
EZ STEP-BY-STEP METHOD: Apply the following step(s) to change an improper fraction into a mixed number:

STEP 1: Divide the numerator by the denominator. Since the numerator is not evenly divisible by the denominator, there will be a remainder.

STEP 2: Write the above result in following way:
   (A) The quotient or the answer becomes the whole number part of the mixed number,
   (B) The remainder becomes the numerator of the fractional part of the mixed number, and
   (C) The divisor becomes the denominator of the fractional part of the mixed number. Or simply, the denominator remains the same as that of the original fraction.

Example #1: $\dfrac{9}{7} = 1\dfrac{2}{7}$ **Example #2:** $\dfrac{19}{7} = 2\dfrac{5}{7}$

EZ NOTE: Only improper fractions, i.e., whose numerators are greater than their denominators can be converted into mixed numbers and vice versa. Proper fraction, i.e., fractions whose numerators are less than their denominators cannot be converted into mixed numbers and vice versa.

2.3: INVERSE & RECIPROCALS:

2.3.1: INVERSE:

(A) ADDITIVE INVERSE: **(i)** The additive inverse is the opposite (negative) of the number.

EZ RULE #1:   The additive inverse of a is $(-a)$ **For Example:**   The additive inverse of 7 is (-7)

                                 (ii) The addition of any number and its additive inverse is zero.

EZ RULE #2: $a + (-a) = 0$ **For Example:** $7 + (-7) = 0$

(B) MULTIPLICATIVE INVERSE: **(i)** The multiplicative inverse is the reciprocal of the number.

EZ RULE #1:   Multiplicative inverse of "a" is $\dfrac{1}{a}$ **For Example:**   Multiplicative inverse of 7 is $\dfrac{1}{7}$

                         (ii) The product of any number and its reciprocal (multiplicative inverse) is one.

EZ RULE #2: $a \times \dfrac{1}{a} = 1$; therefore a & $\dfrac{1}{a}$ are inverses.   **For Example:** $7 \times \dfrac{1}{7} = 1$; therefore 7 & $\dfrac{1}{7}$ are inverses

2.3.2: RECIPROCALS:

A fraction is said to be inverted when its numerator and denominator are interchanged $\Rightarrow \dfrac{b}{a}$ is the inverted form of $\dfrac{a}{b}$

(A) RECIPROCAL OF INTEGER: The reciprocal of any given integer is 1 divided by that number.

EZ RULE: Reciprocal of any integer $a = \dfrac{1}{a}$ and $-a = -\dfrac{1}{a}$ **For Example:**   Reciprocal of $7 = \dfrac{1}{7}$ & $-7 = -\dfrac{1}{7}$

(B) RECIPROCAL OF FRACTIONS: The reciprocal of any nonzero fraction can be found by interchanging (switching) its numerator and the denominator; the new fraction formed is called the reciprocal of the original fraction.

EZ RULE: Reciprocal of any fraction $\dfrac{a}{b} = \dfrac{b}{a}$ **For Example:**   Reciprocal of $\dfrac{5}{7} = \dfrac{1}{\frac{5}{7}} = \dfrac{7}{5}$

(C) RECIPROCAL OF MIXED NUMBERS: To find reciprocal of mixed numbers – first convert them to improper fractions, and then follow the same rule given above, i.e., interchange its numerator and the denominator.

EZ RULE: Reciprocal of any fraction $a\dfrac{b}{c} = \dfrac{a \times c + b}{c} = \dfrac{c}{a \times c + b}$ **For Example:**   Reciprocal of $1\dfrac{2}{5} = \dfrac{7}{5} = \dfrac{5}{7}$

(D) RECIPROCAL OF ZERO: Since the reciprocal of any given number is 1 divided by that number, reciprocal of 0 is $\dfrac{1}{0}$, which is not defined. Therefore, "zero" has no reciprocal.

EZ RULE: Reciprocal of $0 = \dfrac{1}{0}$ = undefined

(E) RECIPROCAL OF ONE: Reciprocal of 1 and -1 is itself. The number 1 and -1 is its own reciprocal.

EZ RULE: Reciprocal of $1 = \dfrac{1}{1} = 1$ and Reciprocal of $-1 = -\dfrac{1}{1} = -1$

Product of a Number and its Reciprocal is One: The product of any given number and its reciprocal is always 1. In other words, it's a pair of numbers whose product is 1.

EZ RULE: Product of any fraction "$\dfrac{a}{b}$" and its reciprocal "$\dfrac{b}{a}$" is $1 \Rightarrow \dfrac{a}{b} \times \dfrac{b}{a} = 1$

For Example: $7 \times \dfrac{1}{7} = 1$ **For Example:** $\dfrac{5}{7} \times \dfrac{7}{5} = 1$

Quotient of a Number and its Negative is –1: The quotient of any given number and its negative is always -1.

For Example: $\dfrac{2}{5} \div \left(-\dfrac{2}{5}\right) = \dfrac{2}{5} \times \left(-\dfrac{5}{2}\right) = -1$

2.4: SIMPLIFYING FRACTIONS:

2.4.1: EQUIVALENT FRACTIONS:

Since fractions represent the relationship of part to whole, if the part and the whole are both changed by the same multiple, the relationship between the part and the whole will not be changed. Two fractions are said to be equivalent if multiplying or dividing both the numerator and the denominator of one of the fraction by the same number results in the other fraction. If the numerator and the denominator of a fraction are both multiplied or divided by the same nonzero number, the overall value of the fraction will not change.

For instance, if two people shared a pie, one person had $\frac{1}{2}$ of a pie and the second person had $\frac{5}{10}$ of a pie, they both

had exactly the same amount of the pie. We express this concept by saying that $\frac{1}{2}$ and $\frac{5}{10}$ are equivalent fractions; that

is, they both have the exact same numeric value.

Likewise, are $\frac{2}{7}$ and $\frac{16}{56}$ equivalent fractions? There is a number, that when multiplied by 2, gives 16, and there is a

number that, when multiplied by 7, gives 56. If these numbers are the same, the fractions are equivalent. Since they are the same number, $2 \times 8 = 16 = 7 \times 8 = 56$, the fractions are equivalent.

Are, $\frac{2}{5}$ and $\frac{12}{20}$ equivalent? Since $2 \times 6 = 12$, but $5 \times 6 \neq 20$, they are not equivalent. Alternately, since $12 \div 6 = 2$, but

$20 \div 6 \neq 5$, they are not equivalent.

To compute Equivalent Fractions, either multiply or divide the numerator and the denominator of the fraction by the same number.

For Example: $\frac{1}{2} \times \frac{5}{5} = \frac{5}{10}$ & $\frac{5}{10} \div \frac{5}{5} = \frac{1}{2}$

$\Rightarrow$ If we multiply both the numerator and the denominator of $\frac{1}{2}$ by 5, we get $\frac{5}{10}$; and if we divide

both the numerator and denominator of $\frac{5}{10}$ by 5, we get $\frac{1}{2}$.

Logic behind Equivalent Fractions: The value of a number is unchanged if the number is multiplied by 1. Similarly, in a fraction, multiplying the numerator and the denominator by the same nonzero number is the same as multiplying the fraction by 1; i.e., the value of the fraction is unchanged.

Any two or more fractions that represent the same number value or ratio, i.e., when divided results in the same number or ratio, but uses different numbers in the numerator and denominator are known as Equivalent Fractions.

For Example: $\frac{1}{2} = \frac{2}{4} = \frac{4}{8} = \frac{8}{16} = \frac{16}{32} = \frac{32}{64} = \frac{64}{128}$

The final value of the fraction does not change when the numerator and the denominator of the fraction are multiplied or divided by the same number, hence they are known as Equivalent Fractions. All the above fractions are equivalent fractions because they all represent the same quantity. The value of these fractions remains the same since both the numerator and the denominator are being multiplied by the same number. Notice that the denominator is twice as large as the numerator in every case. Any fraction that has a denominator that is exactly twice as large as the numerator is equivalent to ½.

Importance of Equivalent Fractions: To perform operations with fractions, you should be able to write equivalent fractions in higher or lower terms. In a multiple-choice test, there will be five answer choices to each question and your answer to a problem may not be the same as any of the given choices. Therefore, you may have to express a fraction as an equivalent fraction.

CONVERTING A FRACTION INTO AN EQUIVALENT FRACTION WITH A KNOWN NUMERATOR OR DENOMINATOR:
A given fraction can be expressed as another fraction of which the numerator or denominator is any multiple of the numerator or denominator of the given fraction.

EZ STEP-BY-STEP METHOD: Apply the following step(s) to find a fraction with a known numerator or denominator equivalent to a given fraction:

STEP 1: First, divide the numerator or denominator of the given fraction into the known numerator or denominator.

STEP 2: Next, multiply the result by the numerator or denominator of the given fraction $\Rightarrow$ this will give the numerator or denominator of the required equivalent fraction

Example #1: Find a fraction with a denominator of 25 which is equivalent to $\frac{2}{5}$.

Solution: Equivalent fraction $\Rightarrow \frac{10}{25}$ [Since 5 goes into 25, 5 times, the numerator is 2 × 5 = 10]

Example #2: Find a fraction with a numerator of 10 which is equivalent to $\frac{2}{5}$.

Solution: Equivalent fraction $\Rightarrow \frac{10}{25}$ [Since 2 goes into 10, 5 times, the denominator is 5 × 5 = 25]

HOW TO FIND EQUIVALENT FRACTIONS:

Since we have already learned that the value of a number does not change when that number is multiplied or divided by 1, fractions can be either scaled-up (raised) or scaled-down (reduced), respectively, through the multiplication (to scale-up) or the division (to scale-down) of both the numerator and the denominator by the same non-zero number.

(A) SCALING-UP FRACTIONS:

- Equivalent Fractions can be written in higher terms by Scaling-Up.
- Scaling-Up fractions means to multiply both numerator and denominator of the fraction by the same number.
- Scaling-Up is used to write an equivalent fraction with a bigger or magnified numerator and denominator.
- Scaling-Up a fraction only changes the outside appearance of the fraction, not its value.

Note: While scaling-Up a fraction, the fraction is multiplied by 2/2, 3/3, 4/4, 5/5, 6/6 and so on, the value of all these is 1, and any number times 1 equals itself.

For Example: $\frac{1}{2} = \frac{2}{4} = \frac{4}{8} = \frac{8}{16} = \frac{16}{32} = \frac{32}{64} = \frac{64}{128}$

$\Rightarrow$ Since we multiplied both the numerator and the denominator by the same number, the value of the fraction remains the same, which is ½ or 0.5

(B) SCALING-DOWN FRACTIONS:

- Equivalent Fractions can be written in lower terms by Scaling-Down.
- Scaling-Down a fraction means to divide both numerator and denominator of the fraction by the same number.
- Scaling-Down is used to write an equivalent fraction with a smaller or understated numerator and denominator.
- Scaling-Down a fraction only changes the outside appearance of the fraction, not its value.

Note: While Scaling-Down a fraction, the fraction is divided by 2/2, 3/3, 4/4, 5/5, 6/6 and so on, the value of all these is 1, and any number divided by 1 equals itself.

For Example: $\frac{64}{128} = \frac{32}{64} = \frac{16}{32} = \frac{8}{16} = \frac{4}{8} = \frac{2}{4} = \frac{1}{2}$

$\Rightarrow$ Since we divided both the numerator and the denominator by the same number, the value of the fraction remains the same, which is ½ or 0.5

$\Rightarrow$ Therefore, $\frac{5}{10}$ is $\frac{1}{2}$ reduced to its lowest terms and $\frac{5}{10}$ is $\frac{10}{20}$ raised to a higher term.

EZ TIP: The quickest way to determine whether two or more fractions are equivalent is to convert them to decimals by dividing. For the fractions to be equivalent, the two quotients must be the same.

2.4.2: REDUCING FRACTIONS:

REDUCING A FRACTION TO ITS LOWEST TERMS:
Most fractions that you will be dealing with will be proper fractions, that is, they will already be reduced to their lowest terms, $\frac{5}{7}$ is such a fraction. However, often times you will be required to reduce fractions to their lowest terms. The method we use to take a fraction and put it in its lowest terms is called **simplifying** or **reducing**. To reduce means to divide out any common multiples from both the numerator and denominator. This process is also commonly referred to as **canceling**. To simplify a fraction is to write that same fraction in its lowest possible terms without changing the value of the fraction.

HOW TO SIMPLIFY FRACTIONS:
A given fraction can be simplified or reduced to its lowest form by applying the Scaling-Down process until it reach's its lowest form and the fractions cant be reduced any further. As a thumb rule, whenever you are dealing with fractions, you'll need to put them in lowest terms. A fraction is said to be in its lowest terms when its numerator and denominator are not divisible by any common integer greater than 1.

For example, the fraction ½ is in lowest terms, but the fraction $\frac{5}{10}$ is not, since 5 and 10 are both divisible by 5.

Every fraction can be simplified or reduced to its lowest terms by applying one of the following two methods:

METHOD #1: To reduce a fraction to lowest terms, divide the numerator and the denominator by their Greatest Common Factor (GCF).

METHOD #2: To reduce a fraction to lowest terms, cancel all the common factors of the numerator and the denominator until there is no common factor other than 1.

CANCELING: The division of both numerator and denominator by common factors is called canceling. Canceling common factors does not change the value of the fraction.

For Example: Reduce $\frac{10}{14}$ to its lowest terms.

$\Rightarrow$ First, determine the largest common factor of the numerator and denominator, and then divide the top and bottom by that number to reduce:

$\Rightarrow \frac{10}{14} = \frac{5 \times 2}{7 \times 2} = \frac{5 \times 2 \div 2}{7 \times 2 \div 2} = \frac{5}{7}$

HOW TO CHECK IF A FRACTION IS IN ITS LOWEST TERMS:
A fraction is said to be in its lowest terms when the GCF of the numerator and the denominator is 1. In other words, if the GCF is 1, the fraction is already in lowest terms, and it can't be reduced any further. A fraction is in lowest terms if no positive integer greater than 1 is a factor of both the numerator and the denominator.

For Example: $\frac{80}{96} = \frac{5}{6}$ or $\frac{80}{96} = \frac{40}{48} = \frac{20}{24} = \frac{10}{12} = \frac{5}{6}$

$\Rightarrow$ This is the lowest term of the given fraction since it can't be reduced any further. The GCF of 80 and 96 is 16 so divide the numerator and the denominator by 16. Or cancel all the common factors of the numerator and the denominator until there is no common factor other than 1. The lowest form is 5/6; since the GCF of 5 & 6 is 1, the fraction can no longer be reduced.

EZ NOTE: Reduce all fractions before doing any work with them. Doing so will save a lot of time and prevent errors in computation.

2.5: COMMON AND LEAST COMMON DENOMINATORS:

2.5.1: COMMON DENOMINATORS (CD):

Common denominator is a number into which the denominators of all the fractions can be divided evenly without leaving any remainder. In other words, a common denominator is a common multiple of the denominators of two or more fractions. Common denominator is a useful tool while adding or subtracting fractions or while comparing the relative sizes of fractions.

HOW TO FIND COMMON DENOMINATOR (CD): To find a common denominator of two or more fractions, multiply all the denominators of the fractions. This denominator is just a common denominator, not necessarily the lowest common denominator (LCD).

For Example: Common Denominator of $\frac{1}{5}$ and $\frac{1}{10}$:

Multiply both the denominators: $5 \times 10 = 50$
Common Denominator = 50

2.5.2: LEAST COMMON DENOMINATOR (LCD):

The Least Common Multiple (LCM) of the denominators of a number of fractions is called their Least or Lowest Common Denominator (LCD). The Lowest Common Denominator (LCD) is the least common multiple of the denominators of two or more fractions. Least Common Denominator (LCD) is a useful tool while adding or subtracting fractions or while comparing the relative sizes of fractions.

HOW TO FIND LEAST OR LOWEST COMMON DENOMINATOR (LCD):

EZ STEP-BY-STEP METHOD: Apply the following step(s) to find the Least Common Denominator of two or more fractions:

STEP 1: List all the multiples of the denominator of the first fraction.

STEP 2: List all the multiples of the denominator of the second fraction.

STEP 3: The multiple that is smallest and common to both the denominators is the LCD.

Note: Simply list all the multiples of each of the denominators until there is a multiple that is common to all the denominators, this is also known as LCD.

EZ REFERENCE: For more in-depth knowledge about LCD and different methods to find LCD, refer to Least Common Multiple section of the chapter on Integers.

For Example: Lowest Common Denominators of 1/2 and 1/5:

Multiples of 2	2	4		6	8	10	12	14		16	18	20	22	24	
Multiples of 5			5			10			15			20			25

The above table shows that 10 and 20 are common denominators.
LCD: 10

DIFFERENCE BETWEEN CD & LCD:

A CD (common denominator) is just a common multiple of the denominators of the fractions. The LCD (lowest common denominator) is the least common multiple, i.e., the smallest positive number that is a multiple of all the terms.

In general, multiplying the denominators to find a common denominator (CD) will yield larger and harder to manage numbers. It's always better to find the lowest common denominator (LCD), especially while adding or subtracting large unlike fractions.

2.6: ARITHMETIC OPERATIONS WITH FRACTIONS:

2.6.1: ADDITION OF FRACTIONS:

2.6.1.1: ADDITION OF FRACTIONS WITH COMMON DENOMINATORS:
EZ STEP-BY-STEP METHOD: Apply the following step(s) to add fractions with same/common denominators:

STEP 1: Add together all the numerators of the given fractions to find the numerator of the result.

STEP 2: Use the same common denominator as the denominator of the result.

STEP 3: Finally, if possible, simplify/reduce the resulting fraction to its lowest terms to get the final answer.

EZ CAUTION: Do not add the denominators.

EZ RULE: $\dfrac{A}{C} + \dfrac{B}{C} = \dfrac{A+B}{C}$ **For Example:** $\dfrac{1}{9} + \dfrac{7}{9} = \dfrac{1+7}{9} = \dfrac{8}{9}$ (1 ninths + 7 ninths = 8 ninths)

2.6.1.2: ADDITION OF FRACTIONS WITH DIFFERENT DENOMINATORS:
METHOD #1: CRISS-CROSS METHOD:
(Suitable for adding fractions with small numbers)

EZ STEP-BY-STEP METHOD: Apply the following step(s) to add fractions with different denominators:

STEP 1: Multiply the numerator of first fraction with the denominator of the second fraction, i.e., from lower left to upper right

STEP 2: Multiply the numerator of second fraction with the denominator of the first fraction, i.e., from lower right to upper left.

STEP 3: Add the above two products and write that as the numerator of the result.

STEP 4: Multiply the denominator of the first fraction with the denominator of the second fraction and write that as the denominator of the result.

STEP 5: Finally, if possible, simplify/reduce the resulting fraction to its lowest terms to get the final answer.

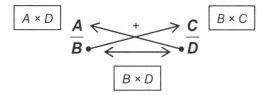

EZ RULE: $\dfrac{A}{B} + \dfrac{C}{D} = \dfrac{(A \times D) + (B \times C)}{(B \times D)}$ **For Example:** $\dfrac{5}{2} + \dfrac{8}{9} = \dfrac{(5 \times 9) + (8 \times 2)}{(2 \times 9)} = \dfrac{45 + 16}{18} = \dfrac{61}{18}$

METHOD #2: TRADITIONAL COMMON DENOMINATOR METHOD:
(Suitable for adding fractions with larger numbers)

EZ STEP-BY-STEP METHOD: Apply the following step(s) to add fractions with different denominators:

STEP 1: First, find the lowest common denominator (LCD) using any of the methods explained in the earlier section.
   Note: We can't add or subtract two fractions directly unless they have the same denominator. Therefore, before adding, we must first find the lowest common denominator (LCD).

STEP 2: Once the LCD has been found, all the numerators must be brought up to parity or equivalence.
   Note: Use the lowest common denominator (LCD) and convert (scale up) each fraction to equivalent fractions so that all the fractions has the lowest common denominator. In order to do that, multiply numerator and denominator of each fraction by the value that raises each denominator to the LCD. In other words, multiply each numerator by the number that raises its respective denominator to the LCD. (This number can be arrived at by dividing the LCD by the old or original denominator.)

STEP 3: Since the new like fractions, being equivalent to the originals, now have the common denominator, are now ready to be added, simply combine or add the fractions as usual, i.e., combine the numerators by adding and keep the LCD as the denominator.

STEP 4: Finally, if possible, simplify/reduce the resulting fraction to its lowest terms to get the final answer.
Note: This method is best suited for adding fractions with larger numbers.

For Example: $\dfrac{5}{2}+\dfrac{8}{9}=\left(\dfrac{5}{2}\times\dfrac{9}{9}\right)+\left(\dfrac{8}{9}\times\dfrac{2}{2}\right)=\dfrac{45}{18}+\dfrac{16}{18}=\dfrac{45+16}{18}=\dfrac{61}{18}$

EZ HINT: The easiest common denominator to find is the product of the denominators, but the best denominator to use is the least common denominator (LCD), which is the least common multiple of all the denominators. Using the least common denominator minimizes the amount of reducing that is necessary to express the final answer in lowest terms.

2.6.1.3: ADDITION OF FRACTION & INTEGER:

To add a fraction and any other number, write that number as a fraction whose denominator is 1, and then follow the same rules as given above.

EZ RULE: $\dfrac{A}{B}+n=\dfrac{A}{B}+\dfrac{n}{1}$

Example #1: $\dfrac{5}{6}+2=\dfrac{5}{6}+\dfrac{2}{1}=\dfrac{5}{6}+\dfrac{12}{6}=\dfrac{17}{6}$ **Example #2:** $\dfrac{7}{8}+2=\dfrac{7}{8}+\dfrac{2}{1}=\dfrac{7}{8}+\dfrac{16}{8}=\dfrac{23}{8}$

2.6.1.4: ADDITION OF MIXED NUMBER:

To add mixed numbers, add the integers separately, and add the fractions separately, using the rules given above.
EZ NOTE: If the addition of the fraction part results in an improper fraction, convert it into a mixed number and again add the whole part to the integer part.

Example #1: $1\dfrac{1}{2}+1\dfrac{1}{4}=(1+1)+\left(\dfrac{1}{2}+\dfrac{1}{4}\right)=2+\left(\dfrac{2}{4}+\dfrac{1}{4}\right)=2+\dfrac{3}{4}=2\dfrac{3}{4}$

Example #2: $5\dfrac{1}{2}+2\dfrac{3}{4}=(5+2)+\left(\dfrac{1}{2}+\dfrac{3}{4}\right)=7+\left(\dfrac{2}{4}+\dfrac{3}{4}\right)=7+\dfrac{5}{4}=7+1\dfrac{1}{4}=(7+1)\dfrac{1}{4}=8\dfrac{1}{4}$

EZ ALTERNATE METHOD: We can also add mixed numbers by first changing them to improper fractions, and then adding them using the rules given above, and then again changing them to mixed numbers.

Example #1: $1\dfrac{1}{2}+1\dfrac{1}{4}=\dfrac{3}{2}+\dfrac{5}{4}=\dfrac{6}{4}+\dfrac{5}{4}=\dfrac{11}{4}=2\dfrac{3}{4}$

Example #2: $5\dfrac{1}{2}+2\dfrac{3}{4}=\dfrac{11}{2}+\dfrac{11}{4}=\dfrac{22}{4}+\dfrac{11}{4}=\dfrac{33}{4}=8\dfrac{1}{4}$

2.6.2: SUBTRACTION OF FRACTIONS:

2.6.2.1: SUBTRACTION OF FRACTIONS WITH COMMON DENOMINATORS:

EZ STEP-BY-STEP METHOD: Apply the following step(s) to subtract fractions with the same/common denominators:
STEP 1: Subtract the numerators of the given fractions to find the numerator of the result.
STEP 2: Use the same common denominator as the denominator of the result.
STEP 3: Finally, if possible, simplify/reduce the resulting fraction to its lowest terms to get the final answer.
EZ NOTE: Do not subtract the denominators.

EZ RULE: $\dfrac{A}{C}-\dfrac{B}{C}=\dfrac{A-B}{C}$ **For Example:** $\dfrac{7}{9}-\dfrac{1}{9}=\dfrac{7-1}{9}=\dfrac{6}{9}$ (7 ninths – 1 ninths = 6 ninths)

2.6.2.2: SUBTRACTION OF FRACTIONS WITH DIFFERENT DENOMINATORS:

EZ METHOD #1: CRISS-CROSS METHOD:
(Suitable for subtracting only two fractions with small numbers)
EZ STEP-BY-STEP METHOD: Apply the following step(s) to subtract fractions with different denominators:

STEP 1: Multiply the numerator of first fraction with the denominator of the second fraction.

STEP 2: Multiply the numerator of second fraction with the denominator of the first fraction.

STEP 3: Subtract the above two products and write that as the numerator of the result.

STEP 4: Multiply the denominator of the first fraction with the denominator of the second fraction and write that as the denominator of the result.

STEP 5: Finally, if possible, simplify/reduce the resulting fraction to its lowest terms to get the final answer.

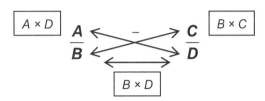

EZ RULE: $\dfrac{A}{B} - \dfrac{C}{D} = \dfrac{(A \times D) - (B \times C)}{(B \times D)}$ **For Example:** $\dfrac{5}{2} - \dfrac{8}{9} = \dfrac{(5 \times 9) - (8 \times 2)}{(2 \times 9)} = \dfrac{45 - 16}{18} = \dfrac{29}{18}$

EZ METHOD #2: TRADITIONAL COMMON DENOMINATOR METHOD:
(Suitable for subtracting fractions with larger numbers)

EZ STEP-BY-STEP METHOD: Apply the following step(s) to subtract fractions with different denominators:

STEP 1: First, find the lowest common denominator (LCD).
   Note: We can't add or subtract two fractions directly unless they have the same denominator. Therefore, before subtracting, we must first find the lowest common denominator (LCD). For more information on how to find LCD, refer to the previous section on LCD.

STEP 2: Once the LCD has been found, the numerators must be brought up to parity or equivalence.
   Note: Use the lowest common denominator (LCD) and convert (scale up) each fraction to equivalent fractions so that all the fractions has the lowest common denominator. In order to do that, multiply numerator and denominator of each fraction by the value that raises each denominator to the LCD. In other words, multiply each numerator by the number that raises its respective denominator to the LCD. (This number can be arrived at by dividing the LCD by the old or original denominator.)

STEP 3: Since the new like fractions, being equivalent to the originals, now have the common denominator, are now ready to be subtracted, simply combine or subtract the fractions as usual, i.e., combine the numerators by subtracting and keep the LCD as the denominator.

STEP 4: Finally, if possible, simplify/reduce the resulting fraction to its lowest terms to get the final answer.

Note: This method is best suited for subtracting fractions with larger numbers.

For Example: $\dfrac{5}{2} - \dfrac{8}{9} = \left(\dfrac{5}{2} \times \dfrac{9}{9}\right) - \left(\dfrac{8}{9} \times \dfrac{2}{2}\right) = \dfrac{45}{18} - \dfrac{16}{18} = \dfrac{45 - 16}{18} = \dfrac{29}{18}$

EZ HINT: The easiest common denominator to find is the product of the denominators, but the best denominator to use is the least common denominator (LCD), which is the least common multiple of all the denominators. Using the least common denominator minimizes the amount of reducing that is necessary to express the final answer in lowest terms.

2.6.2.3: SUBTRACTION OF FRACTION & INTEGER:
To subtract a fraction and any other number, write that number as a fraction whose denominator is 1, and then follow the same rules as given above.

EZ RULE: $\dfrac{A}{B} - n = \dfrac{A}{B} - \dfrac{n}{1}$

Example #1: $2 - \dfrac{5}{6} = \dfrac{2}{1} - \dfrac{5}{6} = \dfrac{12}{6} - \dfrac{5}{6} = \dfrac{7}{6}$ **Example #2:** $2 - \dfrac{7}{8} = \dfrac{2}{1} - \dfrac{7}{8} = \dfrac{16}{8} - \dfrac{7}{8} = \dfrac{9}{8}$

2.6.2.4: SUBTRACTION OF MIXED NUMBER:
To subtract mixed numbers, subtract the integers separately and subtract the fractions separately, using the rules given above.

EZ NOTE: If, however, the fraction in the second number is greater than the fraction in the first number, we first have to borrow 1 from the integer part, and then do the subtraction.

Example #1: $1\dfrac{1}{2} - 1\dfrac{1}{4} = (1-1) + \left(\dfrac{1}{2} - \dfrac{1}{4}\right) = 0 + \left(\dfrac{2}{4} - \dfrac{1}{4}\right) = 0 + \dfrac{1}{4} = \dfrac{1}{4}$

Example #2: $9\dfrac{1}{2} - 2\dfrac{3}{4}$ $\Rightarrow$ Since ¾ > ½, we have to borrow 1 from 9:

$$9\dfrac{1}{2} = 9 + \dfrac{1}{2} = (8+1) + \dfrac{1}{2} = 8\left(1 + \dfrac{1}{2}\right) = 8 + \dfrac{3}{2} = 8\dfrac{3}{2}$$

$$\Rightarrow 9\dfrac{1}{2} - 2\dfrac{3}{4} = 8\dfrac{3}{2} - 2\dfrac{3}{4} = (8-2) + \left(\dfrac{3}{2} - \dfrac{3}{4}\right) = 6\left(\dfrac{6}{4} - \dfrac{3}{4}\right) = 6\dfrac{3}{4}$$

EZ ALTERNATE METHOD: We can also subtract mixed numbers by first changing them to improper fractions, and then subtracting them using the rules given above, and then again changing them to mixed numbers.

Example #1: $1\dfrac{1}{2} - 1\dfrac{1}{4} = \dfrac{3}{2} - \dfrac{5}{4} = \dfrac{6}{4} - \dfrac{5}{4} = \dfrac{1}{4}$

Example #2: $9\dfrac{1}{2} - 2\dfrac{3}{4} = \dfrac{19}{2} - \dfrac{11}{4} = \dfrac{38}{4} - \dfrac{11}{4} = \dfrac{27}{4} = 6\dfrac{3}{4}$

2.6.3: MULTIPLICATION OF FRACTIONS:

2.6.3.1: MULTIPLICATION OF TWO FRACTIONS:

EZ STEP-BY-STEP METHOD: Apply the following step(s) to multiply any two given fractions:

STEP 1: Multiply the numerators straight across ⇒ i.e., multiply the numerator of first fraction with the numerator of the second fraction and write that as the numerator of the result.

STEP 2: Multiply the denominators straight across ⇒ i.e., multiply the denominator of first fraction with the denominator of the second fraction and write that as the denominator of the result.

STEP 3: Finally, if possible, simplify/reduce the resulting fraction to its lowest terms to get the final answer.

Note: You don't have to find a common denominator to multiply fractions.

EZ RULE: To multiply two simple fractions, multiply the numerators together to get the new numerator and multiply the denominators together to get the new denominator.

$$\dfrac{A}{B} \quad \underset{\xleftarrow{\hspace{2em}}}{\overset{\xrightarrow{\hspace{2em}}}{}} \quad \dfrac{C}{D} \qquad \boxed{A \times C} \\ \boxed{B \times D}$$

EZ RULE: $\dfrac{A}{B} \times \dfrac{C}{D} = \dfrac{(A \times C)}{(B \times D)}$

Example #1: $\dfrac{2}{7} \times \dfrac{5}{8} = \dfrac{(2 \times 5)}{(7 \times 8)} = \dfrac{10}{56} = \dfrac{5}{28}$ **Example #2:** $\dfrac{1}{9} \times \dfrac{7}{8} = \dfrac{(1 \times 7)}{(9 \times 8)} = \dfrac{7}{72}$

2.6.3.2: MULTIPLICATION OF FRACTION AND INTEGER:

To multiply a fraction by any other number, write that number as a fraction whose denominator is 1, and then follow the same rules as given above. We can also multiply the numerator by the whole number and leave the denominator as it is.

EZ RULE: $\dfrac{A}{B} \times n = \dfrac{A}{B} \times \dfrac{n}{1}$

Example #1: $\dfrac{6}{7} \times 2 = \dfrac{6}{7} \times \dfrac{2}{1} = \dfrac{12}{7}$ **Example #2:** $\dfrac{8}{9} \times 2 = \dfrac{8}{9} \times \dfrac{2}{1} = \dfrac{16}{9}$

2.6.3.3: MULTIPLICATION OF MIXED NUMBERS:

To multiply mixed numbers, first change them to improper fractions, and then multiply using the rules given above, and then again changing them to mixed numbers.

For Example: $1\dfrac{1}{2} \times 1\dfrac{1}{4} = \dfrac{3}{2} \times \dfrac{5}{4} = \dfrac{15}{8} = 1\dfrac{7}{8}$

EZ CAUTION: $2 \times 5\dfrac{1}{2}$ = is not equal to $10\dfrac{1}{2}$; Instead: $2 \times 5\dfrac{1}{2} = 2(5 + \dfrac{1}{2}) = 10 + 1 = 11$

MULTIPLICATION SHORTCUT: REDUCE FRACTIONS BEFORE MULTIPLYING:

Before multiplying any fractions, first cancel the common factors. Canceling before multiplying fractions eliminates complex multiplication and the need to reduce the answer, both of which can sometimes get very complicated.

EZ STEP-BY-STEP METHOD: Apply the following step(s) to cancel fractions while multiplying:

STEP 1: Find a common factor between any of the numerators and denominators, i.e., a number that divides evenly into either one of the numerators and either one of the denominators.

STEP 2: Next, divide each of them, the numerator and the denominator by that common factor.

STEP 3: Keep on repeating step 1 & 2 until you can't find anymore common factors to cancel.

EZ NOTE: While multiplying fractions, we can cancel vertically and diagonally, i.e., up-and-down or cross-cancel.

For Example: By Canceling: Without Canceling:

$$\Rightarrow \frac{9}{\cancel{8}} \times \frac{\cancel{8}}{\cancel{7}} \times \frac{\cancel{7}}{\cancel{6}} \times \frac{\cancel{6}}{5} = \frac{9}{5} \qquad\qquad \Rightarrow \frac{9}{8} \times \frac{8}{7} \times \frac{7}{6} \times \frac{6}{5} = \frac{3024}{1680} = \frac{9}{5}$$

$$\Rightarrow \frac{\cancel{25}^{\,5}}{\cancel{12}^{\,2}} \times \frac{\cancel{6}^{\,1}}{\cancel{5}^{\,1}} = \frac{5}{2} \qquad\qquad \Rightarrow \frac{25}{12} \times \frac{6}{5} = \frac{150}{60} = \frac{5}{2}$$

$\Rightarrow$ As you can notice from the above examples, it can be very time-consuming to reduce an answer after multiplication. Therefore, to make things easy, always reduce before multiplying.

EZ TIP: Cross-canceling the fractions can only be done when multiplying, not when adding/subtracting.

Product of Fractions can be equal to 1:   **For Example:** $\dfrac{11}{2} \times \dfrac{2}{5} \times \dfrac{5}{7} \times \dfrac{7}{9} \times \dfrac{9}{11} = 1$

Note: When all the factors of the numerator and denominator cancel each other, the result is 1, not 0.

2.6.4: DIVISION OF FRACTIONS:

2.6.4.1: DIVISION OF TWO FRACTIONS:

EZ STEP-BY-STEP METHOD: Apply the following step(s) to divide any two given fractions:

STEP 1: Before dividing one fraction (the dividend) by another fraction (the divisor), first invert (flip-over) or take the reciprocal of the divisor (the second fraction).

STEP 2: Change the operation sign from division sign to a multiplication sign and multiply the fractions as usual.

STEP 3: Multiply the numerators straight across $\Rightarrow$ i.e., multiply the numerator of first fraction with the numerator of the second fraction and write that as the numerator of the result.

STEP 4: Multiply the denominators straight across $\Rightarrow$ i.e., multiply the denominator of first fraction with the denominator of the second fraction and write that as the denominator of the result.

STEP 5: Finally, if possible, simplify/reduce the resulting fraction to its lowest terms to get the final answer.

EZ NOTE: We don't have to find a common denominator to divide fractions.

EZ RULE: To divide two simple fractions, invert the second fraction (the divisor), and then multiply straight across, i.e., multiply the numerators together to get the new numerator and multiply the denominators together to get the new denominator.

Note: Dividing by a fraction is the same as multiplying by its reciprocal.

EZ RULE: $\dfrac{A}{B} \div \dfrac{C}{D} = \dfrac{A}{B} \times \dfrac{D}{C} = \dfrac{(A \times D)}{(B \times C)}$

Example #1: $\dfrac{2}{7} \div \dfrac{8}{5} = \dfrac{2}{7} \times \dfrac{5}{8} = \dfrac{(2 \times 5)}{(7 \times 8)} = \dfrac{10}{56} = \dfrac{5}{28}$ **Example #2:** $\dfrac{1}{9} \div \dfrac{8}{7} = \dfrac{1}{9} \times \dfrac{7}{8} = \dfrac{(1 \times 7)}{(9 \times 8)} = \dfrac{7}{72}$

2.6.4.2: DIVISION OF FRACTION AND INTEGER:

(A) To divide a fraction by any other whole number, write that whole number as a fraction whose denominator is 1, and then multiply the reciprocal of the fraction by that number following the same rules as given above in 2.6.4.1.

EZ RULE: $\dfrac{A}{B} \div n = \dfrac{A}{B} \div \dfrac{n}{1} = \dfrac{A}{B} \times \dfrac{1}{n}$

Example #1: $\dfrac{5}{6} \div 2 = \dfrac{5}{6} \div \dfrac{2}{1} = \dfrac{5}{6} \times \dfrac{1}{2} = \dfrac{5}{12}$ **Example #2:** $\dfrac{7}{8} \div 2 = \dfrac{7}{8} \div \dfrac{2}{1} = \dfrac{7}{8} \times \dfrac{1}{2} = \dfrac{7}{16}$

(B) To divide any whole number by a fraction, write that whole number as a fraction whose denominator is 1, and then multiply that number by the reciprocal of the fraction following the same rules as given above in 2.6.4.1.

EZ RULE: $n \div \dfrac{A}{B} = \dfrac{n}{1} \div \dfrac{A}{B} = \dfrac{n}{1} \times \dfrac{B}{A}$

Example #1: $2 \div \dfrac{5}{6} = \dfrac{2}{1} \div \dfrac{5}{6} = \dfrac{2}{1} \times \dfrac{6}{5} = \dfrac{12}{5}$ **Example #2:** $2 \div \dfrac{7}{8} = \dfrac{2}{1} \div \dfrac{7}{8} = \dfrac{2}{1} \times \dfrac{8}{7} = \dfrac{16}{7}$

2.6.4.3: DIVISION OF MIXED NUMBERS:

EZ RULE: To divide mixed numbers, first change them to improper fractions, and then multiply using the rule given above, and then again changing them to mixed numbers.

For Example: $1\dfrac{1}{2} \div 1\dfrac{1}{4} = \dfrac{3}{2} \div \dfrac{5}{4} = \dfrac{3}{2} \times \dfrac{4}{5} = \dfrac{12}{10} = \dfrac{6}{5} = 1\dfrac{1}{5}$

2.6.4.4: DOUBLE DIVISIONS:

Sometimes double division can be confusing because of the way it is written. Don't get confused. When there is a double division fraction, that is, a fraction written with four terms, just rewrite it as the top fraction divided by the bottom fraction, and solve it normally (by using the reciprocal of the divisor and then multiplying).

For Example: $\dfrac{\frac{1}{2}}{\frac{5}{7}} = \dfrac{1}{2} \div \dfrac{5}{7} = \dfrac{1}{2} \times \dfrac{7}{5} = \dfrac{7}{10}$

MULTIPLE OPERATIONS WITH FRACTIONS:

To apply multiple operations in fractions, apply the same PEMDAS rules.

Example #1: Simplify $\dfrac{1}{2} + \left[\left(\dfrac{1}{2} \div \dfrac{1}{2} \right) \times \dfrac{1}{2} \right] - \dfrac{1}{2}$ **Example #2:** Simplify $\dfrac{1}{2} + \left[\left(\dfrac{2}{5} \div \dfrac{2}{7} \right) \times \dfrac{1}{2} \right] - \dfrac{1}{5}$

Solution:

$\Rightarrow \dfrac{1}{2} + \left[\left(\dfrac{1}{2} \times \dfrac{2}{1} \right) \times \dfrac{1}{2} \right] - \dfrac{1}{2}$ $\Rightarrow \dfrac{1}{2} + \left[\left(\dfrac{2}{5} \times \dfrac{7}{2} \right) \times \dfrac{1}{2} \right] - \dfrac{1}{5}$

$\Rightarrow \dfrac{1}{2} + \left[(1) \times \dfrac{1}{2} \right] - \dfrac{1}{2}$ $\Rightarrow \dfrac{1}{2} + \left[\left(\dfrac{7}{5} \right) \times \dfrac{1}{2} \right] - \dfrac{1}{5}$

$\Rightarrow \dfrac{1}{2} + \dfrac{1}{2} - \dfrac{1}{2}$ $\Rightarrow \dfrac{1}{2} + \dfrac{7}{10} - \dfrac{1}{5}$

$\Rightarrow \dfrac{1}{2}$ $\Rightarrow \dfrac{5}{10} + \dfrac{7}{10} - \dfrac{2}{10}$

                                         $\Rightarrow \dfrac{10}{10}$

                                         $\Rightarrow 1$

2.7: FACTS ABOUT FRACTIONS:

DISTRIBUTING FRACTIONS:

DISTRIBUTIVE LAWS WITH FRACTIONS:
The laws of operations that you learned in the chapter on integers are also applicable to fraction.

For Example: $\frac{1}{2}\left(\frac{1}{3}+\frac{1}{4}\right) \Rightarrow \frac{1}{2}\left(\frac{1}{3}+\frac{1}{4}\right) = \left(\frac{1}{2}\times\frac{1}{3}\right) + \left(\frac{1}{2}\times\frac{1}{4}\right) = \frac{1}{6}+\frac{1}{8} = \frac{4}{24}+\frac{3}{24} = \frac{7}{24}$

Distribution is not always possible when it comes to distributing compound fractions. A compound fraction is a fraction in which there is a sum or a difference in the numerator and/or the denominator.

DISTRIBUTING (SPLITTING-UP) THE NUMERATORS & DENOMINATORS:
While working with compound fractions, you must always remember the following important rule.

EZ RULE: While simplifying fractions that contain sums or differences in the numerator and/or the denominator
⇒ you may (distribute) split up the terms of the numerator, but you can NEVER (distribute) split the terms of the denominator.

Scenario#1:   When the numerator is expressed as a sum/difference: You can (distribute) split-up the numerator.

$\Rightarrow \frac{a+b}{c} = \frac{a}{c} + \frac{b}{c}$

For Example: $\frac{10+15}{5} = \frac{10}{5} + \frac{15}{5} = 2 + 3 = 5$

Scenario #2:   When the denominator is expressed as a sum/difference: You CAN NOT (distribute) split-up the denominator; instead simplify the denominator first.

$\Rightarrow \frac{a}{b+c} \neq \frac{a}{b} + \frac{a}{c}$

For Example: $\frac{5}{10+15} \neq \frac{5}{10} + \frac{5}{15}$ WRONG!

$\Rightarrow \frac{5}{10+15} = \frac{5}{25} = \frac{1}{5}$ CORRECT!

Scenario #3:   When both the numerator and the denominator are expressed as sums/difference: You CAN NOT (distribute) split-up either the numerator or the denominator; instead simplify the numerator and the denominator first.

$\Rightarrow \frac{a+b}{c+d} \neq \frac{a}{c} + \frac{b}{d}$

For Example: $\frac{15+10}{5+2} \neq \frac{15}{5} + \frac{10}{2}$ WRONG!

$\Rightarrow \frac{15+10}{5+2} = \frac{25}{7}$ CORRECT!

RULES FOR FRACTIONS BETWEEN 0 & 1:

The following rules govern the relationship between the numerator and the denominator of proper fractions between 0 and 1. Be careful, these rules apply only to positive proper fractions, that is, fractions that are between 0 and 1.

EZ RULE #1:   In any fraction between 0 and 1: If the numerator of a fraction is increased, while keeping the denominator constant, the value of the fraction increases as it approaches 1.

For Example: $0 < \dfrac{1}{8} < \dfrac{2}{8} < \dfrac{3}{8} < \dfrac{4}{8} < \dfrac{5}{8} < \dfrac{6}{8} < \dfrac{7}{8} < \dfrac{8}{8} = 1$

Conversely: In any fraction between 0 and 1: If the numerator of a fraction is decreased, while keeping the denominator constant, the value of the fraction decreases as it approaches 0.

For Example: $1 = \dfrac{8}{8} > \dfrac{7}{8} > \dfrac{6}{8} > \dfrac{5}{8} > \dfrac{4}{8} > \dfrac{3}{8} > \dfrac{2}{8} > \dfrac{1}{8} > 0$

EZ RULE #2: In any fraction between 0 and 1: If the denominator of a fraction is increased, while keeping the numerator constant, the value of the fraction decreases as it approaches 0.

For Example: $1 = \dfrac{1}{1} > \dfrac{1}{2} > \dfrac{1}{3} > \dfrac{1}{4} > \dfrac{1}{5} > \dfrac{1}{6} > \dfrac{1}{7} > \dfrac{1}{8} > \dfrac{1}{1000} \approx 0$

Conversely: In any fraction between 0 and 1: If the denominator of a fraction is decreased, while keeping the numerator constant, the value of the fraction increases as it approaches 1.

For Example: $0 \approx \dfrac{1}{1000} < \dfrac{1}{8} < \dfrac{1}{7} < \dfrac{1}{6} < \dfrac{1}{5} < \dfrac{1}{4} < \dfrac{1}{3} < \dfrac{1}{2} < \dfrac{1}{1} = 1$

EZ RULE #3: In any fraction between 0 and 1: Increasing both the numerator and the denominator by the same value makes the fraction closer to 1. If you add the same number to both the numerator and the denominator, the value of the fraction increases as it approaches 1.

For Example: $\dfrac{1}{2} < \dfrac{1+1}{2+1} = \dfrac{2}{3} < \dfrac{2+9}{3+9} = \dfrac{11}{12} < \dfrac{11+100}{12+100} = \dfrac{111}{112} < \dfrac{111+1000}{112+1000} = \dfrac{1111}{1112}$

$\Rightarrow \dfrac{1}{2} < \dfrac{2}{3} < \dfrac{11}{12} < \dfrac{111}{112} < \dfrac{1111}{1112} \approx 1$

Conversely: In any fraction between 0 and 1: Decreasing both the numerator and the denominator by the same value makes the fraction closer to 0. If you subtract the same number from both the numerator and the denominator, the value of the fraction decreases as it approaches 0.

For Example: $\dfrac{1111}{1112} > \dfrac{1111-1000}{1112-1000} = \dfrac{111}{112} > \dfrac{111-100}{112-100} = \dfrac{11}{12} > \dfrac{11-9}{12-9} = \dfrac{2}{3} > \dfrac{2-1}{3-1} = \dfrac{1}{2}$

$\Rightarrow \dfrac{1111}{1112} > \dfrac{111}{112} > \dfrac{11}{12} > \dfrac{2}{3} > \dfrac{1}{2} \approx 0$

RULES FOR FRACTIONS BETWEEN –1 AND 1:

EZ RULE #1: The reciprocal of any given number between 0 and 1 is greater than the given number.

$\Rightarrow$ If $0 < n < 1$ $\Rightarrow$ then, $\dfrac{1}{n} > n$

For Example: The reciprocal of $\dfrac{2}{5} = \dfrac{1}{\frac{2}{5}} = \dfrac{5}{2} = 2\dfrac{1}{2}$, which is greater than $\dfrac{2}{5}$ $\qquad \Rightarrow$ Therefore, $\dfrac{2}{5} < \dfrac{5}{2}$

EZ RULE #2: The reciprocal of any given number between –1 and 0 is less than the given number.

$\Rightarrow$ If $-1 < n < 0$ $\Rightarrow$ then, $-\dfrac{1}{n} > -n$

For Example: The reciprocal of $-\dfrac{2}{5} = \dfrac{1}{\left(-\frac{2}{5}\right)} = -\dfrac{5}{2} = -2\dfrac{1}{2}$, which is smaller than $-\dfrac{2}{5}$ $\qquad \Rightarrow$ Therefore, $-\dfrac{2}{5} > -\dfrac{5}{2}$

EZ RULE #3: The square of any given number between 0 and 1 is always smaller than the original given number.
$\Rightarrow$ If $0 < n < 1$ $\Rightarrow$ then, $n^2 < n$

For Example: $\left(\dfrac{1}{2}\right)^2 = \dfrac{1}{2} \times \dfrac{1}{2} = \dfrac{1}{4}$, which is less than ½ $\qquad \Rightarrow$ Therefore, $\dfrac{1}{2} > \dfrac{1}{4}$

EZ RULE #4:   Multiplying any given positive number by a fraction between 0 and 1 gives a product smaller than the given original number.

$\Rightarrow$ If m and n are any positive numbers $\Rightarrow$ then, $m \times \left(\dfrac{1}{n}\right) > q$

For Example: $5 \bullet \left(\dfrac{1}{2}\right) = \dfrac{5}{2} = 2\dfrac{1}{2}$, which is less than 5 $\Rightarrow$ Therefore, $5 > \dfrac{5}{2}$

EZ RULE #5:   Multiplying any given negative number by a fraction between 0 and 1 gives a product greater than the given original number.

$\Rightarrow$ If n is any positive numbers and m is any negative number $\Rightarrow$ then, $-m \times \left(\dfrac{1}{n}\right) > -m$

For Example: $-5 \bullet \left(\dfrac{1}{2}\right) = -\dfrac{5}{2} = -2\dfrac{1}{2}$, which is greater than –5 $\Rightarrow$ Therefore, $-5 < -\dfrac{5}{2}$

FRACTION OPERATIONS FOR POSITIVE PROPER FRACTIONS:

The following rules govern the outcome when performing basic operations – addition, subtraction, multiplication, and division – on proper fractions, that is, fractions that are between 0 and 1. Consider the following rules as they yield some unexpected results.

Adding Two Proper Fractions: Similar to adding positive integers, adding proper fractions increases their value.

For Example: $\dfrac{1}{2} + \dfrac{1}{5} = \dfrac{5+2}{10} = \dfrac{7}{10}$

Subtracting Two Proper Fractions: Similar to subtracting positive integers, subtracting proper fractions decreases their value.

For Example: $\dfrac{1}{2} - \dfrac{1}{5} = \dfrac{5-2}{10} = \dfrac{3}{10}$

Multiplying Two Proper Fractions: Unlike multiplying positive integers, multiplying proper fractions decreases their value.

For Example: $\dfrac{1}{2} \times \dfrac{1}{5} = \dfrac{1}{10}$

Dividing Two Proper Fractions: Unlike dividing positive integers, dividing proper fractions increases their value.

For Example: $\dfrac{1}{2} \div \dfrac{1}{5} = \dfrac{1}{2} \times \dfrac{5}{1} = \dfrac{5}{2}$

EZ NOTE: It's interesting to note that multiplying proper fractions decreases their value, while dividing proper fractions increases their value; something that is exactly the opposite of what happens with integers or even improper fractions.

FRACTION AS PART-WHOLE RELATIONSHIP:

FRACTION OF A NUMBER:

(A) To find a fraction of a number $\Rightarrow$ multiply the fraction by the number. **For Example:** $\dfrac{1}{5}$ of $55 = \dfrac{1}{5} \times 55 = 11$

(B) To find a fraction of a fraction $\Rightarrow$ multiply the fraction by the fraction. **For Example:** $\dfrac{1}{2}$ of $\dfrac{1}{5} = \dfrac{1}{2} \times \dfrac{1}{5} = \dfrac{1}{10}$

For Example: If one-half of the 250 freshmen at a High School are boys, and one-fifth of the boys are athletes, how many freshmen are boy athletes?

Solution: No. of freshmen boys $\Rightarrow \dfrac{1}{2}$ of 250 = 125   No. of freshmen boy athletes $\Rightarrow \dfrac{1}{5} \times 125 = 25$

SUM OF ALL THE PARTS OF THE SAME WHOLE IS 1:

If $\frac{a}{b}$ is the fraction of a whole that satisfies some property, then $1 - \frac{a}{b}$ is the fraction of the same whole that does not satisfy it. All parts of the same whole must sum up to the whole. For Instance: If ¼ of a math class consists of boys, then $1 - ¼ = ¾$ of the same math class consists of girls.

For Example: If one-half of the 250 freshmen at a High School are boys, and one-fifth of the boys are athletes, how many freshmen are boys who are not athletes?

Solution: No. of freshmen boys $\Rightarrow \frac{1}{2}$ of 250 = 125

No. of freshmen boys who are athletes $\Rightarrow \frac{1}{5} \times 125 = 25$

No. of freshmen boys who are not athletes $\Rightarrow 1 - \frac{1}{5} = \frac{4}{5}$ of 125 = 100

DIFFERENCE BETWEEN "OF THE WHOLE" AND "OF THE REMAINING":

There is a clear difference between *"of the whole"* and *"of the remaining or leftover"*; both phrases mean different things, and must be dealt differently. Note the following two examples, which illustrate the difference.

Example #1: If John ate $\frac{1}{3}$ of the pie and Tom ate $\frac{1}{4}$ of it, what fraction of the pie was still uneaten?

Solution: Part of the pie that was eaten $\Rightarrow$ John + Tom = $\frac{1}{3} + \frac{1}{4} = \frac{4}{12} + \frac{3}{12} = \frac{7}{12}$

Remaining Part uneaten $\Rightarrow 1 - \frac{7}{12} = \frac{5}{12}$

Example #2: If John ate $\frac{1}{3}$ of the pie and Tom ate $\frac{1}{4}$ of what was left, what fraction of the pie was still uneaten?

Solution: Part of the pie that John ate $\Rightarrow \frac{1}{3}$

Remaining Part $\Rightarrow 1 - \frac{1}{3} = \frac{2}{3}$

Part of the Pie that Tom ate $\Rightarrow \frac{1}{4} \times \frac{2}{3} = \frac{1}{6}$

Total Part of the pie eaten $\Rightarrow$ John + Tom = $\frac{1}{3} + \frac{1}{6} = \frac{2}{6} + \frac{1}{6} = \frac{3}{6} = \frac{1}{2}$

Total Remaining Part uneaten $\Rightarrow 1 - \frac{1}{2} = \frac{1}{2}$

Note: In the first example, Tom ate ¼ of whole pie, and in the second example, he only ate ¼ of what was left after John got his share, both are different.

2.8: COMPARING FRACTIONS:

2.8.1: UNIVERSAL METHOD:

EZ STEPS: Apply the following step(s) to compare two or more fractions of any type:

STEP 1: First, convert all the given fractions into decimal numbers by dividing the numerator by the denominator.

STEP 2: Next, apply the same rules for comparing decimals (given in the decimal section later in the book).

For Example: Compare and find the smallest and the largest fraction:

$$\frac{5}{6} \qquad \frac{7}{8} \qquad \frac{9}{10} \qquad \frac{8}{9} \qquad \frac{6}{7}$$
$$\downarrow \qquad \downarrow \qquad \downarrow \qquad \downarrow \qquad \downarrow$$
$$0.833 \qquad 0.875 \qquad 0.9 \qquad 0.888 \qquad 0.857$$

Convert all the given fractions into decimals and then apply the same rules for comparing decimals.

Since 0.833 is the smallest number, therefore, $\frac{5}{6}$ is the smallest fraction.

Since 0.9 is the largest number, therefore, $\frac{9}{10}$ is the largest fraction.

Other Methods to Compare Fractions: For a shorter and quicker way to compare fractions, following are the different methods to compare fractions according to the types of fractions.

2.8.2: CROSS MULTIPLICATION METHOD:

Apply this method to compare any two fractions:

EZ STEP-BY-STEP METHOD: Apply the following step(s) to compare any two fractions of any type:

STEP 1: First, cross-multiply the denominator of one fraction by the numerator of the other fraction and mark the product by circling them.
Note: Always cross multiply from the bottom up (like a criss-cross X in which both strokes start from the bottom and mark the product where you end up).

STEP 2: Next, compare the products obtained in the circles – if the number to the right is greater, then fraction on the right is greater; and if the number to the left is greater, then the fraction to the left is greater.

$\Rightarrow$ If $ad > bc$, then $\frac{a}{b} > \frac{c}{d}$ $\qquad$ $\Rightarrow$ If $ad < bc$, then $\frac{a}{b} < \frac{c}{d}$ $\qquad$ $\Rightarrow$ If $ad = bc$, then $\frac{a}{b} = \frac{c}{d}$

For Example: Compare and find the smaller and larger fraction:

$$Smaller \longleftarrow \boxed{54} \quad \frac{6}{7} \quad \times \quad \frac{8}{9} \quad \boxed{56} \longrightarrow Bigger$$

$\Rightarrow$ Since 54 is the smaller number, therefore, $\frac{6}{7}$ is the smaller fraction.

$\Rightarrow$ Since 56 is the larger number, therefore, $\frac{8}{9}$ is the larger fraction.

2.8.3: SAME DENOMINATOR/ NUMERATOR METHOD:

SAME DENOMINATOR METHOD:

Apply this method to compare fractions with the same positive denominator:

EZ STEP-BY-STEP METHOD: Apply the following step(s) to compare fractions with the same positive denominator:

STEP 1: Compare the numerators – the fraction with the smallest numerator is the smallest fraction, and the fraction with the largest numerator is the largest fraction.

EZ HINT: Logically thinking, if we divide a pie into 10 equal pieces, 9 of those pieces are larger than 7 of those pieces. Just like \$9 are more than \$7 or 9 points are more than 7 points. Therefore, 9 tenths is more than 7 tenths $\Rightarrow \dfrac{9}{10} > \dfrac{7}{10}$.

For Example: Compare and find the smallest and the largest fraction:

$$\frac{6}{5} \qquad \frac{7}{5} \qquad \frac{8}{5} \qquad \frac{9}{5} \qquad \frac{11}{5}$$

Since all the fractions have the same denominators, compare the numerators, the fraction with the smallest numerator is the smallest fraction, and the fraction with the largest numerator is the largest fraction. Since 6 is the smallest numerator, 6/5 is the smallest fraction and since 11 is the largest numerator, 11/5 is the largest fraction.

SAME NUMERATOR METHOD:

Apply this method to compare fractions with the same positive numerator:

EZ STEP-BY-STEP METHOD: Apply the following step(s) to compare fractions with the same positive numerator:

STEP 1: Compare the denominators – the fraction with the largest denominator is the smallest fraction, and the fraction with the smallest denominator is the largest fraction.

EZ HINT: Logically thinking, if we cut a pie into 3 equal pieces, each piece is larger than a piece we would get if we had divided the pie into 4 equal pieces. Therefore one-third is more than one-fourth $\Rightarrow \dfrac{1}{3} > \dfrac{1}{4}$. Likewise, if two equal size pizzas are cut, one into 7 equal slices and the other into 9 equal slices, and if you could pick 2 slices from either one of the pizzas, you'll get a bigger share if you pick $\dfrac{2}{7}$ of the first pizza than $\dfrac{2}{9}$ of the second pizza.

For Example: Compare and find the smallest and the largest fraction:

$$\frac{5}{6} \qquad \frac{5}{7} \qquad \frac{5}{8} \qquad \frac{5}{9} \qquad \frac{5}{11}$$

Since all the fractions have the same numerators, compare the denominators, the fraction with the largest denominator is the smallest fraction, and the fraction with the smallest denominator is the largest fraction. Since 11 is the largest denominator, 5/11 is the smallest fraction, and since 6 is the smallest denominator, 5/6 is the largest fraction.

2.8.4: FINDING THE COMMON DENOMINATOR/ NUMERATOR METHOD:

FINDING THE COMMON DENOMINATOR METHOD:

Apply this method to compare fractions with different numerators and denominators.

EZ STEP-BY-STEP METHOD: Apply the following step(s) to compare fractions with different positive denominator or numerator:

STEP 1: First, find the least common denominator (LCD) of all the fraction, then scale-up and express all the fractions over the least common denominator so that now all the fractions have the same (LCD) denominator.

STEP 2: Next, compare the numerators – the fraction with the smallest numerator is the smallest fraction, and the fraction with the largest numerator is largest fraction.

EZ HINT: You can convert given fractions to those with common denominators in order to compare them. For instance, converting ½ to 3/6 may help you determine whether it is greater than or less than 5/6. Similarly, to determine whether ½ is greater than or less than 2/5, convert both numbers to fractions with 10 as the denominator, that is, 5/10 and 4/10.

For Example: Compare and find the smallest and largest fraction:

$$\frac{3}{2} \qquad \frac{5}{3} \qquad \frac{7}{4} \qquad \frac{11}{6} \qquad \frac{19}{12} \quad \Rightarrow \text{Scale-Up} \Rightarrow \quad \frac{18}{12} \qquad \frac{20}{12} \qquad \frac{21}{12} \qquad \frac{22}{12} \qquad \frac{19}{12}$$

Since all the fractions now have the same denominators, compare the numerators, the fraction with the smallest numerator is the smallest fraction and the fraction with the largest numerator is the largest fraction. Therefore, 18/12 or 3/2 is the smallest fraction and 22/12 or 11/6 is the largest fraction.

FINDING THE COMMON NUMERATOR METHOD:

Apply this method to compare fractions with different numerators and denominators.

EZ STEP-BY-STEP METHOD: Apply the following step(s) to compare fractions with different positive denominator or numerator:

STEP 1: First, find the least common numerator (LCN) of all the fraction, then scale-up and express all the fractions under the least common numerator so that now all the fractions have the same numerator.

STEP 2: Next, compare the denominators – the fraction with the smallest denominator is the largest fraction, and the fraction with the largest denominator is the smallest fraction.

EZ HINT: You can convert given fractions to those with common numerators in order to compare them. For instance, converting 2/3 to 5/15 may help you determine whether it is greater than or less than 5/12. Similarly, to determine whether 2/3 is greater than or less than 5/7, convert both numbers to fractions with 10 as the numerator, that is, 10/15 and 10/14.

For Example: Compare and find the smallest and largest fraction:

$$\frac{2}{3} \qquad \frac{3}{5} \qquad \frac{4}{7} \qquad \frac{6}{11} \qquad \frac{12}{19} \quad \Rightarrow \text{Scale-up} \Rightarrow \quad \frac{12}{18} \qquad \frac{12}{20} \qquad \frac{12}{21} \qquad \frac{12}{22} \qquad \frac{12}{19}$$

Since all the fractions now have the same numerators, compare the denominators, the fraction with the smallest denominator is the largest fraction and the fraction with the largest denominator is the smallest fraction. Therefore, 12/22 or 6/11 is the smallest fraction and 12/18 or 2/3 is the largest fraction.

OTHER METHODS:

EYEBALLING METHOD:

Apply this method to compare fractions that are so distinct that the differences are clearly visible. Sometimes the fractions are so distinct and the difference is so clearly visible that it can easily be determined by eyeballing. In such cases, you may not need to perform time-consuming calculations to answer the question.

For instance: while comparing $\frac{9}{20}$ and $\frac{26}{50}$, we can very easily figure out which one of the fraction is bigger and which one is smaller without doing any calculations, by simply eyeballing the two given fractions. If you eyeball the fractions by taking a closer look, you'll realize that the first fraction $\frac{9}{20}$ is slightly less than ½ and the second fraction $\frac{26}{50}$ is slightly greater than ½. Therefore, it is clear that $\frac{26}{50}$ is the bigger fraction and $\frac{9}{20}$ is the smaller fraction.

EZ TIPS: Use the following tips while Eyeballing:
$\Rightarrow$ If in any fraction, the numerator is bigger than the denominator, then the value of that fraction is greater than 1.
$\Rightarrow$ If in any fraction, the denominator is bigger than the numerator, then the value of that fraction is less than 1.
$\Rightarrow$ Sometimes the fractions are so familiar or easy to work with that you already know the answer without doing any calculations.
For Example: ½, ¼, ¾, 1/3, 2/3 are some of the fractions that you are already familiar with.

Example #1: Compare and find the largest fraction: $\quad \frac{5}{6} \qquad \frac{6}{7} \qquad \frac{7}{6} \qquad \frac{7}{8} \qquad \frac{8}{9}$

There is only one fraction in which the numerator is bigger than the denominator, and in all the rest of the fractions, the numerator is smaller than the denominator. Therefore, 7/6 is the largest fraction.

Example #2: Compare and find the smallest fraction: $\quad \frac{9}{8} \qquad \frac{8}{7} \qquad \frac{6}{7} \qquad \frac{7}{6} \qquad \frac{6}{5}$

There is only one fraction in which the numerator is smaller than the denominator, and in all the rest of the fractions, the numerator is bigger than the denominator. Therefore, 6/7 is the smallest fraction.

COMPARING NEGATIVE FRACTIONS:

While comparing negative fractions, keep in mind the following tips:

EZ TIP #1: Any positive fraction is greater than any negative fraction, and any negative fraction is less than any positive fraction.

EZ TIP #2: While comparing negative fractions, use the fact that, if $a > b$, then $-a < -b$.

For Example: If $\frac{1}{2} > \frac{1}{5}$, then it implies that $\Rightarrow -\frac{1}{2} < -\frac{1}{5}$

2.9: COMPLEX FRACTIONS:

Complex fractions are fractions of fractions. A complex fraction is a fraction whose numerator and/or denominator are themselves fractions. In other words, a complex fraction is a fraction that contains one or more fractions in its numerator and/or denominator.

EZ NOTE: The numerator should be separated from the denominator by a long thick line.

$$\frac{\frac{a}{b}}{\frac{c}{d}} = \frac{a}{b} \div \frac{c}{d} = \frac{a}{b} \times \frac{d}{c} = \frac{ad}{bc}$$

The following are the two ways to simplify a complex fraction:

SIMPLIFYING METHOD:

EZ STEP-BY-STEP METHOD: Apply the following step(s) to simplify a complex fraction:

STEP 1: Simplify the numerator separately, and combine the terms to get a single fraction on the top.

STEP 2: Simplify the denominator separately, and combine the terms to get a single fraction on the bottom.

STEP 3: Now we are left with the division of two fractions, so divide the resulting top fraction by the bottom fraction by multiplying the top fraction by the reciprocal of the bottom one.

STEP 4: Finally, if possible, simplify/reduce the resulting fraction to its lowest terms to get the final answer.

EZ TIP: This method is preferable when it is difficult to get an LCM for all the denominators.

Example #1: $\Rightarrow \dfrac{1 + \dfrac{2}{9}}{2 + \dfrac{1}{7}}$

$\Rightarrow \dfrac{\dfrac{9}{9} + \dfrac{2}{9}}{\dfrac{14}{7} + \dfrac{1}{7}}$ [In the numerator & denominator, scale-up the fractions to the LCD]

$\Rightarrow \dfrac{\dfrac{11}{9}}{\dfrac{15}{7}}$ [Add the fractions in the numerator and the denominator]

$\Rightarrow \dfrac{11}{9} \div \dfrac{15}{7}$ [Divide the fraction in numerator by the fraction in denominator]

$\Rightarrow \dfrac{11}{9} \times \dfrac{7}{15}$ [Switch the division to multiplication sign and flip the second fraction]

$\Rightarrow \dfrac{77}{135}$ [Multiply the two fractions straight across]

Example #2: $\dfrac{\dfrac{1}{2} + \dfrac{2}{3}}{\dfrac{3}{4} + \dfrac{4}{5}}$

$\Rightarrow \dfrac{\dfrac{3}{6} + \dfrac{4}{6}}{\dfrac{15}{20} + \dfrac{16}{20}}$ [In the numerator & denominator, scale-up the fractions to the LCD]

$\Rightarrow \dfrac{\dfrac{7}{6}}{\dfrac{31}{20}}$ [Add the fractions in the numerator and the denominator]

$$\Rightarrow \frac{7}{6} \div \frac{31}{20}$$ [Divide the fraction in numerator by the fraction in denominator]

$$\Rightarrow \frac{7}{6} \times \frac{20}{31}$$ [Switch the division to multiplication sign and flip the second fraction]

$$\Rightarrow \frac{140}{186}$$ [Multiply the two fractions straight across]

$$\Rightarrow \frac{70}{93}$$ [Reduce the fraction to its lowest terms by cancelling by 2]

LCM METHOD:

EZ STEP-BY-STEP METHOD: Apply the following step(s) to simplify a complex fraction:

STEP 1: Multiply each and every term in the numerator and denominator of the complex fraction by the least common multiple (LCM) of all the denominators that appears in the complex fractions. Doing so will eliminate all the denominators, greatly simplifying the calculations.

STEP 2: Finally, if possible, simplify/reduce the resulting fraction to its lowest terms to get the final answer.

Example #1: $\dfrac{1+\dfrac{2}{9}}{2+\dfrac{1}{7}}$ (LCM of 9 & 7 is 63, multiply each term by 63, and then simplify.)

$$\Rightarrow \frac{63 \bullet \left(1 + \dfrac{2}{9}\right)}{63 \bullet \left(2 + \dfrac{1}{7}\right)}$$ [Multiply numerator & denominator by the LCD of all denominators]

$$\Rightarrow \frac{63(1) + 63\left(\dfrac{2}{9}\right)}{63(2) + 63\left(\dfrac{1}{7}\right)}$$ [Apply distributive property in the numerator and denominator]

$$\Rightarrow \frac{63 + 14}{126 + 9}$$ [Do the multiplications in the numerator and denominator]

$$\Rightarrow \frac{77}{135}$$ [Add the numbers in the in the numerator and denominator]

Example #2: $\dfrac{\dfrac{1}{2}+\dfrac{2}{3}}{\dfrac{3}{4}+\dfrac{4}{5}}$ (LCM of 2, 3, 4, & 5 is 60, multiply each term by 60, and then simplify.)

$$\Rightarrow \frac{60 \bullet \left(\dfrac{1}{2} + \dfrac{2}{3}\right)}{60 \bullet \left(\dfrac{3}{4} + \dfrac{4}{5}\right)}$$ [Multiply numerator & denominator by the LCD of all denominators]

$$\Rightarrow \frac{60\left(\dfrac{1}{2}\right) + 60\left(\dfrac{2}{3}\right)}{60\left(\dfrac{3}{4}\right) + 60\left(\dfrac{4}{5}\right)}$$ [Apply distributive property in the numerator and denominator]

$$\Rightarrow \frac{30 + 40}{45 + 48}$$ [Do the multiplications in the numerator and denominator]

$$\Rightarrow \frac{70}{93}$$ [Add the numbers in the in the numerator and denominator]

PRACTICE EXERCISE – QUESTIONS AND ANSWERS WITH EXPLANATIONS: FRACTIONS:

CONVERSION OF MIXED FRACTION INTO IMPROPER FRACTION: Convert the following mixed numbers to improper fractions:

Question #1: $2\dfrac{7}{9}$

Solution: $\Rightarrow \dfrac{(9 \times 2) + 7}{9}$ [Multiply the integer with the denominator and add the numerator]

           $\Rightarrow \dfrac{25}{9}$ [Simplify the expression]

Question #2: $5\dfrac{7}{9}$

Solution: $\Rightarrow \dfrac{(9 \times 5) + 7}{9}$ [Multiply the integer with the denominator and add the numerator]

           $\Rightarrow \dfrac{52}{9}$ [Simplify the expression]

Question #3: $7\dfrac{8}{9}$

Solution: $\Rightarrow \dfrac{(9 \times 7) + 8}{9}$ [Multiply the integer with the denominator and add the numerator]

           $\Rightarrow \dfrac{71}{9}$ [Simplify the expression]

Question #4: $9\dfrac{5}{7}$

Solution: $\Rightarrow \dfrac{(7 \times 9) + 5}{7}$ [Multiply the integer with the denominator and add the numerator]

           $\Rightarrow \dfrac{68}{7}$ [Simplify the expression]

Question #5: $17\dfrac{6}{5}$

Solution: $\Rightarrow \dfrac{(5 \times 17) + 6}{5}$ [Multiply the integer with the denominator and add the numerator]

           $\Rightarrow \dfrac{91}{5}$ [Simplify the expression]

CONVERSION OF IMPROPER FRACTION INTO MIXED FRACTION: Convert the following improper fractions to mixed numbers:

Question #6: $\dfrac{15}{7}$

Solution: $\Rightarrow 2\dfrac{1}{7}$ [Divide the numerator by denominator and write as a mixed number]

Question #7: $\dfrac{27}{5}$

Solution: $\Rightarrow 5\dfrac{2}{5}$ [Divide the numerator by denominator and write as a mixed number]

Question #8: $\dfrac{51}{7}$

Solution: $\Rightarrow 7\dfrac{2}{7}$ [Divide the numerator by denominator and write as a mixed number]

Question #9: $\dfrac{79}{8}$

Solution: $\Rightarrow 9\dfrac{7}{8}$ [Divide the numerator by denominator and write as a mixed number]

Question #10: $\dfrac{87}{5}$

Solution: $\Rightarrow 17\dfrac{2}{5}$ [Divide the numerator by denominator and write as a mixed number]

ADDITION OF FRACTIONS: Add the following fractions and simplify:

Question #11: $\dfrac{1}{12}+\dfrac{5}{12}$

Solution: $\Rightarrow \dfrac{6}{12}$ [Add the numbers in the numerator with common denominator]

                     $\Rightarrow \dfrac{1}{2}$ [Reduce the fraction to its lowest terms]

Question #12: $\dfrac{5}{18}+\dfrac{9}{18}$

Solution: $\Rightarrow \dfrac{14}{18}$ [Add the numbers in the numerator with common denominator]

                     $\Rightarrow \dfrac{7}{9}$ [Reduce the fraction to its lowest terms]

Question #13: $\dfrac{1}{8}+\dfrac{5}{8}+\dfrac{11}{8}$

Solution: $\Rightarrow \dfrac{17}{8}$ [Add the numbers in the numerator with common denominator]

Question #14: $\dfrac{1}{7}+\dfrac{2}{7}+\dfrac{8}{7}+\dfrac{9}{7}$

Solution: $\Rightarrow \dfrac{20}{7}$ [Add the numbers in the numerator with common denominator]

Question #15: $22\dfrac{2}{11}+55\dfrac{5}{11}$

Solution: $\Rightarrow (22+55)\left(\dfrac{2}{11}+\dfrac{5}{11}\right)$ [Add the whole number part and the fraction part separately]

                     $\Rightarrow 77\dfrac{7}{11}$ [Simplify the expression]

Question #16: $\dfrac{1}{8} + \dfrac{2}{9}$

Solution: $\Rightarrow \dfrac{9}{72} + \dfrac{16}{72}$ [Scale up the fractions in the numerator their LCD]

          $\Rightarrow \dfrac{25}{72}$ [Add the numbers in the numerator with common denominator]

Question #17: $\dfrac{2}{5} + \dfrac{5}{2}$

Solution: $\Rightarrow \dfrac{4}{10} + \dfrac{25}{10}$ [Scale up the fractions in the numerator their LCD]

          $\Rightarrow \dfrac{29}{10}$ [Add the numbers in the numerator with common denominator]

Question #18: $\dfrac{5}{2} + \dfrac{7}{8}$

Solution: $\Rightarrow \dfrac{20}{8} + \dfrac{7}{8}$ [Scale up the fractions in the numerator their LCD]

          $\Rightarrow \dfrac{27}{8}$ [Add the numbers in the numerator with common denominator]

Question #19: $\dfrac{7}{2} + \dfrac{5}{6}$

Solution: $\Rightarrow \dfrac{21}{6} + \dfrac{5}{6}$ [Scale up the fractions in the numerator their LCD]

          $\Rightarrow \dfrac{26}{6}$ [Add the numbers in the numerator with common denominator]

          $\Rightarrow \dfrac{13}{3}$ [Reduce the fraction to its lowest terms]

Question #20: $\dfrac{6}{2} + \dfrac{1}{9}$

Solution: $\Rightarrow \dfrac{54}{18} + \dfrac{2}{18}$ [Scale up the fractions in the numerator their LCD]

          $\Rightarrow \dfrac{56}{18}$ [Add the numbers in the numerator with common denominator]

          $\Rightarrow \dfrac{28}{9}$ [Reduce the fraction to its lowest terms]

SUBTRACTION OF FRACTIONS: Subtract the following fractions and simplify:

Question #21: $\dfrac{17}{25} - \dfrac{12}{25}$

Solution: $\Rightarrow \dfrac{5}{25}$ [Subtract the numbers in the numerator with common denominator]

          $\Rightarrow \dfrac{1}{5}$ [Reduce the fraction to its lowest terms]

Question #22: $17\dfrac{6}{7} - 5\dfrac{1}{7}$

Solution: $\Rightarrow (17-5)\left(\dfrac{6}{7}-\dfrac{1}{7}\right)$ [Subtract the whole number part and the fraction part separately]

$\Rightarrow 12\dfrac{5}{7}$ [Simplify the expression]

Question #23: $27\dfrac{8}{9}-12\dfrac{1}{9}$

Solution: $\Rightarrow (27-12)\left(\dfrac{8}{9}-\dfrac{1}{9}\right)$ [Subtract the whole number part and the fraction part separately]

$\Rightarrow 15\dfrac{7}{9}$ [Simplify the expression]

Question #24: $95\dfrac{7}{19}-17\dfrac{2}{19}$

Solution: $\Rightarrow (95-17)\left(\dfrac{7}{19}-\dfrac{2}{19}\right)$ [Subtract the whole number part and the fraction part separately]

$\Rightarrow 78\dfrac{5}{19}$ [Simplify the expression]

Question #25: $97\dfrac{9}{11}-28\dfrac{2}{11}$

Solution: $\Rightarrow (97-28)\left(\dfrac{9}{11}-\dfrac{2}{11}\right)$ [Subtract the whole number part and the fraction part separately]

$\Rightarrow 69\dfrac{7}{11}$ [Simplify the expression]

Question #26: $\dfrac{2}{9}-\dfrac{1}{8}$

Solution: $\Rightarrow \dfrac{16}{72}-\dfrac{9}{72}$ [Scale up the fractions in the numerator their LCD]

$\Rightarrow \dfrac{7}{72}$ [Subtract the numbers in the numerator with common denominator]

Question #27: $\dfrac{9}{2}-\dfrac{2}{9}$

Solution: $\Rightarrow \dfrac{81}{18}-\dfrac{4}{18}$ [Scale up the fractions in the numerator their LCD]

$\Rightarrow \dfrac{77}{18}$ [Subtract the numbers in the numerator with common denominator]

Question #28: $\dfrac{1}{6}-\dfrac{1}{8}$

Solution: $\Rightarrow \dfrac{4}{24}-\dfrac{3}{24}$ [Scale up the fractions in the numerator their LCD]

$\Rightarrow \dfrac{1}{24}$ [Subtract the numbers in the numerator with common denominator]

Question #29: $\dfrac{9}{2}-\dfrac{2}{6}$

Solution: $\Rightarrow \dfrac{27}{6} - \dfrac{2}{6}$ [Scale up the fractions in the numerator their LCD]

$\Rightarrow \dfrac{25}{6}$ [Subtract the numbers in the numerator with common denominator]

Question #30: $\dfrac{5}{2} - \dfrac{9}{8}$

Solution: $\Rightarrow \dfrac{20}{8} - \dfrac{9}{8}$ [Scale up the fractions in the numerator their LCD]

$\Rightarrow \dfrac{11}{8}$ [Subtract the numbers in the numerator with common denominator]

MULTIPLICATION OF FRACTIONS: Multiply the following fractions and simplify:

Question #31: $\dfrac{2}{9} \times \dfrac{8}{2}$

Solution: $\Rightarrow \dfrac{2^{1}}{9} \times \dfrac{8}{2^{1}}$ [Cancel-out the common factors in numerator and denominator]

$\Rightarrow \dfrac{8}{9}$ [Multiply the numbers in the numerator and denominator]

Question #32: $\dfrac{7}{8} \times \dfrac{8}{9}$

Solution: $\Rightarrow \dfrac{7}{8^{1}} \times \dfrac{8^{1}}{9}$ [Cancel-out the common factors in numerator and denominator]

$\Rightarrow \dfrac{7}{9}$ [Multiply the numbers in the numerator and denominator]

Question #33: $\dfrac{2}{8} \times \dfrac{6}{9}$

Solution: $\Rightarrow \dfrac{2^{1}}{8^{4^{2}}} \times \dfrac{6^{3^{1}}}{9^{3}}$ [Cancel-out the common factors in numerator and denominator]

$\Rightarrow \dfrac{1}{6}$ [Multiply the numbers in the numerator and denominator]

Question #34: $\dfrac{5}{6} \times \dfrac{8}{9}$

Solution: $\Rightarrow \dfrac{5}{6^{3}} \times \dfrac{8^{4}}{9}$ [Cancel-out the common factors in numerator and denominator]

$\Rightarrow \dfrac{20}{27}$ [Multiply the numbers in the numerator and denominator]

Question #35: $\dfrac{2}{5} \times \dfrac{7}{8}$

Solution: $\Rightarrow \dfrac{2^{1}}{5} \times \dfrac{7}{8^{4}}$ [Cancel-out the common factors in numerator and denominator]

$\Rightarrow \dfrac{7}{20}$ [Multiply the numbers in the numerator and denominator]

DIVISION OF FRACTIONS: Divide the following fractions and simplify:

Question #36: $\dfrac{2}{8} \div \dfrac{2}{9}$

Solution: $\Rightarrow \dfrac{2}{8} \times \dfrac{9}{2}$ [Switch the division to multiplication sign and flip the second fraction]

$\Rightarrow \dfrac{2^1}{8} \times \dfrac{9}{2^1}$ [Cancel-out the common factors in numerator and denominator]

$\Rightarrow \dfrac{9}{8}$ [Multiply the numbers in the numerator and denominator]

Question #37: $\dfrac{5}{6} \div \dfrac{8}{9}$

Solution: $\Rightarrow \dfrac{5}{6} \times \dfrac{9}{8}$ [Switch the division to multiplication sign and flip the second fraction]

$\Rightarrow \dfrac{5}{6^2} \times \dfrac{9^3}{8}$ [Cancel-out the common factors in numerator and denominator]

$\Rightarrow \dfrac{15}{16}$ [Multiply the numbers in the numerator and denominator]

Question #38: $\dfrac{8}{4} \div \dfrac{16}{2}$

Solution: $\Rightarrow \dfrac{8}{4} \times \dfrac{2}{16}$ [Switch the division to multiplication sign and flip the second fraction]

$\Rightarrow \dfrac{8^1}{4^2} \times \dfrac{2^1}{16^2}$ [Cancel-out the common factors in numerator and denominator]

$\Rightarrow \dfrac{1}{4}$ [Multiply the numbers in the numerator and denominator]

Question #39: $\dfrac{20}{8} \div \dfrac{7}{2}$

Solution: $\Rightarrow \dfrac{20}{8} \times \dfrac{2}{7}$ [Switch the division to multiplication sign and flip the second fraction]

$\Rightarrow \dfrac{20^5}{8^{2^1}} \times \dfrac{2^1}{7}$ [Cancel-out the common factors in numerator and denominator]

$\Rightarrow \dfrac{5}{7}$ [Multiply the fractions straight across]

Question #40: $\dfrac{2}{7} \div \dfrac{8}{9}$

Solution: $\Rightarrow \dfrac{2}{7} \times \dfrac{9}{8}$ [Switch the division to multiplication sign and flip the second fraction]

$\Rightarrow \dfrac{2^1}{7} \times \dfrac{9}{8^4}$ [Cancel-out the common factors in numerator and denominator]

$\Rightarrow \dfrac{9}{28}$ [Multiply the numbers in the numerator and denominator]

COMPARING FRACTION: Find out the LARGEST fraction:

Question #41: (A) $\dfrac{51}{50}$ (B) $\dfrac{70}{71}$ (C) $\dfrac{20}{21}$ (D) $\dfrac{90}{91}$ (E) $\dfrac{10}{11}$

Solution: There is only one fraction in which the numerator is bigger than the denominator, in all the rest of the fractions the numerator is smaller than the denominator. Therefore, 51/50 is the largest fraction.

Question #42: (A) $\dfrac{25}{26}$ (B) $\dfrac{56}{55}$ (C) $\dfrac{15}{16}$ (D) $\dfrac{95}{96}$ (E) $\dfrac{75}{76}$

Solution: There is only one fraction in which the numerator is bigger than the denominator, in all the rest of the fractions the numerator is smaller than the denominator. Therefore, 56/55 is the largest fraction.

Question #43: (A) $\dfrac{6}{11}$ (B) $\dfrac{6}{13}$ (C) $\dfrac{6}{7}$ (D) $\dfrac{6}{19}$ (E) $\dfrac{6}{17}$

Solution: Since all the fractions have the same numerators, compare the denominators, the fraction with the smallest denominator is the largest fraction. Since 7 is the smallest denominator, 6/7 is the largest fraction.

Question #44: (A) $\dfrac{7}{15}$ (B) $\dfrac{7}{11}$ (C) $\dfrac{7}{12}$ (D) $\dfrac{7}{9}$ (E) $\dfrac{7}{17}$

Solution: Since all the fractions have the same numerators, compare the denominators, the fraction with the smallest denominator is the largest fraction. Since 9 is the smallest denominator, 7/9 is the largest fraction.

Question #45: (A) $\dfrac{11}{8}$ (B) $\dfrac{9}{8}$ (C) $\dfrac{15}{8}$ (D) $\dfrac{13}{8}$ (E) $\dfrac{17}{8}$

Solution: Since all the fractions have the same denominators, compare the numerators, the fraction with the largest numerator is the largest fraction. Since 17 is the largest numerator, 17/8 is the largest fraction.

Question #46: (A) $\dfrac{13}{9}$ (B) $\dfrac{11}{9}$ (C) $\dfrac{17}{9}$ (D) $\dfrac{15}{9}$ (E) $\dfrac{19}{9}$

Solution: Since all the fractions have the same denominators, compare the numerators, the fraction with the largest numerator is the largest fraction. Since 19 is the largest numerator, 19/9 is the largest fraction.

Question #47: (A) $\dfrac{1}{2}$ (B) $\dfrac{9}{8}$ (C) $\dfrac{3}{4}$ (D) $\dfrac{7}{6}$ (E) $\dfrac{2}{3}$

Solution: $\Rightarrow$ LCM of 2, 8, 4, 6, and 3 = 24 $\Rightarrow \dfrac{12}{24} \quad \dfrac{27}{24} \quad \dfrac{18}{24} \quad \dfrac{28}{24} \quad \dfrac{16}{24}$

Since all the fractions now have the same denominators, compare the numerators, the fraction with the larger numerator is the greatest fraction. Therefore, 28/24 or 7/6 is the largest fraction.

Question #48: (A) $\dfrac{25}{9}$ (B) $\dfrac{11}{4}$ (C) $\dfrac{17}{6}$ (D) $\dfrac{5}{2}$ (E) $\dfrac{8}{3}$

Solution: $\Rightarrow$ LCM of 9, 4, 6, 2, and 3 = 36 $\Rightarrow \dfrac{100}{36} \quad \dfrac{99}{36} \quad \dfrac{102}{36} \quad \dfrac{90}{36} \quad \dfrac{96}{36}$

Since all the fractions now have the same denominators, compare the numerators, the fraction with the larger numerator is the greatest fraction. Therefore, 102/36 or 17/6 is the largest fraction.

Question #49: (A) $\dfrac{7}{6}$ (B) $\dfrac{11}{8}$ (C) $\dfrac{5}{4}$ (D) $\dfrac{21}{16}$ (E) $\dfrac{1}{2}$

Solution: $\Rightarrow$ LCM of 6, 8, 4, 16, and 2 = 48 $\Rightarrow \dfrac{56}{48} \quad \dfrac{66}{48} \quad \dfrac{60}{48} \quad \dfrac{63}{48} \quad \dfrac{24}{48}$

Since all the fractions now have the same denominators, compare the numerators, the fraction with the larger numerator is the greatest fraction. Therefore, 66/48 or 11/8 is the largest fraction.

Question #50: (A) $\dfrac{9}{8}$ (B) $\dfrac{1}{2}$ (C) $\dfrac{10}{9}$ (D) $\dfrac{3}{4}$ (E) $\dfrac{5}{6}$

Solution: $\Rightarrow$ LCM of 8, 2, 9, 4, and 6 = 72 $\Rightarrow$ $\dfrac{81}{72}$ $\dfrac{36}{72}$ $\dfrac{80}{72}$ $\dfrac{54}{72}$ $\dfrac{60}{72}$

Since all the fractions now have the same denominators, compare the numerators, the fraction with the larger numerator is the greatest fraction. Therefore, 81/72 or 9/8 is the largest fraction.

COMPARING FRACTIONS: Find out the SMALLEST fraction:

Question #51: (A) $\dfrac{11}{10}$ (B) $\dfrac{71}{70}$ (C) $\dfrac{21}{20}$ (D) $\dfrac{91}{90}$ (E) $\dfrac{50}{51}$

Solution: There is only one fraction in which the numerator is smaller than the denominator; in all the rest of the fractions the numerator is bigger than the denominator. Therefore, 50/51 is the smallest fraction.

Question #52: (A) $\dfrac{26}{25}$ (B) $\dfrac{16}{15}$ (C) $\dfrac{76}{75}$ (D) $\dfrac{55}{56}$ (E) $\dfrac{96}{95}$

Solution: There is only one fraction in which the numerator is smaller than the denominator; in all the rest of the fractions the numerator is bigger than the denominator. Therefore, 55/56 is the smallest fraction.

Question #63: (A) $\dfrac{9}{17}$ (B) $\dfrac{9}{11}$ (C) $\dfrac{9}{19}$ (D) $\dfrac{9}{13}$ (E) $\dfrac{9}{15}$

Solution: Since all the fractions have the same numerators, compare the denominators, the fraction with the largest denominator is the smallest fraction. Since 19 is the largest denominator, 9/19 is the smallest fraction.

Question #54: (A) $\dfrac{8}{11}$ (B) $\dfrac{8}{17}$ (C) $\dfrac{8}{13}$ (D) $\dfrac{8}{15}$ (E) $\dfrac{8}{9}$

Solution: Since all the fractions have the same numerators, compare the denominators, the fraction with the largest denominator is the smallest fraction. Since 17 is the largest denominator, 8/17 is the smallest fraction.

Question #55: (A) $\dfrac{9}{7}$ (B) $\dfrac{17}{7}$ (C) $\dfrac{12}{7}$ (D) $\dfrac{15}{7}$ (E) $\dfrac{11}{7}$

Solution: Since all the fractions have the same denominators, compare the numerators, the fraction with the smallest numerator is the smallest fraction. Since 9 is the smallest numerator, 9/7 is the smallest fraction.

Question #56: (A) $\dfrac{7}{6}$ (B) $\dfrac{17}{6}$ (C) $\dfrac{13}{6}$ (D) $\dfrac{19}{6}$ (E) $\dfrac{11}{6}$

Solution: Since all the fractions have the same denominators, compare the numerators, the fraction with the smallest numerator is the smallest fraction. Since 7 is the smallest numerator, 7/6 is the smallest fraction.

Question #57: (A) $\dfrac{3}{2}$ (B) $\dfrac{7}{6}$ (C) $\dfrac{5}{4}$ (D) $\dfrac{11}{8}$ (E) $\dfrac{4}{3}$

Solution: $\Rightarrow$ LCM of 2, 6, 4, 8, and 3 = 24 $\Rightarrow$ $\dfrac{36}{24}$ $\dfrac{28}{24}$ $\dfrac{30}{24}$ $\dfrac{33}{24}$ $\dfrac{32}{24}$

Since all the fractions now have the same denominators, compare the numerators, the fraction with the smaller numerator is the smallest fraction. Therefore, 28/24 or 7/6 is the smallest fraction.

Question #58: (A) $\dfrac{26}{9}$ (B) $\dfrac{13}{4}$ (C) $\dfrac{17}{6}$ (D) $\dfrac{7}{2}$ (E) $\dfrac{10}{3}$

Solution: $\Rightarrow$ LCM of 9, 4, 6, 2, and 3 = 36 $\Rightarrow$ $\dfrac{104}{36}$ $\dfrac{117}{36}$ $\dfrac{102}{36}$ $\dfrac{126}{36}$ $\dfrac{120}{36}$

Since all the fractions now have the same denominators, compare the numerators, the fraction with the smaller numerator is the smallest fraction. Therefore, 102/36 or 17/6 is the smallest fraction.

Question #59:   (A) $\dfrac{5}{2}$ (B) $\dfrac{23}{16}$ (C) $\dfrac{7}{4}$ (D) $\dfrac{11}{8}$ (E) $\dfrac{13}{6}$

Solution: $\Rightarrow$ LCM of 2, 16, 4, 8, and 6 = 48 $\Rightarrow \dfrac{120}{48} \quad \dfrac{69}{48} \quad \dfrac{84}{48} \quad \dfrac{66}{48} \quad \dfrac{104}{48}$

Since all the fractions now have the same denominators, compare the numerators, the fraction with the smaller numerator is the smallest fraction. Therefore, 66/48 or 11/8 is the smallest fraction.

Question #60:   (A) $\dfrac{11}{9}$ (B) $\dfrac{3}{2}$ (C) $\dfrac{7}{6}$ (D) $\dfrac{5}{4}$ (E) $\dfrac{9}{8}$

Solution: $\Rightarrow$ LCM of 9, 2, 6, 4, and 8 = 72 $\Rightarrow \dfrac{88}{72} \quad \dfrac{108}{72} \quad \dfrac{84}{72} \quad \dfrac{90}{72} \quad \dfrac{81}{72}$

Since all the fractions now have the same denominators, compare the numerators, the fraction with the smaller numerator is the smallest fraction. Therefore, 81/72 or 9/8 is the smallest fraction.

THIS PAGE HAS BEEN INTENTIONALLY LEFT BLANK

PART 3.0: DECIMALS:

TABLE OF CONTENTS:

EZ REFERENCE: -To practice easy-to-medium level questions, please refer to our EZ Practice Basic Workbook.
      -To practice medium-to-difficult level questions, please refer to our EZ Practice Advanced Workbook.

3.1: BASICS ABOUT DECIMALS:

Decimals are numbers that use place value to show quantities less than one. Just like fraction is one way of expressing the numbers that fall in between the whole numbers, decimals is another way of expressing these numbers. In other words, decimals are just another way of writing fractions by using a decimal point. For instance, the decimal 7.1 falls between the integers 7 and 8. Decimals express fractions using tenths, hundredths, thousandths, and so on. When a fraction is divided, meaning when the numerator is divided by the denominator, the result is a decimal. Decimal is a fraction that has 10 or any power of 10 for its denominator, and is expressed in the decimal system of notation.

We use two different systems of notation for fractions and decimals: a fraction is denoted with a fraction bar, whereas, a decimal is denoted with a decimal point. For instance, $\frac{5}{2}$ in terms of a fraction name is the same as 2.5 in terms of a decimal name. Therefore, in our number system, all numbers can be expressed in fractional or decimal form.

PARTS OF DECIMAL NUMBERS:
A decimal consists of two parts, a whole number, which is to the left of the decimal point, plus a decimal fraction part, which is to the right of the decimal point.
In other words, the decimal point separates the whole number part of the number from the decimal fractional part.

For Example: $\frac{50}{8} = 6.25$

⇒ In the number 6.25, 6 is the whole number part of the number and .25 is the decimal fraction part.

6	.	25
↓	↓	↓
Whole Number Part	Decimal Point	Decimal Fraction Part

For Example: 7,925.579 is a decimal number which represents 7,925 added to the decimal fraction .579

DECIMAL USE IN DAILY LIFE: We use decimals in our daily life without even realizing. For instance, while working with money, in the amount $6.25, we are already dealing with decimals. We know that the digits to the left represent dollars and digits to the right of the decimal point represent cents, or hundredths of a dollar. Since decimals are used to express money in terms of dollars and cents, think of the 6.25 as 6 dollars and 25 cents. 100 pennies or 4 quarters make a dollar. 25 cents or 1 quarter, then, is $\frac{25}{100}$ or $\frac{1}{4}$ of a dollar. However, not all decimals look like sums of money, so there are other ways of determining just what common fraction a decimal fraction represents.

DECIMAL FRACTION:
A decimal fraction is a decimal with zero as the whole number. Decimal fractions represent common fractions.
A collection of digits after the decimal point is called a decimal fraction.
For Example: .257, .169, .25, .19 are all decimal fractions.
To find the fraction that a decimal fraction represents: Write the numerator of the fraction as the number represented by the digits to the right of the decimal point, i.e., the decimal fraction without any decimal point.
Write the denominator as 10 × 10 × 10 × 10 ….. × 10. The number of copies (or times) of 10 is equal to the number of digits to the right of the decimal point.

For instance, the decimal fraction .25 represents the common fraction $\frac{25}{100}$ or $\frac{1}{4}$.

Therefore, 6.25 is the same thing as the mixed number $6\frac{1}{4}$.

ADDING OR REMOVING ZEROS BEFORE THE DECIMAL POINT:
Placing (or removing) a zero before the decimal point does not change the value of the decimal. A zero to the left of the decimal point is optional in a decimal fraction.
EZ RULE: For any real numbers a, b, c, d, e, .abcde = 0.abcde = .abcde
For Example: .257 = 0.257 = 00.257 = .257

ADDING OR REMOVING ZEROS AFTER THE DECIMAL POINT:
A decimal fraction is not altered by adding or removing zeros to the right of the last figure. So we can add or remove any number of zeros to the right of a decimal fraction without changing its value.

EZ RULE: For any real numbers *a*, *b*, *c*, *d*, *e*, and *n*, *n.abcde* = *a.bcde*00000 = *n.abcde*
For Example: 1.57 = 1.570 = 1.5700 = 1.57000 = 1.570000 = 1.57
                    0.257 = 0.2570 = 0.25700 = 0.257000 = 0.2570000 = 0.257

EZ TIP: For decimals less than 1, use 0 to the left of the decimal point to make it more noticeable and less confusing.

EZ CAUTION: Be careful, not to add or remove any zeros from within a number. Doing so will alter the value of the number.
For Example: 7.01 ≠ 7.1   &   127.609 ≠ 127.69

ELIMINATE ZEROS TO THE FAR RIGHT OF DECIMAL NUMBERS:
Zeros to the far right of a decimal fraction do not affect the value of a decimal fraction; however, they do affect conversions.

For instance, 6.25 = 6.2500, but $6\frac{25}{100}$ does not equal $6\frac{2,500}{100}$.

When converting decimal numbers with a zero or several zeros to the far right, we either must eliminate the zeros before the conversion, or apply them consistently.

For instance, if we were converting .2500 to a common fraction, and we decided to keep the zeros, we would end up with a denominator of 10,000 (since there are 4 digits to the right of the decimal), and a numerator of 2500. The whole fraction would be $\frac{2500}{10000}$ which reduces to $\frac{25}{100}$.

Eliminating the zeros from the beginning would give us $\frac{25}{100}$ straight away.

Therefore, it is always best to first eliminate any unwanted zeros that appear towards the far right of a decimal number before doing anything with it. Those zeros have no value and hence must be eliminated before any conversions.

Fractions whose denominators are multiples of ten can be converted to decimals by employing a reverse of the above.

For instance, $\frac{25}{100}$ thus becomes 0.25 because there are two zeros after the 1 in the denominator, and the numerator is 25.

WRITING INTEGERS AS DECIMALS:
Any integer can be treated and written as a decimal – just add a decimal point after it and a zero. So, any integer may be expressed as a decimal by writing zeros in the decimal part.
EZ RULE: For any real number *n*, *n* = *n*.0000000
For Example: 7 = 7.0 = 7.00 = 7.000 = 7.0000 = 7.00000.......
89 = 89.0 = 89.00.......

HOW TO READ DECIMALS:
To read a decimal number, read the whole number, then the decimal part, and then the place value of the last decimal digit.
For Example:
5.1   ⇒ five point one   ⇒ "five and one-tenths"
5.12   ⇒ five point one two   ⇒ "five and twelve-hundredths"
5.123   ⇒ five point one two three ⇒ "five and one-hundredths and twenty-three-thousandths"
5.1234   ⇒ five point one two three four   ⇒ "five and one-thousandths two-hundredths & thirty-four ten-thousandths"

3.2: PLACE VALUE AND DECIMALS:

It's important to recognize that 5/10 or 0.5 is ten times greater than 5/100 or 0.05, which is in turn ten times greater than 0.005 or 5/1000. Similarly, 5/1000 or 0.005 is ten times less than 5/100 or 0.05, which is in turn ten times less than 5/10 or 0.5. These relationships demonstrate a fundamental principle regarding the significance of the place value system. The place value system is based on the simple principle that each place in a number is worth ten times more than the place to its immediate right and ten times less than the place to its immediate left. Each place value is at a decrement of 10 from left to right and at an increment of 10 from right to left. For that same reason, 0.05 is ten times more than 0.005, and ten times less than 0.5. Therefore, number places are named according to the value they hold in the decimal numbers. The number of figures that follow the decimal point is called the number of decimal places. For instance: 0.1 has 1 decimal place, 0.12 has 2 decimal places, 0.123 has 3 decimal places, 0.1234 has 4 decimal places, 0.12345 has 5 decimal places, and so on.

A decimal point is used, and the place value for each digit depends on its position relative to the decimal point. Therefore, every digit in a decimal number has a specific place-value based on the specific place that it occupies. A decimal number uses place value based on powers of 10 and with a denomination of 10, such as, 10, 100, 1,000, 10,000, etc. For instance: in the number $95.72 \Rightarrow 95$ means $(9 \times 10) + (5 \times 1)$ and .72 means $(7 \times 1/10) + (2 \times 1/100)$. In the decimal system, the position of the decimal point determines the place value of each of the digits in a given number.

NAMING PLACE VALUES: Each position, or digit, in the decimal number, regardless of its location, whether it's to the left or right of the decimal point, has a different name associated with it, which is called its *"place value"*. The name of each location corresponds to the place value of that place. It is important that you get familiar with this naming convention. The following chart shows the place value of the digits in a decimal number:

Ten Thousands	Thousands	Hundreds	Tens	Ones/ Units	Decimal Point	Tenths	Hundredths	Thousandths	Ten Thousandths	Hundred Thousandths
10000	1000	100	10	1	.	0.1	0.01	0.001	0.0001	0.00001

EZ NOTE: Any place value to the right of the decimal point ends with a *"ths"*. Any place value to the left of the decimal point ends just with an *"s"*.

```
1        2        3        4        5        .        6        7        8        9
T        T        H        T        O        .        T        H        T        T
E        H        U        E        N                 E        U        H        E
N        O        N        N        E                 N        N        O        N
-        U        D        S        S                 T        D        U        -
T        S        R                                   H        R        S        T
H        A        E                                   S        E        A        H
O        N        D                                            D        N        O
U        D        S                                            T        D        S
S        S                                                     H        T        A
A                                                              S        H        N
N                                                                       S        D
D                                                                                T
S                                                                                H
                                                                                 S
```

DIGITS TO THE LEFT OF THE DECIMAL POINT:

Ten-Thousands   ⇒ 5th position to the left of the decimal point is the *"ten-thousands"* place.
Thousands   ⇒ 4th position to the left of the decimal point is the *"thousands"* place.
Hundreds   ⇒ 3rd position to the left of the decimal point is the *"hundreds"* place.
Tens   ⇒ 2nd position to the left of the decimal point is the *"tens"* place.
Ones   ⇒ 1st position to the left of the decimal point is the *"ones"* place.
.   ⇒ Decimal Point

DIGITS TO THE RIGHT OF THE DECIMAL POINT:

Tenths   ⇒ 1st position to the right of the decimal point is the *"tenths"* place.
                     -The digit in this position tells you how many *tenths* you should take.
                     -It is the numerator of a fraction whose denominator is 10.
Hundredths   ⇒ 2nd position to the right of the decimal point is the *"hundredths"* place.

	-The digit in this position tells you how many *hundredths* you should take.
	-It is the numerator of a fraction whose denominator is 100.
Thousandths	⇒ 3rd position to the right of the decimal point is the *"thousandths"* place.
	-The digit in this position tells you how many *thousandths* you should take.
	-It is the numerator of a fraction whose denominator is 1,000.
Ten-Thousandths	⇒ 4th position to the right of the decimal point is the *"ten-thousandths"* place.
	-The digit in this position tells you how many *ten-thousandths* you should take.
	-It is the numerator of a fraction whose denominator is 10,000.

EZ TIP: The various digits represent different numbers depending on their position.

Example #1:   In the decimal 12,345.6789, determine the place value of each digit.

Digit			Place Value	
1	1 ten-thousands	$1 \times 10,000$	Ten Thousands	10,000.0000
2	2 thousands	$2 \times 1,000$	Thousands	2,000.0000
3	3 hundreds	3×100	Hundreds	300.0000
4	4 tens	4×10	Tens	40.0000
5	5 ones	5×1	Ones	5.0000
.			Decimal Point	00000.0000
6	6 tenths	6×0.1	Tenths	00000.6
7	7 hundredths	7×0.01	Hundredths	00000.07
8	8 thousandths	8×0.001	Thousandths	00000.008
9	9 ten-thousandths	9×0.0001	Ten Thousandths	00000.0009
				12345.6789

Therefore, the number 12,345.6789 can be written as:

$$\Rightarrow (1 \times 10,000) + (2 \times 1,000) + (3 \times 100) + (4 \times 10) + (5 \times 1) + (6 \times \frac{1}{10}) + (7 \times \frac{1}{100}) + (8 \times \frac{1}{1,000}) + (9 \times \frac{1}{10,000})$$

$$\Rightarrow (1 \times 10^4) + (2 \times 10^3) + (3 \times 10^2) + (4 \times 10^1) + (5 \times 1) + (6 \times 10^{-1}) + (7 \times 10^{-2}) + (8 \times 10^{-3}) + (9 \times 10^{-4})$$

$$\Rightarrow 10,000 + 2,000 + 300 + 40 + 5 + 0.6 + 0.07 + 0.008 + 0.0009$$

⇒ 1 ten-thousands + 2 thousands + 3 hundreds + 4 tens + 5 ones + 6 tenths + 7 hundredths + 8 thousandths + 9 ten-thousandths

The above number in words: Twelve thousand, three hundred forty five, six thousandths, seven hundredths and eighty nine ten-thousandths.

Example #2:   In the decimal 95,728.6341, determine the place value of each digit.

Digit			Place Value	
9	9 ten-thousands	$9 \times 10,000$	Ten Thousands	90,000.0000
5	5 thousands	$5 \times 1,000$	Thousands	5,000.0000
7	7 hundreds	7×100	Hundreds	700.0000
2	2 tens	2×10	Tens	20.0000
8	8 ones	8×1	Ones	8.0000
.			Decimal Point	00000.0000
6	6 tenths	6×0.1	Tenths	00000.6
3	3 hundredths	3×0.01	Hundredths	00000.03
4	4 thousandths	4×0.001	Thousandths	00000.004
1	1 then-thousandths	1×0.0001	Ten Thousandths	00000.0001
				95,728.6241

Therefore, the number 95,728.6341 can be written as:

$$\Rightarrow (9 \times 10,000) + (5 \times 1,000) + (7 \times 100) + (2 \times 10) + (8 \times 1) + (6 \times \frac{1}{10}) + (3 \times \frac{1}{100}) + (4 \times \frac{1}{1,000}) + (1 \times \frac{1}{10,000})$$

$$\Rightarrow (9 \times 10^4) + (5 \times 10^3) + (7 \times 10^2) + (2 \times 10^1) + (8 \times 1) + (6 \times 10^{-1}) + (3 \times 10^{-2}) + (4 \times 10^{-3}) + (1 \times 10^{-4})$$

$$\Rightarrow 90,000 + 5,000 + 700 + 20 + 8 + 0.6 + 0.03 + 0.004 + 0.0001$$

⇒ 9 ten-thousands + 5 thousands + 7 hundreds + 2 tens + 8 ones + 6 tenths + 3 hundredths + 4 thousandths + 1 ten-thousandths

The above number in words: Ninety five thousand, seven hundred twenty eight, six thousand three hundred and forty one ten-thousandths.

3.3: DIFFERENT TYPES OF DECIMALS:

When a rational number $\dfrac{a}{b}$ is divided, meaning when the numerator is divided by the denominator, the result is a decimal, which can be, rational or irrational number, terminating, or repeating decimal.

3.3.1: TERMINATING DECIMALS:

When a rational number "$\dfrac{a}{b}$" is divided, meaning when the numerator "a" is divided by the denominator "b", the result is a decimal. If "b" divides "a" with a remainder of "0" after reaching a certain point, the result is a **terminating** decimal.

Example #1: $\dfrac{1}{2}$ = 0.5   **Example #2:** $\dfrac{1}{5}$ = 0.2

3.3.2: NON-TERMINATING OR REPEATING DECIMALS:

When a rational number "$\dfrac{a}{b}$" is divided, meaning when the numerator "a" is divided by the denominator "b", the result is a decimal. If "b" continues to divide "a" indefinitely so that the decimal forms a repeating pattern of integers, the result is a **non-terminating** or **repeating** or **recurring** or **periodic** or **circulating** decimal. In other words, the division does not terminate after one, two, three, four, or five decimal places; rather it goes on forever with a digit or set of digits repeating continually. The repeated figures or set of figures is called the Period of the decimal. Repeating decimals are represented by dots (.......)

3.3.2.1: PURE RECURRING DECIMAL:

Decimals in which all the figures after the decimal point recur is called a **pure recurring decimal**.

Example #1: $\dfrac{1}{3}$ = 0.333333333.......

⇒ Here we see that on performing division, the remainder is always 1, and in the quotient the figure 3 is continually repeated.

Example #2: $\dfrac{7}{9}$ = 0.77777.......

⇒ Here we see that on performing division, the remainder is always 7, and in the quotient the figure 7 is continually repeated.

Example #3: $\dfrac{7}{11}$ = 0.6363636363.......

⇒ Here we find that after 2 digits after the quotient have been obtained, the remainder left is 7, which is the same as that with which we started. Now, if we continue the division, we shall get the same set of figures 63 again and again and in the same order.

Example #4: $\dfrac{1}{7}$ = 0.142857,142857,142857,142857.......

⇒ Here we find that after 6 digits of the quotient have been obtained, the remainder left is 1, which is the same as that with which we started. Now, if we continue the division, we shall get the same set of figures 142857 again and again and in the same order.

3.3.2.2: MIXED RECURRING DECIMAL:

Decimals in which some but not all the figures after the decimal point recur, is called a **mixed recurring decimal**.

Example #1: $\dfrac{1}{6}$ = 0.1666666.......

⇒ Here we find that after two digits in the quotient have been obtained the remainder left is 4, which is the same as what was left after the first digit had been obtained; therefore, the digit 4 will be continuously repeated.

Example #2: $\dfrac{11}{12}$ = 0.91666666.......

⇒ Here we find that after two digits in the quotient have been obtained the remainder left is 8, which is the same as what was left after the first two digits had been obtained; therefore, the digit 6 will be continuously repeated.

Example #3: $\dfrac{13}{44}$ = 0.295454545454.......

⇒ Here we find that after four digits in the quotient have been obtained the remainder left is 24, which is the same as what was left after the first two digits had been obtained; therefore, the digits 54 will be continuously repeated.

3.3.3: NON-TERMINATING & NON-REPEATING:

When an irrational number "$\dfrac{a}{b}$" is divided, meaning when the numerator "a" is divided by the denominator "b", the result is a decimal. If "b" continues to divide "a" indefinitely so that the decimal form is **non-terminating** and **non-repeating**, the result is an **irrational number**. In other words, the division does not terminate after one, two, three, four, or five decimal places; rather it goes on forever. The irrational number cannot be expressed as the quotient of two integers but can be written as non-terminating and non-repeating decimals. In other words, an irrational number is a number that can't be represented by a fraction whose numerator and denominator are both integers.

Example #1: $\sqrt{2}$ = 1.414213562373095048801.......

Example #2: $\sqrt{5}$ = 2.2360679774997896964091.......

3.4: ROUNDING-OFF DECIMALS:

Often times an approximation of a number or an answer can be found much more quickly and easily, and it may even be more useful than the exact number. For instance, if a company had sales of 998,975 for a particular year, it is a lot easier to remember that the sales were about $1 million.

Rounding-off numbers can help you quickly and easily get approximate answers. Since many questions require only approximate answers, you can save some valuable time on the test by rounding-off numbers. Therefore, it's often useful to round off awkward or unwieldy decimals to the nearest tenth, hundredth, thousandths, and so on.

MEANING OF ROUNDING-OFF:
Rounding-off a number to a decimal place means finding the multiple of the representative of that decimal place which is closest to the original number.

⇒ Rounding off a number to the nearest *thousands* means ⇒ finding the multiple of 1,000 which is closest to the original number

⇒ Rounding off a number to the nearest *hundreds* means ⇒ finding the multiple of 100 which is closest to the original number

⇒ Rounding off a number to the nearest *tens* means ⇒ finding the multiple of 10 which is closest to the original number

⇒ Rounding off a number to the nearest *ones* means ⇒ finding the multiple of 1 which is closest to the original number

⇒ Rounding off a number to the nearest *tenths* means ⇒ finding the multiple of 1/10 which is closest to the original number

⇒ Rounding off a number to the nearest *hundredths* means ⇒ finding the multiple of 1/100 which is closest to the original number

EZ HINT: Most problems dealing with money are rounded off to the nearest ones if the answer is only in dollars and no cents and to the nearest hundredths or cent if the answer contains dollars and a fractional part of a dollar.

EZ STEP-BY-STEP METHOD: Apply the following step(s) to round off a decimal number to the *n*th decimal place:

STEP 1: Underline the digit in the *n*th place value to which the number is being rounded-off to.

STEP 2: Keep all the preceding digits or the digits to the left of the specified *n*th place to be the same.
   Note: the digit in the *n*th place and all the digits to its right may change.

STEP 3: Look up at the digit to the immediate right (one place) of the specified underlined *n*th place value to which the number needs to be rounded off to:
   (A) If the digit to the right of the *n*th place is less than 5 (i.e., 1, 2, 3, or 4), then round-down, that is, leave the underlined digit in the *n*th place value the same, and change all the other digits to its right to zeros or simply drop the digit to the right.
   Note: If you are at or beyond the decimal point, then there is no need to add any more 0's, just eliminate those numbers.
   (B) If the digit to the right of the *n*th place is equal to or greater than 5, (i.e., 5, 6, 7, 8, 9) then round-up, that is, increase the underlined digit in the *n*th place by 1, and change all the digits to its right to zeros (9 increased by 1 is 10: put down the 0 and carry the 1) or simply drop the digit to the right.
   Note: If there are still digits to the left of the decimal point, then convert them to 0's and eliminate the decimal point as well as everything that is after the decimal point.

EZ HINT: ROUND-UP OR ROUND-DOWN:
The key to rounding off decimal number is to look up at the digit to the right of the specified place to which the number needs to be rounded off:
Round-Up: ⇒ If the digit to the right is equal to or greater than 5, then round-up.
Round-Down: ⇒ If the digit to the right is less than 5, then round-down.

ROUNDING-OFF A DECIMAL NUMBER TO DIFFERENT PLACES:
A decimal number can be rounded-off to its nearest thousands, hundreds, tens, ones, tenths, hundredths, thousandth, ten thousandths, millionths place and so on.

Example #1:   Round-off 7,915.71869 to all the places.

ROUNDING	PROCEDURE	ANSWER
Thousands	The digit in the thousands place is 7; keep everything to the left of it the same, and increase the 7 to 8 since the next digit (9) is ≥ 5; fill in with 0's to the left of the decimal point	8000
Hundreds	The digit in the hundreds place is 9; keep everything to the left of it the same, and keep the 9 as same since the next digit (1) is ≤ 5; fill in with 0's to the left of the decimal point.	7900
Tens	The digit in the tens place is 1; keep everything to the left of it the same, and increase the 1 to 2 since the next digit (5) is ≥ 5; fill in with 0's to the left of the decimal point.	7920
Ones	The digit in the ones place is 5; keep everything to the left of it the same, since the next digit (7) is ≥ 5, increase the 5 to 6; there are no more places to the left of the decimal point, so stop.	7916
Tenths	The digit in the tenths place is 7; keep everything to the left of it the same, and keep the 7 as same since the next digit (1) is ≤ 5; since we are beyond the decimal point, there is no need to add any more 0's	7915.7
Hundredths	The digit in the hundredth place is 1; keep everything to the left of it, the same, and increase the 1 to 2 since the next digit (8) is ≥ 5; since we are beyond the decimal point, there is no need to add any more 0's	7915.72
Thousandths	The digit in the thousandth place is 8; keep everything to the left of it the same, and increase the 8 to 9 since the next digit (6) is ≥ 5; since we are beyond the decimal point, there is no need to add any more 0's	7915.719
Ten Thousandths	The digit in the ten thousandth place is 6; keep everything to the left of it the same, and increase the 6 to 7 since the next digit (9) is ≥ 5; since we are beyond the decimal point, there is no need to add any more 0's.	7915.7187

Example #2:   Round-off 12345.6789 to all the places.

Round to the Nearest	Answer
Thousands	12,000
Hundreds	12,300
Tens	12,350
Ones	12,346
Tenths	12345.7
Hundredths	12345.68
Thousandths	12345.679
Ten Thousandths	12345.6789

3.5: ORDERING & COMPARING DECIMALS:

Ordering decimal numbers means to list them in chronological order starting from smallest to largest or from largest to smallest. This also helps in comparing decimals. Following are the two methods to compare decimals.

3.5.1: BY COMPARING PLACE VALUES:

EZ STEP-BY-STEP METHOD: Apply the following step(s) to order and compare decimals:

STEP 1: List all the decimal numbers so that the decimal points are aligned vertically on top of each other.

STEP 2: Add in zeros to the end of the decimal number that are shorter in length so that each number is equal in length, and have the same number of digits after the decimal point.

STEP 3: Next, compare the place value of each digit of the number, one place value column at a time, and working from left to right:
   (A) First, compare the numbers according to their whole number parts, from smallest to largest or from largest to smallest.
   (B) Next, compare the numbers according to their tenths place.
   (C) Next, compare the numbers according to their hundredths place.
   (D) Next, compare the numbers according to their thousandths place.
   (E) Next, compare the numbers according to their ten-thousandths place.
   (F) Next, compare the numbers according to their hundred-thousandths place.

EZ TIP: The final list would automatically arrange the numbers in order and it can be easily compared.

Example #1:   Following decimals are arranged in increasing and decreasing order:

Increasing Order:		Decreasing Order:	
0.07	⇒ Smallest	0.77	⇒ Largest
0.0707		0.707	
0.077		0.7	
0.7		0.077	
0.707		0.707	
0.77	⇒ Largest	0.07	⇒ Smallest

⇒ 0.07 < 0.0707 < 0.077 < 0.7 < 0.707 < 0.77

Example #2:   Following decimals are arranged in increasing and decreasing order:

Increasing Order		Decreasing Order	
5.9276	⇒ Smallest	7.9257	⇒ Largest
7.2957		7.9168	
7.5759		7.7159	
7.5821		7.5821	
7.7159		7.5759	
7.9168		7.2957	
7.9257	⇒ Largest	5.9276	⇒ Smallest

⇒ 5.9276 < 7.2957 < 7.5759 < 7.5821 < 7.7159 < 7.9168 < 7.9257

3.5.2: BY CONVERTING THE DECIMALS INTO INTEGERS:

EZ STEP-BY-STEP METHOD: Apply the following step(s) to compare decimals:

STEP 1: Stack all the decimal numbers vertically so that the decimal points are aligned vertically on top of each other.

STEP 2: Add in zeros to the end of the decimal numbers (i.e., after the last digit to the right of the decimal point) that are shorter in length than the longest decimal number until all the decimal numbers are of equal length (i.e., they all have the same number of digits).
   Note: doing this will make each decimal number of equal lengths or will give each decimal fraction the same denominator.

STEP 3: Next, move the decimal point equal number of places to the right in all the numbers so that all the decimal numbers are converted into whole numbers.

STEP 4: Now since all the numbers are whole numbers, compare the digits of the number, working from left to right:

EZ NOTE: Since the denominators of all the fractions are the same, the numerators determine the order of values.
(A) First, compare and order the numbers according to their millions place.
(B) Next, compare and order the numbers according to their hundred thousands place.
(C) Next, compare and order the numbers according to their ten thousands place.
(D) Next, compare and order the numbers according to their thousands place.
(E) Next, compare and order the numbers according to their hundreds place.
(F) Next, compare and order the numbers according to their tens place.
(G) Next, compare and order the numbers according to their ones place.

EZ TIP: For some people it's a lot easier to compare whole numbers than decimals. Just think of those whole numbers in dollars ($) and it may now become even easier!

Example #1:   Following decimals are arranged in increasing and decreasing order:
Arranged in Increasing Order: | Arranged in Decreasing Order:

0.07	= 0.0700	$= \dfrac{700}{10,000}$	= 700	⇒ Smallest	0.77	= 0.7700	$= \dfrac{7,700}{10,000}$	= 7,700	⇒ Largest
0.0707	= 0.0707	$= \dfrac{707}{10,000}$	= 707		0.707	= 0.7070	$= \dfrac{7,070}{10,000}$	= 7,070	
0.077	= 0.0770	$= \dfrac{770}{10,000}$	= 770		0.7	= 0.7000	$= \dfrac{7,000}{10,000}$	= 7,000	
0.1	= 0.1000	$= \dfrac{1,000}{10,000}$	= 1,000		0.1	= 0.1000	$= \dfrac{1,000}{10,000}$	= 1,000	
0.7	= 0.7000	$= \dfrac{7,000}{10,000}$	= 7,000		0.077	= 0.0770	$= \dfrac{770}{10,000}$	= 770	
0.707	= 0.7070	$= \dfrac{7,070}{10,000}$	= 7,070		0.0707	= 0.0707	$= \dfrac{707}{10,000}$	= 707	
0.77	= 0.7700	$= \dfrac{7,700}{10,000}$	= 7,700 ⇒ Largest		0.07	= 0.0700	$= \dfrac{700}{10,000}$	= 700	⇒ Smallest

0.07 < 0.0707 < 0.077 < 0.1 < 0.7 < 0.707 < 0.77

Example #2:   Following decimals are arranged in increasing and decreasing order:

Increasing Order:			Decreasing Order:		
5.9276	59276	⇒ Smallest	7.9568	79568	⇒ Largest
7.2957	72957		7.9257	79257	
7.5759	75759		7.7159	77159	
7.5821	75821		7.5821	75821	
7.7159	77159		7.5759	75759	
7.9257	79257		7.2957	72957	
7.9568	79568	⇒ Largest	5.9276	59276	⇒ Smallest

COMPARING NEGATIVE DECIMALS:

EZ TIPS: To compare negative decimals, keep in mind the following tips:

EZ TIP #1:   Any positive decimal is greater than any negative decimal, and any negative decimal is less than any positive decimal.

EZ TIP #2:   While comparing negative decimals, use the fact that, if $a > b$, then $-a < -b$.

For Example: If 0.5 > 0.2, then it implies that ⇒ −0.5 < −0.2

3.6: ARITHMETIC OPERATIONS WITH DECIMALS:

3.6.1: ADDITION OF DECIMALS:

EZ STEP-BY-STEP METHOD: Apply the following step(s) to add decimal numbers:

STEP 1: First, stack up all the decimal numbers vertically under one another in a place-value column order so that all the decimal points are vertically aligned on top of each other, and then draw a line under the last number.
Note: Proper alignment will ensure that tenths are added to tenths, hundredths to hundredths, etc.

STEP 2: Add in placeholder zeros to the end of the decimal number that are shorter in length so that each decimal number is equal in length and have the same number of decimal places.
Note: Adding zeros to the far right of the decimal point does not change the value of the decimal number. If one of the numbers is a whole number, put the decimal point after the whole number and add placeholder zeros so that its length is the same as of other numbers.

STEP 3: Next, begin at the top of each column and add the numbers downwards, as usual, also start from the right most column, and add each column while still maintaining the location of the decimal point.
Note: If you want, instead of adding the columns downwards, i.e., from top to bottom, you can also add the columns upwards, i.e., from bottom to top.
Note: Regroup, or carry, as needed, as you would with whole numbers.

STEP 4: Place the decimal point in the sum (answer) directly below the decimal points in the problem so that it is still in alignment with decimal point of the given numbers.

EZ HINT: Adding decimals is much like adding whole numbers. The rules you use to add whole numbers can be used to add decimals. The trick is to line up the place-value column correctly. In other words, make sure that the decimal points are in line and that the digits are added vertically, i.e., digits in the tenths, hundredths, and so on places are added and be careful not to mix (add) the digits in the tenths place with the digits in the hundredths place and so on.

Example #1: Add the following two decimal numbers.   **Example #2:** Add the following two decimal numbers.

$$\begin{array}{r} 1.6776 \\ +1.1221 \\ \hline 2.7997 \end{array}$$

$$\begin{array}{r} 1.1659 \\ +1.1298 \\ \hline 2.2957 \end{array}$$

3.6.2: SUBTRACTION OF DECIMALS:

EZ STEP-BY-STEP METHOD: Apply the following step(s) to subtract decimal numbers:

STEP 1: First, stack up the decimal numbers vertically with the greater number on top of the smaller number in a column order so that all the decimal points are vertically aligned on top of each other, and then draw a line under the last number.
Note: Proper alignment will ensure that tenths are subtracted from tenths, hundredths from hundredths, etc.

STEP 2: Next, add in placeholder zeros to the end of the decimal number that are shorter in length so that each decimal number is equal in length and have the same number of decimal places.
Note: Adding zeros to the far right of the decimal point does not change the value of the decimal number. If one of the numbers is a whole number, put the decimal point after the whole number and add placeholder zeros so that its length is the same as of other numbers.

STEP 3: Next, begin at the top of each column and subtract the numbers downwards, as usual, also start from the right most column, and subtract each column while still maintaining the location of the decimal point.
Note: Regroup, or borrow, as needed, as you would with whole numbers.

STEP 4: Finally, place the decimal point in the sum (answer) directly below the decimal points in the problem so that it is still in alignment with decimal point of the given numbers.

EZ HINT: Subtracting decimals is much like subtracting whole numbers. The rules you use to subtract whole numbers can be used to subtract decimals. The trick is to line up the place-value column correctly. In other words, make sure that the decimal points are in line and that the digits are subtracted vertically, i.e., digits in the tenths, hundredths, and so on places are subtracted, and be careful not to mix (subtract) the digits in the tenths place from the digits in the hundredths place and so on.

Example #1:   Subtract the following two decimal nos.   **Example #2:**   Subtract the following two decimal nos.
                            7.8976   7.1751
                          −5.1751   −5.8976
                            2.7225   1.2775

3.6.3: MULTIPLICATION OF DECIMALS:

EZ STEP-BY-STEP METHOD: Apply the following step(s) to multiply decimal numbers:

STEP 1: First, set up the problem as though you were multiplying whole numbers

STEP 2: Ignore the decimal point and multiply the decimal numbers, as usual, as you would integers.

STEP 3: After finding the product, count the total number of decimal places in each of the numbers you've multiplied (i.e., all digits to the right of the decimal point in the multiplier and the multiplicand put together) and then starting from the right, count those many places to the left of the product and insert the decimal point, prefixing zeros, if necessary.
In other words, the decimal point of the product is placed in such a way so that the number of decimal places in the product is equal to the sum of the total number of decimal places in the factors that are multiplied together, i.e., the multiplier and the multiplicand.

EZ HINT: Multiplying decimals is much like multiplying whole numbers except that you must figure out where to place the decimal point in the product. The rules you use to multiply whole numbers can be used to multiply decimals. You don't even have to line up the decimal points. The trick is to wait until you are finished multiplying before you place the decimal point in the answer. Make sure to place the decimal point in the product so that the number of decimal places in the product is equal to the total number of decimal places in the numbers you multiplied.

Example #1:   Multiply the following two decimal nos.   **Example #2:**   Multiply the following two decimal nos.
                   5.6   (1 decimal place)   5.65   (2 decimal places)
                 × 2.9   (1 decimal place)   × 2.25   (2 decimal places)
                   504   2825
                 112×   1130×
                 16.24   (1 + 1 = 2 decimal place)   1130××
                                                                                 12.7125   (2 + 2 = 4 decimal places)

MULTIPLYING A NUMBER BY MULTIPLES OF 10:

If the decimal point is moved one place to the right, the place value of each digit is increased by ten-folds, i.e., its units place become tens, tens become hundreds and so on. In other words, if we place a zero on the right of a number, its value increases ten folds, i.e., its units place become tens, tens become hundreds and so on.

EZ RULE: To multiply any decimal or whole number by a power of 10, such as, 10, 100, 1000, etc., move the decimal point as many places to the right as there are 0's in the multiple of 10, i.e., move the decimal point to the right, a number of places equal to the number of 0's in the multiplier, filling in with 0's if necessary.

For instance, to multiply a number by 10, move the decimal point one place to the right, to multiply a number by 100, move the decimal point two places to the right, and so on.

EZ NOTE: If necessary, push the decimal point to the right by inserting the appropriate number of zeros. You would definitely have to add 0's if the number being multiplied is a whole number.

TABLE OF EXAMPLES:

To multiply by 1	⇒Move the decimal pt 0 place	⇒1.23456 × 1 = 1.23456
To multiply by 10	⇒Move the decimal pt 1 place to the right	⇒1.23456 × 10 = 12.3456
To multiply by 100	⇒Move the decimal pt 2 places to the right	⇒1.23456 × 100 = 123.456
To multiply by 1,000	⇒Move the decimal pt 3 places to the right	⇒1.23456 × 1,000 = 1234.56
To multiply by 10,000	⇒Move the decimal pt 4 places to the right	⇒1.23456 × 10,000 = 12345.6
To multiply by 100,000	⇒Move the decimal pt 5 places to the right	⇒1.23456 × 100,000 = 123456.0
To multiply by 1000,000	⇒Move the decimal pt 6 places to the right	⇒1.23456 × 1000,000 = 1234560.0

3.6.4: DIVISION OF DECIMALS:

EZ STEP-BY-STEP METHOD: Apply the following step(s) to divide decimal numbers:

STEP 1: Since one or both the numbers you are dividing are decimals, its best to get rid of the decimal points and convert them into whole numbers.

Note: Keep moving the decimal places equal number of places to the right in both (or multiply each by a power of 10), the divisor and the dividend until they both become whole numbers. In doing so, you may have to add zeros onto the end of the divisor or the dividend. Adding zeros to the far right of a decimal point does not change the value of the decimal number.

$\Rightarrow$ This can be done by moving the decimal point of the divisor all the way to the right and then moving the decimal point of the dividend the exact same number of places to the right.

(A) First make the divisor (the number you are dividing by) a whole number by moving the decimal point the appropriate number of places to the right. (This is the same as multiplying the divisor by a multiple of 10).

(B) Next, it is necessary that the decimal point of the dividend (the number you are dividing) is also moved the same number of places to the right. (This is the same as multiplying the dividend by the same multiple of 10 as the divisor).

STEP 2: Now that both the divisor and dividend are whole numbers, just carry out the division as usual, as you would with integers, and find out the quotient (answer).

Note: In case you didn't convert the dividend into a whole number, then place the decimal point in the quotient directly above the decimal point in the dividend. Oftentimes, your division will go on and on and you will have to stop at some point and round off the quotient. When you take a figure from the decimal part (if there is any) of the dividend so altered, set down the decimal point in the quotient.

EZ HINT: Dividing decimals is much like dividing whole numbers except that you must first convert the divisor into a whole number. The rules you use to divide whole numbers can be used to divide decimals. Before actually dividing decimals, it's always better to first get rid of the decimal points from the divisor and the dividend, by moving the decimal point the equal number of places to the right. The trick is that both the decimal numbers – divisor and the dividend should be equally multiplied by 10, 100, 100, 10000 or so on, so that they both become whole numbers.

Example #1: $8.5 \div 1.7 = \dfrac{8.5}{1.7} = \dfrac{8.5 \times 10}{1.7 \times 10} = \dfrac{85}{17} = 5$ **Example #2:** $9.5 \div 1.9 = \dfrac{9.5}{1.9} = \dfrac{9.5 \times 10}{1.9 \times 10} = \dfrac{95}{19} = 5$

DIVIDING A NUMBER BY MULTIPLES OF 10:

If the decimal point is moved one place to the left, the place value of each digit is decreased by ten-folds, i.e., its tens place become units, hundreds become tens and so on. For instance, to divide a number by 10, move the decimal point one place to the left, to divide a number by 100, move the decimal point two places to the left, and so on.

EZ RULES: To divide any decimal or whole number by a power of 10, such as, 10, 100, 1000, etc., move the decimal point as many places to the left as there are 0's in the power of 10, i.e., move the decimal point to the left, a number of places equal to the number of 0's in the divisor, filling in with 0's if necessary.

TABLE OF EXAMPLES:

To divide by 1	$\Rightarrow$Move the decimal pt 0 place	$\Rightarrow 1.23456 \div 1 = 1.23456$
To divide by 10	$\Rightarrow$Move the decimal pt 1 place to the left	$\Rightarrow 1.23456 \div 10 = 0.123456$
To divide by 100	$\Rightarrow$Move the decimal pt 2 places to the left	$\Rightarrow 1.23456 \div 100 = 0.0123456$
To divide by 1,000	$\Rightarrow$Move the decimal pt 3 places to the left	$\Rightarrow 1.23456 \div 1,000 = 0.00123456$
To divide by 10,000	$\Rightarrow$Move the decimal pt 4 places to the left	$\Rightarrow 1.23456 \div 10,000 = 0.000123456$
To divide by 100,000	$\Rightarrow$Move the decimal pt 5 places to the left	$\Rightarrow 1.23456 \div 100,000 = 0.0000123456$
To divide by 1000,000	$\Rightarrow$Move the decimal pt 6 places to the left	$\Rightarrow 1.23456 \div 1000,000 = 0.00000123456$

DISTRIBUTIVE LAWS WITH DECIMALS:

The laws of operations that you learned in the chapter on integers are also applicable to decimals.
For Example: $0.9(0.2 + 0.6) = 0.9(0.8) = 0.72$

PRACTICE EXERCISE – QUESTIONS AND ANSWERS WITH EXPLANATIONS:
DECIMALS:

PLACE VALUE AND DECIMALS: Find the place value:

Question #1:   What is the place value of the digit 5 in the decimal number 75,291.0068?
Solution: Place Value of 5 in the decimal 75,291.0068 ⇒ Thousands
[The 4th position to the left of the decimal is the thousands place ⇒ 5 × 1000 = 5,000]

Question #2:   What is the place value of the digit 1 in the decimal number 9,157.269?
Solution: Place Value of 1 in the decimal 9,157.269 ⇒ Hundreds
[The 3rd position to the left of the decimal is the hundreds place ⇒ 1 × 100 = 100]

Question #3:   What is the place value of the digit 2 in the decimal number 821.589?
Solution: Place Value of 2 in the decimal 821.589 ⇒ Tens
[The 2nd position to the left of the decimal is the tens place ⇒ 2 × 10 = 20]

Question #4:   What is the place value of the digit 9 in the decimal number 19.526?
Solution: Place Value of 9 in the decimal 19.526 ⇒ Ones
[The 1st position to the left of the decimal is the ones place ⇒ 9 × 1 = 9]

Question #5:   What is the place value of the digit 7 in the decimal number 51.796?
Solution: Place Value of 7 in the decimal 51.796 ⇒ Tenths
[The 1st position to the right of the decimal is the tenths place ⇒ 7 × 0.1 = 0.7]

Question #6:   What is the place value of the digit 0 in the decimal number 256.907?
Solution: Place Value of 0 in the decimal 256.907 ⇒ Hundredths
[The 2nd position to the right of the decimal is the hundredths place ⇒ 0 × 0.01 = 0.00]

Question #7:   What is the place value of the digit 6 in the decimal number 128.7961?
Solution: Place Value of 6 in the decimal 128.7961 ⇒ Thousandths
[The 3rd position to the right of the decimal is the thousandths place ⇒ 6 × 0.001 = 0.006]

Question #8:   What is the place value of the digit 8 in the decimal number 670.52689?
Solution: Place Value of 8 in the decimal 670.52689 ⇒ Ten-Thousandths
[The 4th position to the right of the decimal is the ten-thousandths place ⇒ 8 × 0.0001 = 0.0008]

Question #9:   Write a numeral in which the value of 6 is in tens place, the value of 2 is in tenths place, the value of 8 is in ones place, the value of 7 is in hundredths place, the value of 9 is in thousands place, the value of 5 is in hundreds place, and the rest of the digits if any are zeros.
Solution: ⇒ 9,568.27

Question #10:   Write a numeral in which the value of 6 is in tens place, the value of 8 is in tenths place, the value of 5 is in ones place, the value of 9 is in ten thousandths place, the value of 7 is in thousands place, the value of 2 is in hundreds place, and the rest of the digits if any are zeros.
Solution: ⇒ 7,265.8009

ROUNDING-OFF DECIMALS: Round-off 976,185.87159 to the nearest x place.

Question #11:   Round off 976,185.87159 to the nearest hundred-thousands place.
Solution: ⇒ 1,000,000 [The digit in the hundred-thousands place is 9; keep everything to the left of it the same, and increase the 9 to 10 since the next digit (7) is ≥ 5; fill in with 0's to the left of the decimal point.]

Question #12:   Round off 976,185.87159 to the nearest ten-thousands place.
Solution: ⇒ 980,000 [The digit in the ten-thousands place is 7; keep everything to the left of it the same, and increase the 7 to 8 since the next digit (6) is ≥ 5; fill in with 0's to the left of the decimal point.]

Question #13: Round off 976,185.87159 to the nearest thousands place.
Solution: ⇒ 976,000 [The digit in the thousands place is 6; keep everything to the left of it the same, and keep the 6 as same since the next digit (1) is ≤ 5; fill in with 0's to the left of the decimal point.]

Question #14: Round off 976,185.87159 to the nearest hundreds place.
Solution: ⇒ 976,200 [The digit in the hundreds place is 1; keep everything to the left of it the same, and increase the 1 to 2 since the next digit (8) is ≥ 5; fill in with 0's to the left of the decimal point.]

Question #15: Round off 976,185.87159 to the nearest tens place.
Solution: ⇒ 976,190 [The digit in the tens place is 8; keep everything to the left of it the same, and increase the 8 to 9 since the next digit (5) is ≥ 5; fill in with 0's to the left of the decimal point.]

Question #16: Round off 976,185.87159 to the nearest ones place.
Solution: ⇒ 976,186 [The digit in the ones place is 5; keep everything to the left of it the same, and increase the 5 to 6 since the next digit (8) is ≥ 5; drop everything else to the right.]

Question #17: Round off 976,185.87159 to the nearest tenths place.
Solution: ⇒ 976,185.9 [The digit in the tenths place is 8; keep everything to the left of it the same, and increase the 8 to 9 since the next digit (7) is ≥ 5; drop everything else to the right.]

Question #18: Round off 976,185.87159 to the nearest hundredths place.
Solution: ⇒ 976,185.87 [The digit in the hundredth place is 7; keep everything to the left of it, the same, and keep 7 as same since the next digit (1) is ≤ 5; drop everything else to the right.]

Question #19: Round off 976,185.87159 to the nearest thousandths place.
Solution: ⇒ 976,185.872 [The digit in the thousandth place is 1; keep everything to the left of it the same, and increase the 1 to 2 since the next digit (5) is ≥ 5; drop everything else to the right.]

Question #20: Round off 976,185.87159 to the nearest ten-thousandths place.
Solution: ⇒ 976,185.8716 [The digit in the ten thousandth place is 5; keep everything to the left of it the same, and increase the 5 to 6 since the next digit (9) is ≥ 5; drop everything else to the right.]

COMPARISON OF DECIMALS: Compare the following sets and find the LARGEST decimal number.

Question #21: {7.9, 7.5, 7.8, 7.2, 7.1}
Solution: ⇒ 7.9   [Compare place value of each digit of the number, from left to right]

Question #22: {5.72, 5.71, 5.79, 5.76, 5.75}
Solution: ⇒ 5.79   [Compare place value of each digit of the number, from left to right]

Question #23: {8.621, 8.698, 8.691, 8.611, 8.689}
Solution: ⇒ 8.698   [Compare place value of each digit of the number, from left to right]

Question #24: {6.819, 6.817, 6.897, 6.879, 6.829}
Solution: ⇒ 6.897   [Compare place value of each digit of the number, from left to right]

Question #25: {0.7198, 0.7251, 0.7919, 0.7219, 0.7989}
Solution: ⇒ 0.7989   [Compare place value of each digit of the number, from left to right]

Question #26: {0.9127, 0.9121, 0.9869, 0.9819, 0.9618}
Solution: ⇒ 0.9869   [Compare place value of each digit of the number, from left to right]

Question #27: {0.5651, 0.5291, 0.5218, 0.5721, 0.5719}
Solution: ⇒ 0.5721   [Compare place value of each digit of the number, from left to right]

Question #28: {0.6512, 0.6869, 0.6289, 0.6152, 0.6728}
Solution: ⇒ 0.6869   [Compare place value of each digit of the number, from left to right]

Question #29: {0.57987, 0.52912, 0.57919, 0.57169, 0.52128}
Solution: ⇒ 0.57987   [Compare place value of each digit of the number, from left to right]

Question #30: {0.85189, 0.85198, 0.87519, 0.86899, 0.87628}
Solution: ⇒ 0.87628   [Compare place value of each digit of the number, from left to right]

COMPARISON OF DECIMALS: Compare the following sets and find the SMALLEST decimal number.

Question #31: {7.9, 7.5, 7.8, 7.2, 7.1}
Solution: ⇒ 7.1   [Compare place value of each digit of the number, from left to right]

Question #32: {5.72, 5.71, 5.79, 5.76, 5.75}
Solution: ⇒ 5.71   [Compare place value of each digit of the number, from left to right]

Question #33: {8.621, 8.698, 8.691, 8.611, 8.689}
Solution: ⇒ 8.611   [Compare place value of each digit of the number, from left to right]

Question #34: {6.819, 6.817, 6.897, 6.879, 6.829}
Solution: ⇒ 6.817   [Compare place value of each digit of the number, from left to right]

Question #35: {0.7198, 0.7251, 0.7919, 0.7219, 0.7989}
Solution: ⇒ 0.7198   [Compare place value of each digit of the number, from left to right]

Question #36: {0.9127, 0.9121, 0.9869, 0.9819, 0.9618}
Solution: ⇒ 0.9121   [Compare place value of each digit of the number, from left to right]

Question #37: {0.5651, 0.5291, 0.5218, 0.5721, 0.5719}
Solution: ⇒ 0.5218   [Compare place value of each digit of the number, from left to right]

Question #38: {0.6512, 0.6869, 0.6289, 0.6152, 0.6728}
Solution: ⇒ 0.6152   [Compare place value of each digit of the number, from left to right]

Question #39: {0.57987, 0.52912, 0.57919, 0.57169, 0.52128}
Solution: ⇒ 0.52128   [Compare place value of each digit of the number, from left to right]

Question #40: {0.85189, 0.85198, 0.87519, 0.86899, 0.87628}
Solution: ⇒ 0.85189   [Compare place value of each digit of the number, from left to right]

ADDITION OF DECIMALS: Add the following decimal numbers.

Question #41: 1.2812 + 1.5256
Solution: ⇒ 2.8068   [Align the decimals and add vertically down starting from right]

Question #42: 2.6215 + 7.2581
Solution: ⇒ 9.8796   [Align the decimals and add vertically down starting from right]

Question #43: 1.2915 + 5.9861
Solution: ⇒ 7.2776   [Align the decimals and add vertically down starting from right]

Question #44: 1.9717 + 6.7851
Solution: ⇒ 8.7568   [Align the decimals and add vertically down starting from right]

Question #45: 6.72 + 1.2698
Solution: ⇒ 7.9898   [Align the decimals and add vertically down starting from right]

Question #46: 5.6 + 2.9278
Solution: ⇒ 8.5278   [Align the decimals and add vertically down starting from right]

Question #47: 1.5211 + 1.1241 + 5.2545
Solution: ⇒ 7.8997   [Align the decimals and add vertically down starting from right]

Question #48: 1.9225 + 1.2512 + 5.5161
Solution: ⇒ 8.6898   [Align the decimals and add vertically down starting from right]

Question #49: 1.7187 + 1.251 + 2.12 + 2.5
Solution: ⇒ 7.5897   [Align the decimals and add vertically down starting from right]

Question #50: 1,000.7257 + 700.821 + 50.25 + 7.1
Solution: ⇒ 1,758.8967   [Align the decimals and add vertically down starting from right]

SUBTRACTION OF DECIMALS: Subtract the following decimal numbers.

Question #51: 7.98 – 5.27
Solution: ⇒ 2.71   [Align the decimals and subtract vertically down starting from right]

Question #52: 9.79 – 2.52
Solution: ⇒ 7.27   [Align the decimals and subtract vertically down starting from right]

Question #53: 7.27 – 1.58
Solution: ⇒ 5.69   [Align the decimals and subtract vertically down starting from right]

Question #54: 9.79 – 1.27
Solution: ⇒ 8.52   [Align the decimals and subtract vertically down starting from right]

Question #55: 97.12 – 21.97
Solution: ⇒ 75.15   [Align the decimals and subtract vertically down starting from right]

Question #56: 78.57 – 12.79
Solution: ⇒ 65.78   [Align the decimals and subtract vertically down starting from right]

Question #57: 100 – 17.29
Solution: ⇒ 82.71   [Align the decimals and subtract vertically down starting from right]

Question #58: 100 – 72.19
Solution: ⇒ 27.81   [Align the decimals and subtract vertically down starting from right]

Question #59: 10,000 – 2,782.79
Solution: ⇒ 7,217.21   [Align the decimals and subtract vertically down starting from right]

Question #60: 10,000 – 728.19
Solution: ⇒ 9,271.81   [Align the decimals and subtract vertically down starting from right]

MULTIPLICATION OF DECIMALS: Multiply the following decimal numbers.

Question #61: 1.5 × 7.5
Solution: ⇒ 11.25   [Multiply the decimals and put the decimal at the appropriate place]

Question #62: 1.7 × 5.1
Solution: ⇒ 8.67   [Multiply the decimals and put the decimal at the appropriate place]

Question #63: 1.25 × 6.25
Solution: ⇒ 7.8125   [Multiply the decimals and put the decimal at the appropriate place]

Question #64: 1.19 × 8.15

Solution: $\Rightarrow$ 9.6985   [Multiply the decimals and put the decimal at the appropriate place]

Question #65:   1.05 × 2.5
Solution: $\Rightarrow$ 2.625   [Multiply the decimals and put the decimal at the appropriate place]

Question #66:   1.09 × 2.1
Solution: $\Rightarrow$ 2.289   [Multiply the decimals and put the decimal at the appropriate place]

Question #67:   7 × 9.8
Solution: $\Rightarrow$ 68.6   [Multiply the decimals and put the decimal at the appropriate place]

Question #68:   27 × 9.51
Solution: $\Rightarrow$ 256.77   [Multiply the decimals and put the decimal at the appropriate place]

Question #69:   0.7 × 0.8
Solution: $\Rightarrow$ 0.56   [Multiply the decimals and put the decimal at the appropriate place]

Question #70:   0.69 × 0.96
Solution: $\Rightarrow$ 0.6624   [Multiply the decimals and put the decimal at the appropriate place]

DIVISION OF DECIMALS: Divide the following decimal numbers.

Question #71:   9 ÷ 1.2
Solution: $\Rightarrow$ 7.5   [Divide the decimals and put the decimal at the appropriate place]

Question #72:   18 ÷ 1.6
Solution: $\Rightarrow$ 11.25   [Divide the decimals and put the decimal at the appropriate place]

Question #73:   78 ÷ 9.6
Solution: $\Rightarrow$ 8.125   [Divide the decimals and put the decimal at the appropriate place]

Question #74:   127 ÷ 2.5
Solution: $\Rightarrow$ 50.8   [Divide the decimals and put the decimal at the appropriate place]

Question #75:   7.5 ÷ 1.2
Solution: $\Rightarrow$ 6.25   [Divide the decimals and put the decimal at the appropriate place]

Question #76:   9.2 ÷ 1.6
Solution: $\Rightarrow$ 5.75   [Divide the decimals and put the decimal at the appropriate place]

Question #77:   22.5 ÷ 1.2
Solution: $\Rightarrow$ 18.75   [Divide the decimals and put the decimal at the appropriate place]

Question #78:   27.9 ÷ 2.5
Solution: $\Rightarrow$ 11.16   [Divide the decimals and put the decimal at the appropriate place]

Question #79:   78.5 ÷ 12.5
Solution: $\Rightarrow$ 6.28   [Divide the decimals and put the decimal at the appropriate place]

Question #80:   96.75 ÷ 11.25
Solution: $\Rightarrow$ 8.6   [Divide the decimals and put the decimal at the appropriate place]

THIS PAGE HAS BEEN INTENTIONALLY LEFT BLANK

PART 4.0: EXPONENTS:

TABLE OF CONTENTS:

EZ REFERENCE: -To practice easy-to-medium level questions, please refer to our EZ Practice Basic Workbook.
                 -To practice medium-to-difficult level questions, please refer to our EZ Practice Advanced Workbook.

4.1: BASICS ABOUT EXPONENTS:

An **"exponent"** is a number that is written by using a special mathematical superscript notation which appears as a little number up and to the right of the mathematical expression. The expression is said to be raised to a power which is represented by the exponent.

An exponent is a number that tells us how many times the number it refers to (known as the base) is used as a factor in a given calculation. In other words, an exponent is a superscripted number that indicates the number of times the base number is multiplied by itself, or how many times the base is a factor. An exponent is a short way of writing the value of a number multiplied several times by itself. Exponent is a shorthand notation of writing some mathematical expressions. For instance, in 5^2, there are 2 factors of 5: $5^2 = 5 \times 5 = 25$. Where 5 is the base, and 2 is the exponent.

PARTS OF EXPONENTIAL EXPRESSIONS:

(A) Base: The Base is the expression or number that appears underneath the exponent. The base is the number multiplied by itself however many times specified by the exponent.

(B) Exponent: The Exponent or the power is the number that appears up and right of the base and it indicates the number of times the base is to be multiplied by itself.

(C) Power: The power is just another way to express a number being raised to an exponent.

MEANING OF EXPONENTS:

The product obtained by multiplying together several factors all of which are equal to the same number is called the power of that number. The base is multiplied by itself as many times as its power.

If a is any number and n is a positive integer, then a^n means the product of n factors each of which is equal to a.

In other words, when a number, a, is to be used n times as a factor in a product, it can be expressed as a^n, which means the nth power of a. In a^n, a is multiplied by itself n times.

If we take the nth root of a number b and the result is a, then b is called the nth power of a.

The exponent tells you how many factors are in the product.

EZ RULE: For any number "a": $a^n = a \times a \times a \times a$ ...."n" number of times $= b \Rightarrow$ i.e., n^{th} root of b is $a \Rightarrow \sqrt[n]{b} = a$

Where "a" is used as a factor n times and where:

"a": is known as a number also known as the base.

"n": is the exponent or the power, a number written slightly above and to the right of the base, that indicates the number of times the base is to be multiplied by itself.

"b": is the result obtained by solving the expression.

Note: The exponent is written to the right and above the base, and to avoid confusion, the exponent is smaller in size.

A number with a positive integer exponent indicates a product, where the positive integer is the number of times that the number is a factor in the product.

For instance, 2^6 means (2)(2)(2)(2)(2)(2); that is, 2 is a factor in the product 6 times.

Example #1: $5^2 \Rightarrow$ 5 is raised to the 2nd power $\Rightarrow$ Where 5 is the base, and 2 is the exponent.

$5^2 = 5 \times 5 = 25$ $\Rightarrow$ since second root of 25 is 5 $\Rightarrow \sqrt[2]{25} = 5$

Example #2: $2^6 \Rightarrow$ 2 is raised to the 6th power $\Rightarrow$ Where 2 is the base, and 6 is the exponent.

$2^6 = 2 \times 2 \times 2 \times 2 \times 2 \times 2 = 64$ $\Rightarrow$ since sixth root of 64 is 2 $\Rightarrow \sqrt[6]{64} = 2$

HOW TO READ EXPONENTS:

EZ RULE: a^n is read as: "*a* raised to the *nth* power" OR "*a* raised to the power of *n*"
a^2 is read as: "*a* squared"   & a^3 is read as: "*a* cubed"
For exponents other that 2 and 3, we use the phrase: "to the ___ power" OR "to the power of ___"
For Example: 7^{11} should be read as: "seven to the eleventh power" OR "seven to the power of eleven"

UNDERSTOOD EXPONENT:

In math, it is customary not to write one as the exponent. When the exponent is not written, as when we write most numbers, the exponent is understood to be equal to 1. So the exponent of all numbers that do not have an exponent should be considered to be one. Since any number to the first power is equivalent to itself, there is no need to write the exponent as one.
EZ RULE: $n^1 = n$
For Example: $10 = 10^1 \Rightarrow$ note that we do not write the exponent as one.

EXPONENTS ARE SPECIAL WAY TO SHOW REPEATED MULTIPLICATION:

Repeated addition of the same number is indicated by multiplication: $\Rightarrow n + n + n + n + n + n + n + n + n = n \times 9$
For Example: $7 + 7 + 7 + 7 + 7 + 7 + 7 + 7 + 7 \Rightarrow 7 \times 9$
Repeated multiplication of the same number is indicated by an exponent: $\Rightarrow n \times n \times n \times n \times n \times n \times n \times n \times n = n^9$
For Example: $7 \times 7 \times 7 \times 7 \times 7 \times 7 \times 7 \times 7 \times 7 \Rightarrow 7^9$
The expression is supposed to be multiplied by itself a specific number of times, which is represented by the exponent.
For Example: To multiply $2 \times 2 \times 2 \times 2 \times 2 \times 2$ $\Rightarrow$ this series of operations can be written at 2^6

EZ CAUTION: 5^2 does not mean that 5 is to be multiplied twice by itself.
"5 multiplied twice by itself" means: $5 \times 5 \times 5$
Instead 5^2 means "product of two fives": 5×5

HOW TO EVALUATE EXPONENTIAL EXPRESSIONS:

To evaluate an exponential expression, perform the multiplication indicated by the exponent.
Expand and multiply the base by the number of times indicated by the exponent.
For Example: To find the value of $2^6 \Rightarrow$ expand and then multiply $2 \times 2 \times 2 \times 2 \times 2 \times 2 = 64$

EXPONENTIAL INCREASE:

When a non-zero positive number increases exponentially, it does not just increase, instead, it increases a whole lot in a short span $\Rightarrow$ the greater the exponent, the faster the rate of increase.
For instance: $10^1 = 10$ $\Rightarrow$
$10^2 = 100$ $\Rightarrow$ increase of 90
$10^3 = 1000$ $\Rightarrow$ increase of 900
$10^4 = 10000$ $\Rightarrow$ increase of 9000
$10^5 = 100000$ $\Rightarrow$ increase of 90000

SOME COMMON USES OF EXPONENTS:

(A) To express scientific notations where very small or very large numbers are involved:
For Example: $10000000 = 10^7$, $0.000000001 = 10^{-9}$
(B) Exponents are frequently used in geometry.
    $\Rightarrow$ Surface Areas are measured in "square units"   **For Example:**   square feet or feet^2, square inch or inch^2
    $\Rightarrow$ Volumes are measured in "cubic units"   **For Example:**   cubic feet or feet^3, cubic inch or inch^3

4.2: SECOND POWER OR SQUARE:

Exponent "2" is read as *"square"* or *"squared"*. A number raised to the power of 2 or whose exponent is 2 is said to be squared or raised to the second power.

The Square of any given number is the process used to find the product of a number times itself. Therefore, to *"square"* a number means to multiply that number by itself. A number multiplied by itself is called the square of that number.

EZ RULE: $a^2 = a \times a$ (read as *a* squared)
Note that once we are able to link between a number and its square, we can apply that knowledge regardless of where the decimal point is located.
For example: if you know $5^2 = 5 \times 5 = 25$
$\Rightarrow$ You should automatically know: $50^2 = 2500$, $0.5^2 = 0.25$, $0.05^2 = 0.0025$, and $(1/5)^2 = 1/25$

EZ TIP: Square of any positive number or square of its negative will always be positive.

4.2.1: SQUARES OF DIFFERENT TYPES OF NUMBERS:

(A) SQUARE OF POSITIVE INTEGERS: To find the square of a positive integer, multiply that integer by itself, the result of which will always be positive.
For Example: $5^2 \Rightarrow 5 \times 5 = 25$

(B) SQUARE OF NEGATIVE INTEGERS: To find the square of any negative number, multiply that negative number by itself, the result of which will always be positive.
For Example: $-5^2 \Rightarrow -5 \times -5 = 25$

(C) SQUARE OF FRACTIONS: To find the square of a fraction, consider the numerator and denominator as separate numbers, and find the square of each number by multiplying its numerator by itself and denominator by itself.
For Example: $\left(\dfrac{5}{9}\right)^2 = \dfrac{5^2}{9^2} = \dfrac{25}{81}$

(D) SQUARE OF DECIMALS: To find the square of a decimal, consider that decimal number as a whole number, find out it's square by multiplying that decimal number by itself, and place the decimal point at the appropriate place.
For Example: $0.5^2 = 0.25$

4.2.2: PERFECT SQUARES:

COMMON PERFECT SQUARES:
Perfect squares are numbers that are the squares of integers. Although you can always figure out the square by working out with paper and pencil, it is recommended that you memorize some of the most common perfect squares so that you can recognize certain common numbers as squares of some of the common numbers, and instantly apply it in a problem as and when needed. Your knowledge of these common squares will be helpful as it can speed up your solution to some of the math problems. Moreover, the most common exponent that appears most often on standardized tests is 2. You must memorize the perfect square of the first 25 numbers. The most common types of problems for which this knowledge will help you is basically used to form squares of numbers in different sections of math, such as:

s^2 $\Rightarrow$ the area of a square
πr^2 $\Rightarrow$ the area of a circle
$a^2 + b^2 = c^0$ $\Rightarrow$ the Pythagorean Theorem
$a^2 - b^2$ $\Rightarrow$ the difference of two squares while factoring or any other factoring and/or simplifying expressions

4.3: THIRD POWER OR CUBE:

Exponent "3" is read as **"cube"** or **"cubed"**.
A number raised to the power of 3 or whose exponent is 3 is said to be cubed or raised to the third power. The cube of any given number is the process used to find the product of a number times itself three times. Therefore, to **"cube"** a number means to multiply that number by itself three times.

EZ RULE: $a^3 = a \times a \times a$ (read as a cubed)

Note that once we are able to link between a number and its cube, we can apply that knowledge regardless of where the decimal point is located.

For Example: if you know $5^3 = 125$

$\Rightarrow$ You should automatically know: $50^3 = 125,000$; $0.5^3 = 0.125$; $0.05^3 = 0.000125$, and $(1/5)^3 = 1/125$

4.3.1: CUBES OF DIFFERENT TYPES OF NUMBERS:

(A) CUBE OF POSITIVE INTEGERS: To find the cube of a positive integer, multiply that integer by itself three times, the result of which will always be positive. In other words, cube of any positive number will always be positive.
For Example: $5^3 \Rightarrow 5 \times 5 \times 5 = 125$

(B) CUBE OF NEGATIVE INTEGERS: To find the cube of any negative number, multiply that negative number by itself three times, the result of which will always be negative. In other words, cube of any negative number will always be negative.
For Example: $-5^3 \Rightarrow -5 \times -5 \times -5 = -125$

(C) CUBE OF FRACTIONS: To find the cube of a fraction, consider the numerator and denominator as separate numbers, and find the cube of each number by multiplying its numerator by itself three times and denominator by itself three times.
For Example: $\left(\dfrac{5}{9}\right)^3 = \dfrac{5^3}{9^3} = \dfrac{125}{729}$

(D) CUBE OF DECIMALS: To find the cube of a decimal, consider that decimal number as a whole number, find its cube by multiplying that decimal number by itself three times, and place the decimal point at the appropriate place.
For Example: $0.5^3 = 0.125$

4.3.2: PERFECT CUBES:

COMMON PERFECT CUBES:

Perfect cubes are numbers that are the cubes of integers. Although you can always figure out the cube by working out with paper and pencil, it is recommended that you memorize some of the most common cubes so that you can recognize certain common numbers as cubes of some of the common numbers, and instantly apply it in a problem as and when needed. Knowing these common cubes will also speed up your solution to some of the math problems.

4.4: PROPERTIES OF EXPONENTS:

Not every base and exponent on your test is going to be a positive integer. Numbers, both positive and negative, integers and fractions, can be raised to a fractional or negative exponent. Even though such numbers follow their own special rules, they adhere to the same general rules of exponents that we had discussed in the previous section in this chapter. Generally speaking, if we raise a number to a power, the number usually gets larger. For instance, $5^2 = 25$. However, raising a number to a power can sometimes have somewhat strange and unexpected results. It actually depends on a lot of factors, such as, if the base number and the exponent is negative or positive, integer or decimal, even or odd. Based on these factors the result can be smaller or bigger than the original number. All these scenarios are discussed in this section of properties of exponents.

4.4.1: PROPERTIES ABOUT EXPONENTS RELATED TO "ZERO" & "ONE":

PROPERTY #1:   POWER OF "ZERO":
⇒ Any non-zero number raised to the power of 0 equals 1 ⇒ $n^0 = 1$ (n is any nonzero number)
Example #1: $7^0 = 1$ **Example #2:** $-25^0 = 1$

PROPERTY #2:   POWER OF "ONE":
⇒ Any number raised to the power of 1 equals that number itself ⇒ $n^1 = n$ (n is any number)
Example #1: $7^1 = 7$ **Example #2:** $-25^1 = -25$

PROPERTY #3:   "ZERO" RAISED TO "ANY POWER":
⇒ Zero raised to the power of any positive number always equals zero ⇒ $0^n = 0$ (n is any +ve no.)
Example #1: $0^7 = 0$ **Example #2:** $0^{25} = 0$

PROPERTY #4:   "ONE" RAISED TO "ANY POWER":
⇒ One raised to the power of any positive number always equals zero ⇒ $1^n = 1$ (n is any number)
Example #1: $1^7 = 1$ **Example #2:** $1^{25} = 1$

PROPERTY #5:   "ZERO" RAISED TO THE "POWER OF ZERO":
⇒ Zero raised to the power of zero is not defined   ⇒ $0^0 =$ **undefined**

EZ TIP: ⇒ If $x^5 = x^7 = x^8$ ⇒Then, x must be either 0 or 1
⇒ If $x^7 = x^9 = x^{15}$ OR   If $x^8 = x^{10} = x^{16}$ ⇒ Then, x must be either 0, 1, or –1.

4.4.2: PROPERTIES ABOUT EXPONENTS OF POSITIVE & NEGATIVE NUMBER:

The sign of the base of an exponential expression may be either positive or negative. With a positive or negative base, multiply the base as many times as the exponent requires.

PROPERTY #1:   EXPONENTS OF POSITIVE NUMBERS:
Any positive number raised to the power of an even or odd positive number will always equal a positive number.
For any positive integer "n": If "a" is positive, then a^n will be positive.
⇒ $a^n = b$ Where "a" is positive, "n" is a positive even or odd number, and "b" is a positive number.
⇒ $n^2 = n \times n = n^2$ or   ⇒ $n^5 = n \times n \times n \times n \times n = n^5$
Example #1: $2^6 \Rightarrow 2 \times 2 \times 2 \times 2 \times 2 \times 2 = 64$ **Example #2:** $2^7 \Rightarrow 2 \times 2 \times 2 \times 2 \times 2 \times 2 \times 2 = 128$

PROPERTY #2:   EXPONENTS OF NEGATIVE NUMBERS:
For any negative integer "n": If "a" is negative, then a^n will be positive if "n" is even, and negative if "n" is odd.

(A) Any negative number in parentheses raised to the power of an even number will always equal a positive number that is bigger than the original number.
⇒ $(-a)^n = b$ Where "a" is negative and "n" is an even number and "b" is a positive number.
⇒ $(-n)^2 = -n \times -n = n^2$
Example #1: $(-5)^2 \Rightarrow -5 \times -5 = 25$ **Example #2:** $(-9)^2 \Rightarrow -9 \times -9 = 81$

(B) Any negative number in parentheses raised to the power of an odd number will always equal a negative number that is smaller than the original number.

$\Rightarrow (-a)^n = b$ Where "a" is negative and "n" is an odd number and "b" is a negative number.

$\Rightarrow (-n)^5 = -n \times -n \times -n \times -n \times -n = -n^5$

Example #1: $(-2)^1 \Rightarrow -2$ **Example #2:** $(-2)^7 \Rightarrow -2 \times -2 \times -2 \times -2 \times -2 \times -2 \times -2 = -128$

(C) Any negative number in parentheses raised to the power of any even number will always be greater than the same negative number in parentheses raised to the power of an odd number.

$\Rightarrow (-a)^m > (-a)^n$ Where "a" is negative, and "m" is an even number and "n" is an odd number.

Example #1: $(-2)^2 > (-2)^7$ **Example #2:** $(-5)^2 > (-5)^7$

EZ CAUTION: A negative number not in parentheses raised to a power of an even or odd number will always remain a negative number.

Example #1: $-9^2 \Rightarrow -(9 \times 9) = -81$ **Example #2:** $-2^7 \Rightarrow -(2 \times 2 \times 2 \times 2 \times 2 \times 2 \times 2) = -128$

EVEN EXPONENTS ARE DANGEROUS; ODD EXPONENTS ARE SAFE:

When an integer is raised to a power, the answer may or may not keep the original sign of the base; this primarily depends if the exponent is even or odd.

Even Exponents: Even exponents are dangerous; they hide the sign of the base. When a base is raised to an even exponent, the resulting answer may either keep or change the original sign of the base. So beware whenever you see an even exponent.

For instance, if $x^2 = 25$, then x can be either 5 or -5. Note that, we cannot answer this question without additional information. If we are told that x is positive, then the answer is that x must be 5. Or, if we are told that x is negative, then the answer is that x must be -5.

Note, any base raised to an even power will always result in a positive answer.

Odd Exponents: Odd exponents are safe; they don't hide the sign of the base. When a base is raised to an odd exponent, the resulting answer keeps the original sign of the base.

For instance, if $x^3 = 125$, then x must be 5, and it cannot be -5 as the cube of -5 is -125. Note that, we can answer this question without additional information.

4.4.3: PROPERTIES ABOUT EXPONENT OF 10:

PROPERTY #1:   10 raised to the power of any positive number equals 1 and add as many zeros as the exponent number to right of 1

Note: The exponent of a power of 10 indicates how many zeros the number would contain if it's written out.

Example #1: $10^2 \Rightarrow 100$ (2 zeros: since 10 multiplied by itself 2 times equals 100)

Example #2: $10^5 \Rightarrow 100,000$ (5 zeros: since 10 multiplied by itself 5 times equals 100,000)

Multiplying a Number by a Power of 10: To multiply a number by a power of 10, move the decimal point to the right, the same number of places as the number of zeros in that power of 10.

Example #1: $0.012579 \times 10^2 \Rightarrow 0.012579 \times 100 = 1.2579$ (Move the decimal point 2 places to the right)

Example #2: $0.012579 \times 10^5 \Rightarrow 0.012579 \times 100,000 = 1257.9$ (Move the decimal point 5 places to the right)

PROPERTY #2:   10 raised to the power of any negative number equals 1 and add as many zeros as the exponent number to the left of 1 and put a decimal point after the first zero.

Example #1: $10^{-2} \Rightarrow 0.01$ **Example #2:** $10^{-5} \Rightarrow 0.00001$

Dividing a Number by a Power of 10: To divide a number by a power of 10, move the decimal point to the left the same number of places as the number of zeros in that power of 10. In other words, move the decimal point the corresponding number of places to the left as many places as the exponent.

Example #1: $12579 \div 10^2 \Rightarrow 12579 \div 100 = 125.79$ (Move the decimal point 2 places to the left)

Example #2: $12579 \div 10^5 \Rightarrow 12579 \div 100,000 = 0.12579$ (Move the decimal point 5 places to the left)

EZ HINT: Dividing by a positive exponent is the same as multiplying by the same negative exponent:

$\Rightarrow a \div 10^n = a \times 10^{-n}$

For Example: $12579 \div 10^5 = 12579 \times 10^{-5}$
$0.12579 = 0.12579$ (Note that diving by 10^5 is the same as multiplying by 10^{-5})

4.4.4: PROPERTIES ABOUT EXPONENTS OF PROPER FRACTIONS:

PROPERTY #1:   Any fraction or decimal of a value between 0 and 1 raised to a positive power always results in a smaller fraction or decimal than the original one.
$\Rightarrow$ If, $0 < n < 1$ Then, $n^2 < n$

Example #1: $\left(\dfrac{1}{2}\right)^2 = \dfrac{1}{4}$ $\Rightarrow \frac{1}{4} < \frac{1}{2}$ **Example #2:** $(0.5)^2 = 0.25$ $\Rightarrow 0.25 < 0.5$

PROPERTY #2:   Any fraction or decimal of a value between 0 and 1 raised to a positive power always results in a smaller fraction or decimal than the same fraction or decimal raised to a smaller positive power.
$\Rightarrow$ If, $0 < n < 1$ Then, $n^5 < n^2$

Example #1: $\left(\dfrac{1}{2}\right)^6 < \left(\dfrac{1}{2}\right)^2$ $\Rightarrow \left(\dfrac{1}{64}\right) < \left(\dfrac{1}{4}\right)$ **Example #2:** $(0.5)^6 < (0.5)^2$ $\Rightarrow 0.015625 < 0.25$

PROPERTY #3:   When any fraction or decimal of a value between 0 and 1 is raised to a positive power, as the exponent increases, the value of the expression decreases. In such cases, power operates as a decreasing instrument.

Example #1: $\left(\dfrac{1}{2}\right)^1 > \left(\dfrac{1}{2}\right)^2 > \left(\dfrac{1}{2}\right)^3 > \left(\dfrac{1}{2}\right)^4$ $\Rightarrow \dfrac{1}{2} > \dfrac{1}{4} > \dfrac{1}{8} > \dfrac{1}{16} > \dfrac{1}{32}$

Example #2: $(0.5)^1 > (0.5)^2 > (0.5)^3 > (0.5)^4 > (0.5)^5 \Rightarrow 0.5 > 0.25 > 0.125 > 0.0625 > 0.03125$
Example #3: $(-0.5)^2 > (-0.5)^3 > (-0.5)^1$ $\Rightarrow 0.25 > -0.125 > -0.5$

4.4.5: PROPERTIES ABOUT EXPONENTS OF NEGATIVE EXPONENTS:

PROPERTY #1:   Any number or expression raised to the negative power equals the reciprocal of that same number or expression raised to the absolute value of the power indicated, which results in a fraction with a numerator of 1; i.e., rewrite the number, without the negative sign in front of the exponent, as the denominator of a fraction with 1 as the numerator of the fraction. In other words, any number raised to the negative exponent "$-n$" is equal to the reciprocal of that same number raised to the positive exponent "n".

$\Rightarrow a^{-n} = \dfrac{1}{a^n}$ and $\dfrac{1}{a^{-n}} = a^n$

Note: A negative exponent indicates a reciprocal. To arrive at an equivalent expression, take the reciprocal of the base and change the sign of the exponent.

Example #1: $5^{-2} = \left(\dfrac{1}{5^2}\right) = \left(\dfrac{1}{5} \times \dfrac{1}{5}\right) = \dfrac{1}{25}$ & $\left(\dfrac{1}{5^{-2}}\right) = 5^2 = 5 \times 5 = 25$

Example #2: $2^{-6} = \left(\dfrac{1}{2^6}\right) = \left(\dfrac{1}{2} \times \dfrac{1}{2} \times \dfrac{1}{2} \times \dfrac{1}{2} \times \dfrac{1}{2} \times \dfrac{1}{2}\right) = \dfrac{1}{64}$ & $\left(\dfrac{1}{2^{-6}}\right) = 2^6 = 2 \times 2 \times 2 \times 2 \times 2 \times 2 = 64$

EZ TIP: Dividing by the positive power (a^n) is the same as multiplying by a negative power (a^{-n})
EZ HINT: When you see a negative exponent, think of reciprocals.

4.4.6: PROPERTIES ABOUT FRACTIONAL EXPONENTS:

PROPERTY #1:   **POSITIVE FRACTIONAL EXPONENTS:**
Any number raised to the power of a fraction, the numerator of that fraction remains the exponent, and the denominator determines which root to take. In other words, raise the base to the power of the numerator of the fractional exponent, and then take the root given by the denominator of the fractional exponent.

$$\Rightarrow a^{\frac{m}{n}} = \sqrt[n]{a^m}$$

Example #1: $2^{\frac{5}{7}} = \sqrt[7]{2^5}$ **Example #2:** $16^{\frac{3}{4}} = 16^{\frac{3}{4}} = \left(\sqrt[4]{16}\right)^3 = 2^3 = 8$

PROPERTY #2: **NEGATIVE FRACTIONAL EXPONENTS:**
Similarly, any number to the power of a negative fraction, the same process needs to be followed, but the result would be a fraction.

$$\Rightarrow a^{-\frac{m}{n}} = \frac{1}{a^{\frac{m}{n}}} = \frac{1}{\left(\sqrt[n]{a}\right)^m}$$

Example #1: $2^{-\frac{5}{7}} = \frac{1}{2^{\frac{5}{7}}} = \frac{1}{\left(\sqrt[7]{2}\right)^5}$ **Example #2:** $16^{-\frac{3}{4}} = \frac{1}{16^{\frac{3}{4}}} = \frac{1}{\left(\sqrt[4]{16}\right)^3} = \frac{1}{2^3} = \frac{1}{8}$

PROPERTY #3: Fractional exponents relate to roots, or they indicate roots.

$$\Rightarrow a^{\frac{1}{n}} = \sqrt[n]{a} \quad \text{(the } n^{th} \text{ root of } a)$$

(A) Any number raised to the power of ½ equals the square root of that number $\Rightarrow n^{\frac{1}{2}} = \sqrt[2]{n}$

Example #1: $25^{\frac{1}{2}} = \sqrt[2]{25} = \sqrt{5 \times 5} = 5$ **Example #2:** $81^{\frac{1}{2}} = \sqrt[2]{81} = \sqrt{9 \times 9} = 9$

(B) Any number raised to the power of 1/3 equals the cube root of that number $\Rightarrow n^{\frac{1}{3}} = \sqrt[3]{n}$

Example #1: $125^{\frac{1}{3}} = \sqrt[3]{125} = 5$ **Example #2:** $729^{\frac{1}{3}} = \sqrt[3]{729} = 9$

Multiplying the Same Number by a Positive & Negative Exponent: Multiplying a number, a, raised to a positive exponent, n, by the same number, a, raised to a negative exponent, $-n$, will always result in 1: $\Rightarrow a^n \times a^{-n} = a^{n-n} = a^0 = 1$
Example #1: $7^5 \times 7^{-5} = 7^{5-5} = 7^0 = 1$ **Example #2:** $2^9 \times 2^{-9} = 2^{9-9} = 2^0 = 1$

4.4.7: MISCELLANEOUS PROPERTIES:
PROPERTY #1: $m^n > n^m$ where m and n are positive integers and $m < n$, and where $m > 2$
For Example: $5^{10} > 10^5$
$9,765,625 > 100,000$

PROPERTY #2: $n^2 > n \times 2$ where n is a positive integer
For Example: $5^2 > 5 \times 2$
$25 > 10$

4.4.8: ROLE OF PARENTHESES IN EXPONENTS:
Parentheses can make a big difference where exponents are involved. Look at the following rules and observe how parentheses can make a big difference:
$\Rightarrow (-n)^2 > -n^2$ where n, is a positive integer $\Rightarrow -n^2 < (-n)^2$ where n, is a positive integer
For Example: $(-10)^2 > -10^2$ **For Example:** $-10^2 < -(10)^2$
$100 > -100$ $-100 < 100$

EZ CAUTION: There are several exponential operations which seem like they ought to work with exponents, however they don't. The following are some such operations, so beware of them and don't let them make you fall in a trap:
$\Rightarrow$ Does $x^2 + x^5 = x^7$ $\Rightarrow$ NO!!
$\Rightarrow$ Does $x^7 - x^5 = x^2$ $\Rightarrow$ NO!!
$\Rightarrow$ Does $\dfrac{\left(x^2 + y^2 + z^2\right)}{\left(x^2 + y^2\right)} = z^2$ $\Rightarrow$ NO!!

4.5: ARITHMETIC OPERATIONS WITH EXPONENTS:

4.5.1: ADDITION OF EXPONENTS:
EZ STEP-BY-STEP METHOD: Apply the following step(s) to add exponential expressions:
STEP 1: First, solve for each individual expressions.
STEP 2: Then, add the results.

EZ RULE: $a^m + b^n$ = multiply a, m times + multiply b, n times (add the results to get the answer).

For Example: $2^6 + 5^2$
$\Rightarrow (2 \times 2 \times 2 \times 2 \times 2 \times 2) + (5 \times 5)$
$\Rightarrow 64 + 25$
$\Rightarrow 89$

EZ CAUTION: While adding exponential expressions, even if the base and/or exponents are same, the terms can't be combined $\Rightarrow a^x + b^x \neq (a + b)^x$

For Example: $\Rightarrow 8^2 + 2^2 \neq (8 + 2)^2$ **For Example:** $\Rightarrow 2^8 + 2^2 \neq 2^{8+2}$
$\Rightarrow (8 \times 8) + (2 \times 2) \neq (10)^2$ $\Rightarrow 256 + 4 \neq 2^{10}$
$\Rightarrow 64 + 4 \neq 100$ $\Rightarrow 160 \neq 1024$
$\Rightarrow 68 \neq 100$

4.5.2: SUBTRACTION OF EXPONENTS:
EZ STEP-BY-STEP METHOD: Apply the following step(s) to subtract exponential expressions:
STEP 1: First, solve for each individual expressions
STEP 2: Then, subtract the results.

EZ RULE: $a^m - b^n$ = multiply a, m times – multiply b, n times (subtract the results to get the answer).

For Example: $2^6 - 5^2$
$\Rightarrow (2 \times 2 \times 2 \times 2 \times 2 \times 2) - (5 \times 5)$
$\Rightarrow 64 - 25$
$\Rightarrow 39$

EZ CAUTION: While subtracting exponential expressions, even if the exponents are same, the terms can't be combined $\Rightarrow a^x - b^x \neq (a - b)^x$

For Example: $\Rightarrow 8^2 - 2^2 \neq (8 - 2)^2$ **For Example:** $\Rightarrow 2^8 - 2^2 \neq 2^{8-2}$
$\Rightarrow (8 \times 8) - (2 \times 2) \neq (6)^2$ $\Rightarrow 256 - 4 \neq 2^6$
$\Rightarrow 64 - 4 \neq 36$ $\Rightarrow 252 \neq 64$
$\Rightarrow 60 \neq 36$

4.5.3: MULTIPLICATION OF EXPONENTS:

4.5.3.1: SAME BASE, SAME/DIFFERENT EXPONENTS:
EZ STEP-BY-STEP METHOD: Apply the following step(s) to multiply exponential expressions with same base and same/different exponents:
STEP 1: Add the exponents, raised to the common base.
STEP 2: Simplify the result if possible.

EZ RULE: $a^m \times a^n = a^{(m+n)}$

Example #1: $2^5 \times 2^7$

$$\Rightarrow (2 \times 2 \times 2 \times 2 \times 2) \times (2 \times 2 \times 2 \times 2 \times 2 \times 2 \times 2)$$
$$\Rightarrow 2^{5+7}$$
$$\Rightarrow 2^{12}$$

Example #2: $7^2 \times 7^9 \Rightarrow 7^{2+9} = 7^{11}$

Example #3: $a^2 \times a^5 \Rightarrow a^{2+5} = a^7$

Example #4: $9^n \times 9^{n+1} \Rightarrow 9^{n+n+1} = 9^{2n+1}$

Note: The above rule also holds for exponents that are not positive integers.

For instance: $a^7 \times a^{-2} \Rightarrow a \times a \times a \times a \times a \times a \times a \times \dfrac{1}{a} \times \dfrac{1}{a} = a^{(7-2)} = a^5$

EZ CAUTION: Let the base remain the same, DO NOT add or multiply the bases. DO NOT multiply the exponents.

For Example: $2^5 \times 2^7 \neq 4^{5+7} \neq 4^{12}$
$2^5 \times 2^7 \neq 4^{5 \times 7} \neq 4^{35}$

4.5.3.2: DIFFERENT BASE, SAME EXPONENTS:

EZ STEP-BY-STEP METHOD: Apply the following step(s) to multiply exponential expressions with different base and same exponents:

STEP 1: First, multiply the bases, and then raise the product to the common exponent.

STEP 2: Simplify the result if possible.

EZ RULE: $a^n \times b^n = (ab)^n$

For Example: $2^5 \times 6^5$
$$\Rightarrow (2 \times 6)^5$$
$$\Rightarrow 12^5$$

EZ CAUTION: Let the exponents remain the same, DO NOT add or multiply the exponents.

For Example: $2^5 \times 6^5 \neq 12^{5+5} \neq 12^{10}$
$2^5 \times 6^5 \neq 12^{5 \times 5} \neq 12^{25}$

4.5.3.3: DIFFERENT BASE, DIFFERENT EXPONENTS:

EZ STEP-BY-STEP METHOD: Apply the following step(s) to multiply exponential expressions with different base and different exponents:

STEP 1: First, solve and find the value of each individual expression.

STEP 2: Then, multiply the results.

EZ RULE: $a^m \times b^n$ = multiply a, m times × multiply b, n times (multiply both the results to get the answer)

For Example: $2^6 \times 5^2$
$$\Rightarrow (2 \times 2 \times 2 \times 2 \times 2 \times 2) \times (5 \times 5)$$
$$\Rightarrow 64 \times 25$$
$$\Rightarrow 1600$$

EZ CAUTION: Let the exponents and the bases remain the same, DO NOT add or multiply the bases or exponents.

For Example: $2^5 \times 5^2 \neq 10^{5+2} \neq 10^7$
$2^5 \times 5^2 \neq 10^{5 \times 2} \neq 10^{10}$

4.5.4: DIVISION OF EXPONENTS:

4.5.4.1: SAME BASE, DIFFERENT EXPONENTS:

EZ STEP-BY-STEP METHOD: Apply the following step(s) to divide exponential expressions with same base and different exponents:

STEP 1: Subtract the exponents $\Rightarrow$ subtract the exponent of the divisor (denominator) from the exponent of the dividend (numerator), raised to the common base.

STEP 2: Simplify the result if possible.

EZ RULE: $a^m \div a^n = a^{(m-n)}$

Example #1: $2^7 \div 2^5$
$\Rightarrow (2 \times 2 \times 2 \times 2 \times 2 \times 2 \times 2) \div (2 \times 2 \times 2 \times 2 \times 2)$
$\Rightarrow \dfrac{2 \cdot 2 \cdot 2 \cdot 2 \cdot 2 \cdot 2 \cdot 2}{2 \cdot 2 \cdot 2 \cdot 2 \cdot 2}$
$\Rightarrow 2^{7-5}$
$\Rightarrow 2^2$

Example #2: $7^9 \div 7^2$
$\Rightarrow 7^{9-2}$
$\Rightarrow 7^7$

Example #3: $a^7 \div a^2$
$\Rightarrow a^{7-2}$
$\Rightarrow a^5$

Example #4: $11^n \div 11^{1-n}$
$\Rightarrow 11^{n-(1-n)}$
$\Rightarrow 11^{n-1+n}$
$\Rightarrow 11^{2n-1}$

EZ CAUTION: Let the base remain the same, DO NOT subtract or divide the bases.
For Example: $2^7 \div 2^5 \neq 1^{7-5} \neq 1^2$

4.5.4.2: DIFFERENT BASE, SAME EXPONENTS:

EZ STEP-BY-STEP METHOD: Apply the following step(s) to divide exponential expressions with different base and same exponents:

STEP 1: First, divide the bases, and then raise the quotient to the common exponent.

STEP 2: Simplify the result if possible.

EZ RULE: $a^n \div b^n = (a/b)^n$

For Example: $10^7 \div 2^7$
$\Rightarrow (10 \div 2)^7$
$\Rightarrow 5^7$

EZ CAUTION: Let the power remain the same, DO NOT subtract or divide the powers.
For Example: $14^5 \div 2^5 \neq 7^{5 \div 5} \neq 7^1$

4.5.4.3: DIFFERENT BASE, DIFFERENT EXPONENTS:

EZ STEP-BY-STEP METHOD: Apply the following step(s) to divide exponential expressions with different base and different exponents:

STEP 1: First, solve and find the value of each individual expression.

STEP 2: Then divide the results.

EZ RULE: $a^m \div b^n$ = multiply a, m times $\div$ multiply b, n times (divide both the results to get the answer.)

Example #1: $2^8 \div 8^2$
$\Rightarrow (2 \times 2 \times 2 \times 2 \times 2 \times 2 \times 2 \times 2) \div (8 \times 8)$
$\Rightarrow 256 \div 64$
$\Rightarrow 4$

EZ CAUTION: Let the exponent and the base remain the same, DO NOT subtract or divide the bases or exponents.

For Example: $10^8 \div 2^2 \neq 5^{8 \div 2} \neq 5^4$

$10^8 \div 2^2 \neq 5^{8-2} \neq 5^6$

4.5.6: DOUBLE EXPONENTS:

A base raised to successive or double exponents means a base raised to one exponent and then that value raised to another exponent.

For instance, to find the value of $(5^2)^6 \Rightarrow$ the base 5 is first squared, and then the result is raised to the sixth power. This computation can be quite tedious; however, with the following rule, the result can be obtained fairly easily without much computations.

EZ RULE: A term raised to an exponent is again raised to an exponent equals that term raised to the exponent which is the product of the two exponents.

$\Rightarrow (a^m)^n = a^{m \times n}$

EZ STEP-BY-STEP METHOD: Apply the following step(s) to solve double exponents:

STEP 1: Multiply the exponents, raised to the same base.

STEP 2: Simplify the result if possible.

Example #1: $(5^2)^6$
$\Rightarrow (5 \times 5)^6$
$\Rightarrow (5^2) \times (5^2) \times (5^2) \times (5^2) \times (5^2) \times (5^2)$
$\Rightarrow (5 \times 5)(5 \times 5)(5 \times 5)(5 \times 5)(5 \times 5)(5 \times 5)$
$\Rightarrow 5^{2 \times 6}$
$\Rightarrow 5^{12}$

Example #2: $(5^7)^8$
$\Rightarrow 5^{7 \times 8}$
$\Rightarrow 5^{56}$

Example #3: $(7^2)^8$
$\Rightarrow 7^{2 \times 8} = 7^{16}$

Example #4: $(7^8)^9$
$\Rightarrow 7^{8 \times 9} = 7^{72}$

Example #5: $(11^{n+1})^2$
$\Rightarrow 11^{2(n+1)} = 11^{2n+2}$

4.5.7: DISTRIBUTIVE LAW OF EXPONENTS:

If there is an exponent outside the parentheses, then the exponent on the outside of the parentheses must be distributed to each individual term within the parentheses.

EZ RULE: $(ab)^m = a^m b^m$

Example #1: $(2 \times 5)^2$
$\Rightarrow 2^2 \times 5^2$
$\Rightarrow 4 \times 25$
$\Rightarrow 100$

Example #2: $(8 \times 9)^2$
$\Rightarrow 8^2 \times 9^2$
$\Rightarrow 64 \times 81$
$\Rightarrow 5,184$

EZ RULE: $\left(\dfrac{a}{b}\right)^m = \dfrac{a^m}{b^m}$

Example #1: $\left(\dfrac{2}{5}\right)^2 = \dfrac{2^2}{5^2} = \dfrac{4}{25}$

Example #2: $\left(\dfrac{8}{9}\right)^2 = \dfrac{8^2}{9^2} = \dfrac{64}{81}$

4.6: COMBINING EXPONENTIAL EXPRESSIONS:

Determining when to combine exponential expression and when not to combine can sometimes be confusing. If two exponential expressions have a base in common or an exponent in common, you may combine them. In other words, you can combine exponential expressions if they have either a base or an exponent in common.
(A) You CAN only combine exponential expressions that are connected by multiplication or division.
⇒ If the bases are the same, then either add or subtract the exponents.
⇒ If the exponents are the same, then either multiply or divide the bases.
(B) You CANNOT combine expressions connected by addition or subtraction.

EZ CAUTION: You may sometimes be tricked into adding or subtracting exponential expressions that have the base or the exponent in common. Always remember, you can only simplify when multiplying or dividing exponential expressions, and not when adding or subtracting.

EZ TABLE FOR COMBINING EXPONENTS: The following table will make it easy for you to remember the combination rules for exponential expressions:

	Same Base	Same Exponent	
Add	When multiplying expressions with the same base, ADD the exponents. EZ Rule: $a^m \times a^n = a^{(m+n)}$ Example: $2^5 \times 2^7 = 2^{5+7} = 2^{12}$	When multiplying expressions with the same exponent, MULTIPLY the bases. EZ Rule: $a^n \times b^n = (ab)^n$ Example: $2^5 \times 6^5 = (2 \times 6)^5 = 12^5$	**Multiply**
Subtract	When dividing expressions with the same base, SUBTRACT the exponents. EZ Rule: $a^m \div a^n = a^{(m-n)}$ Example: $2^7 \div 2^5 = 2^{7-5} = 2^2$	When dividing expressions with the same exponent, DIVIDE the bases. EZ Rule: $a^n \div b^n = (a/b)^n$ Example: $14^5 \div 2^5 = (14 \div 2)^5 = 7^5$	**Divide**
	Same Base	Same Exponent	

EZ TIP: You must remember these rules by heart; however, if you ever forget these rules, you can always derive them by writing out the exponential expressions. For instance: $2^2 \times 2^5 = 2 \times 2 \times 2 \times 2 \times 2 \times 2 \times 2 = 2^{2+5} = 2^7$

Some examples of simplify-able and un-simplify-able expressions:

UN-SIMPLIFY-ABLE EXPRESSIONS
(These expressions can't be simplified)
(A) $2^5 + 2^7$
(B) $2^7 + 5^7$
(C) $2^{12} - 2^5$
(D) $12^7 - 2^7$

SIMPLIFY-ABLE EXPRESSIONS
(These expressions can be simplified)
$2^5 \times 2^7 = 2^{12}$
$2^7 \times 5^7 = 10^7$
$2^{12} \div 2^5 = 2^7$
$12^7 \div 2^7 = 6^7$

SUMMARY OF LAW OF EXPONENTS:

EZ RULE:
(A) $a^m a^n = a^{m+n}$
(B) $(a^m)^n = a^{mn}$
(C) $\dfrac{a^m}{a^n} = a^{m-n}$
(D) $a^n \times b^n = (a \times b)^n$
(E) $a^n \div b^n = (a \div b)^n$
(F) $\left(\dfrac{a}{b}\right)^n = \dfrac{a^n}{b^n} ; b \neq 0$
(G) $a^{-n} = \dfrac{1}{a^n}$

EXAMPLE:
⇒ $2^5 \times 2^7 = 2^{5+7} = 2^{12}$
⇒ $(2^8)^9 = 2^{8 \times 9} = 2^{72}$
⇒ $\dfrac{2^{12}}{2^5} = 2^{12-5} = 2^7$
⇒ $2^2 \times 5^2 = (2 \times 5)^2 = (10)^2 = 100$
⇒ $10^2 \div 2^2 = (10 \div 2)^2 = (5)^2 = 25$
⇒ $\left(\dfrac{5}{9}\right)^2 = \dfrac{5^2}{9^2} = \dfrac{25}{81}$
⇒ $5^{-2} = \dfrac{1}{5^2} = \dfrac{1}{25}$

4.7: SCIENTIFIC NOTATIONS:

Scientific Notation is a special format of writing any given number. Scientific notation means expressing a number as the product of a decimal number between 1 and 10 (i.e., greater than or equal to 1 and less than 10, where there is only one digit to the left of the decimal point) and a power of 10.

It is often difficult to express very large numbers or very small decimal fractions on paper. Such numbers can be more conveniently expressed using scientific notation. Therefore, by using the concept of place value, we can write a very big or small number in a much shorter form.

For instance: $\Rightarrow 2,500,000,000,000 = 2.5 \times 10^{12}$
$\Rightarrow 0.0000000007 = 7 \times 10^{-10}$

EZ STEP-BY-STEP METHOD: Apply the following step(s) to express any given number in form of a scientific notation:

STEP 1: First, re-write that same number and move the decimal point so that there is only one positive number/digit to the left of the decimal point. (Note: Zero is not considered a digit in this case.)

STEP 2: Second, multiply that number by 10 to the power of n, where n is the number of places the decimal point is moved.
      (A) If the decimal point is moved to the left, then n will be positive.
      (B) If the decimal point is moved to the right, then n will be negative.
      (C) If the decimal point is at the correct place, then n will be zero.

FORMAT OF SCIENTIFIC NOTATION: $a.bcde \times 10^{(n)}$
Where: a, b, c, d, and e are any positive numeric digits, such that, $0 < a < 10$, and n is the number of places the decimal point is moved, which can be negative, positive or zero.
For Example: $0.00765 \times 10^{9} = 7.65 \times 10^{6}$

POWER OF 10:

Scientific Notation uses the power of 10. When a number is expressed in Scientific Notation:
(A) The exponent of the 10 indicates the number of places that the decimal point is to be moved in the number that is to be multiplied by a power of 10 in order to obtain the product.
(B) The sign of the exponent of 10 indicates which direction to move in the number that is to be multiplied by a power of 10 in order to obtain the product.
      $\Rightarrow$ If the exponent is positive, then move the decimal point to the right.
      $\Rightarrow$ If the exponent is negative, then move the decimal point to the left.
      $\Rightarrow$ If the exponent is zero, then don't move the decimal point.

In general, the sign of the exponent also indicates the following:
$\Rightarrow$ Positive power of 10 indicates that the value of that exponent is greater than 1.
$\Rightarrow$ Negative power of 10 indicates that the value of that exponent is less than 1.
$\Rightarrow$ Zero power of 10 indicates that the value of that exponent is equal to 1.

$10^{0} = 1$
$10^{1} = 10$ $10^{-1} = 0.1$
$10^{2} = 100$ $10^{-2} = 0.01$
$10^{3} = 1,000$ $10^{-3} = 0.001$
$10^{4} = 10,000$ $10^{-4} = 0.0001$
$10^{5} = 100,000$ $10^{-5} = 0.00001$
$10^{6} = 1,000,000$ $10^{-6} = 0.000001$
$10^{7} = 10,000,000$ $10^{-7} = 0.0000001$
$10^{8} = 100,000,000$ $10^{-8} = 0.00000001$
$10^{9} = 1,000,000,000$ $10^{-9} = 0.000000001$

EZ BASIC TABLE SHOWING SCIENTIFIC NOTATION:

1234567890.0	⇒ Move the decimal point 9 places to the left	⇒ 1.23456789×10^9
123456789.0	⇒ Move the decimal point 8 places to the left	⇒ 1.23456789×10^8
12345678.9	⇒ Move the decimal point 7 places to the left	⇒ 1.23456789×10^7
1234567.89	⇒ Move the decimal point 6 places to the left	⇒ 1.23456789×10^6
123456.789	⇒ Move the decimal point 5 places to the left	⇒ 1.23456789×10^5
12345.6789	⇒ Move the decimal point 4 places to the left	⇒ 1.23456789×10^4
1234.56789	⇒ Move the decimal point 3 places to the left	⇒ 1.23456789×10^3
123.456789	⇒ Move the decimal point 2 places to the left	⇒ 1.23456789×10^2
12.3456789	⇒ Move the decimal point 1 places to the left	⇒ 1.23456789×10^1
1.23456789	⇒ Move the decimal point 0 places	⇒ 1.23456789×10^0
0.123456789	⇒ Move the decimal point 1 places to the right	⇒ $1.23456789 \times 10^{-1}$
0.0123456789	⇒ Move the decimal point 2 places to the right	⇒ $1.23456789 \times 10^{-2}$
0.00123456789	⇒ Move the decimal point 3 places to the right	⇒ $1.23456789 \times 10^{-3}$
0.000123456789	⇒ Move the decimal point 4 places to the right	⇒ $1.23456789 \times 10^{-4}$
0.0000123456789	⇒ Move the decimal point 5 places to the right	⇒ $1.23456789 \times 10^{-5}$
0.00000123456789	⇒ Move the decimal point 6 places to the right	⇒ $1.23456789 \times 10^{-6}$
0.000000123456789	⇒ Move the decimal point 7 places to the right	⇒ $1.23456789 \times 10^{-7}$
0.0000000123456789	⇒ Move the decimal point 8 places to the right	⇒ $1.23456789 \times 10^{-8}$
0.00000000123456789	⇒Move the decimal point 9 places to the right	⇒ $1.23456789 \times 10^{-9}$

DIFFERENT CASES:

(A) When decimal point is moved to the left ⇒ n is positive ⇒ $123456.7 = 1.234567 \times 10^5$

(B) When decimal point is moved to the right ⇒ n is negative ⇒ $0.01234567 = 1.234567 \times 10^{-2}$

(C) When decimal point is not moved ⇒ n is zero ⇒ $1.234567 = 1.234567 \times 10^0$

Example #1: Express 71,956,280 in scientific notation.
Solution: Move the decimal point 7 places to the left and multiply by 10 to the power of 7
⇒ 7.195628×10^7

Example #2: Express 0.000000765 in scientific notation.
Solution: Move the decimal point 7 places to the right and multiply by 10 to the power of −7
⇒ 7.65×10^{-7}

Example #3: Express 7.195628×10^7 in decimal notation.
Solution: Move the decimal point 7 places to the right:
⇒ 71,956,280

Example #4: Express 7.65×10^{-7} in decimal notation.
Solution: Move the decimal point 7 places to the left:
⇒ 0.000000765

PRACTICE EXERCISE – QUESTIONS AND ANSWERS WITH EXPLANATIONS: EXPONENTS:

ADDITION OF EXPONENTS: Add the following exponential expressions and simplify:

Question #1: $2^6 + 2^2$
Solution:
$\Rightarrow (2 \times 2 \times 2 \times 2 \times 2 \times 2) + (2 \times 2)$ [Expand each exponent]
$\Rightarrow 64 + 4$ [Do the multiplication within parentheses]
$\Rightarrow 68$ [Do the addition]

Question #2: $5^4 + 5^2$
Solution:
$\Rightarrow (5 \times 5 \times 5 \times 5) + (5 \times 5)$ [Expand each exponent]
$\Rightarrow 625 + 25$ [Do the multiplication within parentheses]
$\Rightarrow 650$ [Do the addition]

Question #3: $9^2 + 5^2$
Solution:
$\Rightarrow (9 \times 9) + (5 \times 5)$ [Expand each exponent]
$\Rightarrow 81 + 25$ [Do the multiplication within parentheses]
$\Rightarrow 106$ [Do the addition]

Question #4: $9^3 + 6^3$
Solution:
$\Rightarrow (9 \times 9 \times 9) + (6 \times 6 \times 6)$ [Expand each exponent]
$\Rightarrow 729 + 216$ [Do the multiplication within parentheses]
$\Rightarrow 945$ [Do the addition]

Question #5: $2^7 + 7^2$
Solution:
$\Rightarrow (2 \times 2 \times 2 \times 2 \times 2 \times 2 \times 2) + (7 \times 7)$ [Expand each exponent]
$\Rightarrow 128 + 49$ [Do the multiplication within parentheses]
$\Rightarrow 177$ [Do the addition]

Question #6: $2^6 + 5^2$
Solution:
$\Rightarrow (2 \times 2 \times 2 \times 2 \times 2 \times 2) + (5 \times 5)$ [Expand each exponent]
$\Rightarrow 64 + 25$ [Do the multiplication within parentheses]
$\Rightarrow 89$ [Do the addition]

Question #7: $5^0 + 7^0$
Solution:
$\Rightarrow 1 + 1$ [Expand each exponent]
$\Rightarrow 2$ [Do the addition]

Question #8: $9^1 + 8^1$
Solution:
$\Rightarrow 9 + 8$ [Expand each exponent]
$\Rightarrow 17$ [Do the addition]

Question #9: $0^5 + 0^7$
Solution:
$\Rightarrow 0 + 0$ [Expand each exponent]
$\Rightarrow 0$ [Do the addition]

Question #10: $1^9 + 1^7$
Solution:
$\Rightarrow (1 \times 1 \times 1 \times 1 \times 1 \times 1 \times 1 \times 1 \times 1) + (1 \times 1 \times 1 \times 1 \times 1 \times 1 \times 1)$ [Expand each exponent]
$\Rightarrow 1 + 1$ [Do the multiplication within parentheses]
$\Rightarrow 2$ [Do the addition]

SUBTRACTION OF EXPONENTS: Subtract the following exponential expressions and simplify:

Question #11: $2^6 - 2^2$
Solution: $\Rightarrow (2 \times 2 \times 2 \times 2 \times 2 \times 2) - (2 \times 2)$ [Expand each exponent]
$\Rightarrow 64 - 4$ [Do the multiplication within parentheses]
$\Rightarrow 60$ [Do the subtraction]

Question #12: $5^4 - 5^2$
Solution: $\Rightarrow (5 \times 5 \times 5 \times 5) - (5 \times 5)$ [Expand each exponent]
$\Rightarrow 625 - 25$ [Do the multiplication within parentheses]
$\Rightarrow 600$ [Do the subtraction]

Question #13: $9^2 - 5^2$
Solution: $\Rightarrow (9 \times 9) - (5 \times 5)$ [Expand each exponent]
$\Rightarrow 81 - 25$ [Do the multiplication within parentheses]
$\Rightarrow 56$ [Do the subtraction]

Question #14: $9^3 - 6^3$
Solution: $\Rightarrow (9 \times 9 \times 9) - (6 \times 6 \times 6)$ [Expand each exponent]
$\Rightarrow 729 - 216$ [Do the multiplication within parentheses]
$\Rightarrow 513$ [Do the subtraction]

Question #15: $2^7 - 7^2$
Solution: $\Rightarrow (2 \times 2 \times 2 \times 2 \times 2 \times 2 \times 2) - (7 \times 7)$ [Expand each exponent]
$\Rightarrow 128 - 49$ [Do the multiplication within parentheses]
$\Rightarrow 79$ [Do the subtraction]

Question #16: $2^5 - 5^2$
Solution: $\Rightarrow (2 \times 2 \times 2 \times 2 \times 2) - (5 \times 5)$ [Expand each exponent]
$\Rightarrow 32 - 25$ [Do the multiplication within parentheses]
$\Rightarrow 7$ [Do the subtraction]

Question #17: $5^0 - 7^0$
Solution: $\Rightarrow 1 - 1$ [Expand each exponent]
$\Rightarrow 0$ [Do the subtraction]

Question #18: $9^1 - 8^1$
Solution: $\Rightarrow 9 - 8$ [Expand each exponent]
$\Rightarrow 1$ [Do the subtraction]

Question #19: $0^5 - 0^7$
Solution: $\Rightarrow 0 - 0$ [Expand each exponent]
$\Rightarrow 0$ [Do the subtraction]

Question #20: $1^9 - 1^7$
Solution: $\Rightarrow (1 \times 1 \times 1 \times 1 \times 1 \times 1 \times 1 \times 1 \times 1) - (1 \times 1 \times 1 \times 1 \times 1 \times 1 \times 1)$ [Expand each exponent]
$\Rightarrow 1 - 1$ [Do the multiplication within parentheses]
$\Rightarrow 0$ [Do the subtraction]

MULTIPLICATION OF EXPONENTS: Multiply the following exponential expressions and simplify:

Question #21: $2^8 \times 2^2$
Solution: $\Rightarrow 2^{8+2}$ [Add the exponents, raised to the common base]
$\Rightarrow 2^{10}$ [Do the addition of exponents]

Question #22: $2^2 \times 2^5 \times 2^8$
Solution: $\Rightarrow 2^{2+5+8}$ [Add the exponents, raised to the common base]
$\Rightarrow 2^{15}$ [Do the addition of exponents]

Question #23: $2^2 \times 2^5 \times 2^7 \times 2^8$
Solution: $\Rightarrow 2^{2+5+7+8}$ [Add the exponents, raised to the common base]
               $\Rightarrow 2^{22}$ [Do the addition of exponents]

Question #24: $2^1 \times 2^2 \times 2^6 \times 2^8 \times 2^9$
Solution: $\Rightarrow 2^{1+2+6+8+9}$ [Add the exponents, raised to the common base]
               $\Rightarrow 2^{26}$ [Do the addition of exponents]

Question #25: $7^{11} \times 8^{11}$
Solution: $\Rightarrow (7 \times 8)^{11}$ [Multiply the bases, raised to the common exponent]
               $\Rightarrow 56^{11}$ [Do the multiplication of bases]

Question #26: $2^4 \times 8^2$
Solution: $\Rightarrow (2 \times 2 \times 2 \times 2) \times (8 \times 8)$ [Expand each exponent]
               $\Rightarrow 16 \times 64$ [Do the multiplication within each parentheses]
               $\Rightarrow 1024$ [Again, do the multiplication]

Question #27: $a^{11} \times a^{16}$
Solution: $\Rightarrow a^{11+16}$ [Add the exponents, raised to the common base]
               $\Rightarrow a^{27}$ [Do the addition of exponents]

Question #28: $m^2 n^9 \times m^5 n^2$
Solution: $\Rightarrow m^{2+5} n^{9+2}$ [Add the exponents, raised to the common base]
               $\Rightarrow m^7 n^{11}$ [Do the addition of exponents]

Question #29: $xy^9 z^2 \times x^2 yz^2 \times x^5 y^2 z$
Solution: $\Rightarrow x^{1+2+5} y^{9+1+2} z^{2+2+1}$ [Add the exponents, raised to the common base]
               $\Rightarrow x^8 y^{12} z^5$ [Do the addition of exponents]

Question #30: $a^2 b^6 c^5 d^8 \times a^5 b^2 c^7 d^9$
Solution: $\Rightarrow a^{2+5} b^{6+2} c^{5+7} d^{8+9}$ [Add the exponents, raised to the common base]
               $\Rightarrow a^7 b^8 c^{12} d^{17}$ [Do the addition of exponents]

DIVISION OF EXPONENTS: Divide the following exponential expressions and simplify:

Question #31: $5^9 \div 5^2$
Solution: $\Rightarrow 5^{9-2}$ [Subtract the exponents, raised to the common base]
               $\Rightarrow 5^7$ [Do the subtraction of exponents]

Question #32: $7^2 \div 7^{11}$
Solution: $\Rightarrow 7^{2-11}$ [Subtract the exponents, raised to the common base]
               $\Rightarrow 7^{-9}$ [Do the subtraction of exponents]

Question #33: $12^9 \div 2^9$
Solution: $\Rightarrow \left(\dfrac{12}{2} \right)^9$ [Divide the bases, raised to the common exponent]

               $\Rightarrow 6^9$ [Do the division of bases]

Question #34: $18^6 \div 2^6$
Solution: $\Rightarrow \left(\dfrac{18}{2} \right)^6$ [Divide the bases, raised to the common exponent]

               $\Rightarrow 9^6$ [Do the division of bases]

Question #35: $2^4 \div 4^2$
Solution: $\Rightarrow (2 \times 2 \times 2 \times 2) \div (4 \times 4)$ [Expand each exponent]

$\Rightarrow 16 \div 16$ [Do the multiplication within parentheses]

$\Rightarrow 1$ [Do the division]

Question #36: $2^9 \div 8^2$

Solution: $\Rightarrow (2 \times 2 \times 2 \times 2 \times 2 \times 2 \times 2 \times 2 \times 2) \div (8 \times 8)$ [Expand each exponent]

$\Rightarrow 512 \div 64$ [Do the multiplication within parentheses]

$\Rightarrow 8$ [Do the division]

Question #37: $a^{18} \div a^9$

Solution: $\Rightarrow a^{18-9}$ [Subtract the exponents, raised to the common base]

$\Rightarrow a^9$ [Do the subtraction of exponents]

Question #38: $m^9 n^7 \div m^2 n^5$

Solution: $\Rightarrow m^{9-2} n^{7-5}$ [Subtract the exponents, raised to the common base]

$\Rightarrow m^7 n^2$ [Do the subtraction of exponents]

Question #39: $x^9 y^7 z^8 \div x^2 y^5 z^2$

Solution: $\Rightarrow x^{9-2} y^{7-5} z^{8-2}$ [Subtract the exponents, raised to the common base]

$\Rightarrow x^7 y^2 z^6$ [Do the subtraction of exponents]

Question #40: $a^{19} b^8 c^{17} d^9 \div a^{11} b^2 c^{12} d^7$

Solution: $\Rightarrow a^{19-11} b^{8-2} c^{17-12} d^{9-7}$ [Subtract the exponents, raised to the common base]

$\Rightarrow a^8 b^6 c^5 d^2$ [Do the subtraction of exponents]

DOUBLE EXPONENTS: Simplify the following exponential expressions:

Question #41: $(7^6)^2$

Solution: $\Rightarrow 7^{6 \times 2}$ [Multiply the exponents raised to the same base]

$\Rightarrow 7^{12}$ [Do the multiplication of exponents]

Question #42: $(2^7)^8$

Solution: $\Rightarrow 2^{7 \times 8}$ [Multiply the exponents raised to the same base]

$\Rightarrow 2^{56}$ [Do the multiplication of exponents]

Question #43: $(7^9)^0$

Solution: $\Rightarrow 7^{9 \times 0}$ [Multiply the exponents raised to the same base]

$\Rightarrow 7^0$ [Do the multiplication of exponents]

$\Rightarrow 1$ [Any number to the power of zero is 1]

Question #44: $(5^0)^{11}$

Solution: $\Rightarrow 5^{0 \times 11}$ [Multiply the exponents raised to the same base]

$\Rightarrow 5^0$ [Do the multiplication of exponents]

$\Rightarrow 1$ [Any number to the power of zero is 1]

Question #45: $(a^{12})^2$

Solution: $\Rightarrow a^{12 \times 2}$ [Multiply the exponents raised to the same base]

$\Rightarrow a^{24}$ [Do the multiplication of exponents]

Question #46: $(m^6 n^8)^2$

Solution: $\Rightarrow m^{6 \times 2} n^{8 \times 2}$ [Multiply the exponents raised to the same base]

$\Rightarrow m^{12} n^{16}$ [Do the multiplication of exponents]

Question #47: $(x^5 y^9 z^{11})^2$

Solution: $\Rightarrow x^{5 \times 2} y^{9 \times 2} z^{11 \times 2}$ [Multiply the exponents raised to the same base]

$\Rightarrow x^{10} y^{18} z^{22}$ [Do the multiplication of exponents]

Question #48: $(a^6 b^9 c^3 d^4)^2$

Solution: $\Rightarrow a^{6\times2}b^{9\times2}c^{3\times2}d^{4\times2}$ [Multiply the exponents raised to the same base]
$\Rightarrow a^{12}b^{18}c^{6}d^{8}$ [Do the multiplication of exponents]

Question #49: $(11^{n+2})^2$
Solution: $\Rightarrow 11^{2(n+2)}$ [Multiply the exponents raised to the same base]
$\Rightarrow 11^{2n+4}$ [Do the multiplication of exponents]

Question #50: $(11^{n+6})^2$
Solution: $\Rightarrow 11^{2(n+6)}$ [Multiply the exponents raised to the same base]
$\Rightarrow 11^{2n+12}$ [Do the multiplication of exponents]

SCIENTIFIC NOTATION: Write the following in Scientific Notation:

Question #51: 79,586,925
Solution: $\Rightarrow 7.9586925 \times 10^7$ [Move the decimal point 7 places to the left, and multiply by 10^7]

Question #52: 968,175
Solution: $\Rightarrow 9.68175 \times 10^5$ [Move the decimal point 5 places to the left, and multiply by 10^5]

Question #53: 0.068795
Solution: $\Rightarrow 6.7695 \times 10^{-2}$ [Move the decimal point 2 places to the right, and multiply by 10^{-2}]

Question #54: 0.0000815
Solution: $\Rightarrow 8.15 \times 10^{-5}$ [Move the decimal point 5 places to the right, and multiply by 10^{-5}]

Question #55: 5.79681
Solution: $\Rightarrow 5.79681 \times 10^0$ [Move the decimal point 0 places, and multiply by 10^0]

Question #56: 6.97512×100000
Solution: $\Rightarrow 6.97512 \times 10^5$ [Move the decimal point 5 places to the left, and multiply by 10^5]

Question #57: 12.5×1.5
Solution: $\Rightarrow 18.75$ [Multiply the numbers and put the decimal at the appropriate place]
$\Rightarrow 1.875 \times 10^1$ [Move the decimal point 1 place to the left, and multiply by 10^1]

Question #58: 0.002×0.009
Solution: $\Rightarrow 0.000018$ [Multiply the numbers and put the decimal at the appropriate place]
$\Rightarrow 1.8 \times 10^{-5}$ [Move the decimal point 5 places to the right, and multiply by 10^{-5}]

Question #59: 0.15×0.51
Solution: $\Rightarrow 0.0765$ [Multiply the numbers and put the decimal at the appropriate place]
$\Rightarrow 7.65 \times 10^{-2}$ [Move the decimal point 2 places to the right, and multiply by 10^{-2}]

Question #60: 1.95×2.95
Solution: $\Rightarrow 5.7525$ [Multiply the numbers and put the decimal at the appropriate place]
$\Rightarrow 5.7525 \times 10^0$ [Move the decimal point 0 places, and multiply by 10^0]

SCIENTIFIC NOTATION: Write the following in Decimal Notation:

Question #61: 7.9586925×10^7
Solution: $\Rightarrow 79,586,925$ [Move the decimal point 7 places to the right, and eliminate 10^7]

Question #62: 9.68175×10^5
Solution: $\Rightarrow 968,175$ [Move the decimal point 5 places to the right, and eliminate 10^5]

Question #63: 6.7695×10^{-2}

Solution: $\Rightarrow 0.067695$ [Move the decimal point 2 places to the left, and eliminate 10^{-2}]

Question #64: 8.15×10^{-5}
Solution: $\Rightarrow 0.0000815$ [Move the decimal point 5 places to the left, and eliminate 10^{-5}]

Question #65: 5.79681×10^{0}
Solution: $\Rightarrow 5.79681$ [Move the decimal point 0 places, and eliminate 10^{0}]

Question #66: 6.97512×10^{5}
Solution: $\Rightarrow 697512$ [Move the decimal point 5 places the right, and eliminate 10^{5}]

Question #67: 1.875×10^{1}
Solution: $\Rightarrow 18.75$ [Move the decimal point 1 place to the right, and eliminate 10^{1}]

Question #68: 1.8×10^{-5}
Solution: $\Rightarrow 0.000018$ [Move the decimal point 5 places to the left, and eliminate 10^{-5}]

Question #69: 7.65×10^{-2}
Solution: $\Rightarrow 0.0765$ [Move the decimal point 2 places to the left, and eliminate 10^{-2}]

Question #70: 5.7525×10^{0}
Solution: $\Rightarrow 5.7525$ [Move the decimal point 0 places, and eliminate 10^{0}]

PART 5.0: RADICALS:

TABLE OF CONTENTS:

EZ REFERENCE: -To practice easy-to-medium level questions, please refer to our EZ Practice Basic Workbook.
                  -To practice medium-to-difficult level questions, please refer to our EZ Practice Advanced Workbook.

5.1: BASICS ABOUT RADICALS:

A *"radical"* is a number that is written by using a special mathematical radical notation which appears as a little number up and left of the radical sign. A radical is, in some sense, the opposite of an exponent. The radical is also known as the *"root"* of a number or expression.

PARTS OF RADICAL EXPRESSIONS:
(A) Radical Sign: The radical sign indicates that the root of a number or expression is to be taken.
(B) Radicand: The radicand is the number of which the root is to be taken of and it appears inside the radical sign.
(C) Index: The index determines the number of times the root needs to be multiplied by itself in order to equal the Radicand.

$$\sqrt[index]{radicand}$$

MEANING OF RADICALS:

Fractional exponents represent roots $\Rightarrow a^{\frac{1}{n}} = \sqrt[n]{a}$

A root is a number that when taken as a factor a specified number of times give a certain number. If we raise a number m to the nth power and the result is a, then m is called the nth root of a.

EZ RULE: $\sqrt[n]{a} = m \Rightarrow m \times m \times m \times m \times m....... n$ **times** $= a$ $\Rightarrow$ i.e., m to the power of n equals $a \Rightarrow m^n = a$

For instance, $\sqrt[3]{125}$ is an expression that means the number, when multiplied by itself three times, will yield 125; that number is 5, because $5 \times 5 \times 5 = 125$. Therefore, $\sqrt[3]{125} = 5$; and we call this as 5 is the cube root of 125.

For Example: $25^{\frac{1}{2}} = \sqrt[2]{25} = 5$ $\Rightarrow$ Where: 2 is the index, and 25 is the radicand.
                                   $\Rightarrow$ 5 is a square root of 25 because the square of 5 is 25.
                                     $\Rightarrow$ 5 two times equals 25 $\Rightarrow 5^2 = 5 \times 5 = 25$

Rule: If $b = \sqrt{a} = a^{\frac{1}{2}} \Rightarrow$ then, $b^2 = a$

For Example: $4^{\frac{1}{2}} = \sqrt[2]{4} = 2$ $\Rightarrow$ Where: 2 is the index, and 4 is the radicand.
                                     $\Rightarrow$ 2 is a square root of 4 because the square of 2 is 4.
                                     $\Rightarrow$ 2 two times equals 4 $\Rightarrow 2^2 = 2 \times 2 = 4$

Rule: If $b = \sqrt[3]{a} = a^{\frac{1}{3}} \Rightarrow$ then, $b^3 = a$

For Example: $8^{\frac{1}{3}} = \sqrt[3]{8} = 2$ $\Rightarrow$ Where: 3 is the index, and 8 is the radicand.
                                     $\Rightarrow$ 2 is a cube root of 8 because the cube of 2 is 8.
                                     $\Rightarrow$ 2 three times equals 8 $\Rightarrow 2^3 = 2 \times 2 \times 2 = 8$

Rule: If $b = \sqrt[4]{a} = a^{\frac{1}{4}} \Rightarrow$ then, $b^4 = a$

For Example: $16^{\frac{1}{4}} = \sqrt[4]{16} = 2$ $\Rightarrow$ Where: 4 is the index, and 16 is the radicand.
                                     $\Rightarrow$ 2 is a fourth root of 16 because 2 to the power of 4 is 16.
                                     $\Rightarrow$ 2 four times equals 16 $\Rightarrow 2^4 = 2 \times 2 \times 2 \times 2 = 4$

Rule: If $b = \sqrt[5]{a} = a^{\frac{1}{5}} \Rightarrow$ then, $b^5 = a$

For Example: $32^{\frac{1}{5}} = \sqrt[5]{32} = 2$ $\Rightarrow$ Where: 5 is the index, and 32 is the radicand.
                                     $\Rightarrow$ 2 is a fifth root of 32 because 2 to the power of 5 is 32.
                                     $\Rightarrow$ 2 five times equals 32 $\Rightarrow 2^5 = 2 \times 2 \times 2 \times 2 \times 2 = 32$

Rule: If $b = \sqrt[6]{a} = a^{\frac{1}{6}} \Rightarrow$ then, $b^6 = a$

For Example: $64^{\frac{1}{6}} = \sqrt[6]{64} = 2 \Rightarrow$ Where: 6 is the index, and 64 is the radicand.

$\Rightarrow$ 2 is the sixth root of 64 because 2 to the power of 6 is 64
$\Rightarrow$ 2 six times equals 64 $\Rightarrow 2^6 = 2 \times 2 \times 2 \times 2 \times 2 \times 2 = 64$

HOW TO READ RADICALS:

$\Rightarrow \sqrt[n]{a} = m \quad \Rightarrow$ is read as "m is nth root of a"

$\Rightarrow \sqrt{a} = m \quad \Rightarrow$ is read as "m is square-root of a"

$\Rightarrow \sqrt[3]{a} = m \quad \Rightarrow$ is read as "m is cube-root of a"

For radicals other than 2 and 3, we use the phrase: "__ root of __" OR "__ to the root of __"

For Example: $\sqrt[11]{7}$ is read as $\Rightarrow$ "eleventh root of seven" OR $\Rightarrow$ "seven to the root of eleven"

UNDERSTOOD RADICAL:

In math, it is customary not to write two as the index of the radicand. When the index is not written, which is how most radical numbers are written, the index is understood to be equal to 2. So the index of all numbers that do not have an index should be considered to be 2. Since the second root of any number is the square root, radicands without any index numbers express square roots. This is also done due to the fact that square roots are the most common types of roots. So, since the square roots are so common, they are written without the 2 outside the radical sign.

For Example: $\sqrt[2]{100} = \sqrt{100} = 10 \Rightarrow$ note that we do not write the index as 2.

ROOTS OF NUMBER ONE:

1 is the only number whose nth root is also 1.
$\Rightarrow$ The square root of 1 is 1 $\Rightarrow$ The cube root of 1 is 1 $\Rightarrow$ The 4th root of 1 is 1 $\Rightarrow$ The 5th root of 1 is 1 $\Rightarrow$ Etc.......

EXPONENTS AND RADICALS ARE OPPOSITE OPERATIONS:

Roots and exponents are reciprocals of each other. Exponents and radicals are mathematically inverse or opposite operations, just like addition and subtraction, or multiplication and division. In others words, if the power of an exponent and the index of a radical is the same number, then they both will cancel each other. For instance, finding the square root and squaring a number are inverse operations, just like addition and subtraction, or multiplication and division. So the square root of a number (n) is always going to be the number that gives you (n) when the number is squared. The following rule and examples will make this concept clear.

EZ RULE: $\left(\sqrt[m]{n}\right)^m = n$

Example#1: $\left(\sqrt{25}\right)^2 = (5)^2 = 5 \times 5 = 25$ $\Rightarrow$ Squaring a square root results in the same original number

Example#2: $\left(\sqrt[3]{8}\right)^3 = (2)^3 = 2 \times 2 \times 2 = 8$ $\Rightarrow$ Cubing a cube root results in the same original number

5.2: SECOND ROOT OR SQUARE ROOT:

The *"square root"* of any given number is the process used to find a number that when multiplied by itself (or square of that number) results in the original given number.

EZ RULE: A square root of a nonnegative number "n" is equal to a number which when squared or multiplied by itself gives the number "n".

For any positive number "a", there is a positive number "b" that satisfies the equation $b^2 = a$. That number is called the square root of "a": $b = \sqrt{a}$.

Therefore, for any positive number "a": $\sqrt{a} \times \sqrt{a} = \left(\sqrt{a}\right)^2 = a$

Every positive number has two square roots – one positive root, which is its Principal Root, and the other negative root.

5.2.1: SQUARE ROOT OF DIFFERENT TYPES OF NUMBERS:

(A) SQUARE ROOT OF POSITIVE INTEGERS: Every positive integer has two square roots – one positive root, which is its Principal Root, and the other negative root.

For Example: $\sqrt{25} = 5$ $\Rightarrow$ Principal/Positive Square Root (since 5 × 5 = 25)

$\sqrt{25} = -5$ $\Rightarrow$ Negative Square Root (since –5 × –5 = 25)

By convention, if "n" is positive, $\sqrt{n}$ means the positive square root of "n". Whenever there is a $\sqrt{}$ symbol, this means the positive square root.

For Example: $\sqrt{25} = 5$ (since $5^2 = 25$) $\Rightarrow$ As mentioned earlier, even though 25 has two square roots, which are 5 and –5; however, $\sqrt{25}$ means the positive square root of 25, which is 5 only.

(B) SQUARE ROOT OF NEGATIVE NUMBERS: Square root of negative numbers is not defined as a real number. In other words, negative numbers do not have real numbers as their roots.

EZ RULE: $\sqrt{-n}$ = *not defined*   **For Example:** $\sqrt{-25}$ = *not defined*

Note: Zero is the only number that has only one square root, which is 0 itself.

(C) SQUARE ROOT OF FRACTIONS: To find the square root of a fraction, consider the numerator and denominator as separate numbers, and find the square root of each number separately.

EZ RULE: $\sqrt{\dfrac{a^2}{b^2}} = \dfrac{a}{b}$ **For Example:** $\sqrt{\dfrac{25}{81}} = \dfrac{5}{9}$

EZ HINT: In the above example, the numerator and denominator are perfect squares; however, if they were not perfect squares, we would have to either convert the fraction into a decimal and then find its square root or multiply both the numerator and the denominator by such a number that will make numerator and/or denominator into perfect squares.

For Example: $\sqrt{\dfrac{1}{5}} = \sqrt{\dfrac{1 \times 5}{5 \times 5}} = \dfrac{\sqrt{5}}{5}$

Note: The square root of a positive fraction less than 1 is actually larger than the original fraction.

For Example: $\sqrt{\dfrac{1}{4}} = \dfrac{1}{2}$

(D) SQUARE ROOT OF DECIMALS: To find the square root of a decimal, consider the decimal number as a whole number, find its square root and place the decimal point at the appropriate place. Note that once you are able to link between a number and its square root, you can apply that knowledge regardless of where the decimal point is located.

For Example: $\sqrt{0.25} = 0.5$

The square of any decimal number must always contain an even number of decimal places and that the number of decimal places in the square will be double the number of such places in the square root. Therefore, while finding the square root of a decimal number, the number of decimal places should always be made even.

For instance: To find the square root of .04, we must write it as 0.04, and then $\sqrt{0.04} = 0.2$

Note: If a decimal, in its simplest form, has an odd number of places, its square root cannot be found exactly, i.e., its square root will be an irrational number.

5.2.2: PERFECT & IMPERFECT SQUARE ROOTS:

Every positive real number has a square root, which can be a perfect square root, or an *imperfect square root*.

5.2.2.1: PERFECT SQUARE ROOTS:

Numbers whose square roots are whole numbers are known as Perfect Square Roots. Every number that is square of a whole number also has a perfect square root. Each perfect square has a perfect square root.

EZ RULE: If $\sqrt{x}$ yields an integer, then we call x a perfect square.
For instance: 4, 9, 16, 25, etc., are all examples of perfect squares because they all yield an integers.

COMMON PERFECT SQUARE ROOTS:

Although you can always figure out the square root by working out with paper and pencil, it is recommended that you memorize some of the most common square roots so that you can recognize certain common numbers as square roots of some of the common numbers, and instantly apply it in a problem as and when needed. Your knowledge of these common square roots will be helpful as it can speed up your solution to some of the math problems.

5.2.2.2: IMPERFECT SQUARE ROOTS:

EZ RULE: If $\sqrt{x}$ yields a non-integer, then we call x an imperfect square.
For instance: 7, 12, 15, 20, etc., are all examples of imperfect squares because none of them yield an integer.

Numbers whose square roots are not whole numbers are known as Imperfect Square Roots, and in such cases approximation is used.

For instance, $\sqrt{25}$ and $\sqrt{27}$, both have square roots. The only difference between $\sqrt{25}$ and $\sqrt{27}$ is that the square root of 25 is an integer, while the square root of 27 is not an integer.

In other words, $\sqrt{27}$ does not yield an integer answer because no integer multiplied by itself will yield 27.

However, we can still estimate the answer for $\sqrt{27}$ by finding the closest square root that we do know.

Since 27 is a little larger than 25, we should expect that $\sqrt{27}$ is a little more than $\sqrt{25}$, which is 5. In fact, $(5.15)^2 = 26.52$, which is close to 27; and $(5.19)^2 = 26.9361$, which is very close to 27, so $\sqrt{27} \approx 5.19$.

Alternately, another way of getting approximate imperfect square roots is by using perfect square roots as the base. For instance, $\sqrt{25} = 5$ and $\sqrt{36} = 6$; which implies that $\sqrt{27}$ must be somewhere between 5 and 6. The closer the number is to 25, the closer the square root will be to 5, likewise, the closer the number is to 36, the closer the square root will be to 6. So $\sqrt{27}$ must be quite closer to 5 than to 6 because $\sqrt{27}$ is closer to $\sqrt{25}$ than it is to $\sqrt{36}$, and we can estimate it to be 5.2, which is very close to the actual answer, which is 5.19.

Therefore, square roots of integers that aren't perfect square can be approximated as accurately as we want. To get a more accurate answer, you can use your calculator and get much more accuracy than what you need for your test. Moreover, most answers involving square roots use the square root symbol and it will be unlikely that you will have to get an accurate answer, not at least for the purpose of your test.

Example #1:   What is the approximate value of $\sqrt{69}$?
⇒ Since $(8)^2 = 64$ and $(9)^2 = 81$, the square root of 69 must be a number in between 8 and 9, or around 8.5.

Example #2:   What is the approximate value of $\sqrt[3]{-169}$?
⇒ Since $(-5)^3 = -125$ and $(-6)^3 = -216$, the cube root of -169 must be a number in between -5 and -6, or around -5.5

Irrational Number: If the root of a number cannot be exactly obtained, the root is called an irrational number.
The following table shows some of the imperfect square roots:

x	2	3	5	6	7	8	11	17	27	50
$\sqrt[2]{x}$	1.41	1.73	2.24	2.45	2.65	2.83	3.32	4.12	5.20	7.07

EZ HINT: In the expression $5x^2$, only the x is being squared, not the 5. In other words, $5x^2 = 5(x)^2$. If we wanted to square the 5 as well, we would write $(5x)^2$. (Remember that in the order of operations we raise to a power before we multiply, so in $5x^2$ we square x and then multiply by 5.)

SIMPLIFYING IMPERFECT SQUARE ROOTS:

If we do not want to estimate an imperfect square, there is a more accurate method of simplifying it. However, this can only be done if the number inside the radical is any multiple of any perfect square, then the expression can be simplified by factoring out the perfect square.

EZ NOTE: If the number can't be factored into two or more numbers so that one or more of which has a perfect square root, then that radical cannot be simplified.

EZ STEP-BY-STEP METHOD: Apply the following step(s) to simplify imperfect square roots:

STEP 1: Factor the number inside the square root into two or more numbers, such that one or more of them has a perfect square root.

STEP 2: Take the square root of the numbers that has a perfect square root.

STEP 3: Leave the other number that does not have a perfect square root or which cannot be factored anymore so that one of the factors has a perfect square root as it is.

EZ TIP: Look for perfect squares inside the radical sign, factor them out and "square root" them.

EZ RULE: $\sqrt[n]{a \times b} = \sqrt[n]{a} \times \sqrt[n]{b}$

Example #1: $\sqrt{50} = \sqrt{25 \times 2} = \sqrt{25} \times \sqrt{2} = 5\sqrt{2}$ **Example 2:** $\sqrt{20} = \sqrt{4 \times 5} = \sqrt{4} \times \sqrt{5} = 2\sqrt{5}$

SQUARE ROOTS OF BIG NUMBERS:

In some cases, we can find the square root of a number by breaking it into its prime factors.

Example #1: $\sqrt{576}$ $\Rightarrow 4 \times 9 \times 16 = (2 \times 2) \times (3 \times 3) \times (4 \times 4) = 2^2 \times 3^2 \times 4^2 = 2 \times 3 \times 4 = 24$

Example #2: $\sqrt{2916}$ $\Rightarrow 36 \times 81 = (6 \times 6) \times (9 \times 9) = 6^2 \times 9^2 = 6 \times 9 = 54$

Example #3: $\sqrt{5184}$ $\Rightarrow 64 \times 81 = (8 \times 8) \times (9 \times 9) = 8^2 \times 9^2 = 8 \times 9 = 72$

Example #4: $\sqrt{5929}$ $\Rightarrow 49 \times 121 = (7 \times 7) \times (11 \times 11) = 7^2 \times 11^2 = 7 \times 11 = 77$

Example #5: $\sqrt{7056}$ $\Rightarrow 4 \times 36 \times 49 = (2 \times 2) \times (6 \times 6) \times (7 \times 7) = 2^2 \times 6^2 \times 7^2 = 2 \times 6 \times 7 = 84$

Example #6: $\sqrt{9216}$ $\Rightarrow 4 \times 36 \times 64 = (2 \times 2) \times (6 \times 6) \times (8 \times 8) = 2^2 \times 6^2 \times 8^2 = 2 \times 6 \times 8 = 96$

Example #7: $\sqrt{9801}$ $\Rightarrow 81 \times 121 = (9 \times 9) \times (11 \times 11) = 9^2 \times 11^2 = 9 \times 11 = 99$

Example #8: $\sqrt{12544}$ $\Rightarrow 4 \times 49 \times 64 = (2 \times 2) \times (7 \times 7) \times (8 \times 8) = 2^2 \times 7^2 \times 8^2 = 2 \times 7 \times 8 = 112$

Example #9: $\sqrt{15876}$ $\Rightarrow 4 \times 49 \times 81 = (2 \times 2) \times (7 \times 7) \times (9 \times 9) = 2^2 \times 7^2 \times 9^2 = 2 \times 7 \times 9 = 126$

5.3: THIRD ROOT OR CUBE ROOT:

The *"cube root"* of any given number is the process used to find a number that when multiplied twice by itself (or cube of that number) results in the original given number.

Symbol for Cube root: The real cube root is denoted by $\sqrt[3]{}$.
Sign of Cube Root: The sign of the cube root of any number is always the same sign as the number itself.
$\Rightarrow$ Every number, positive or negative, has one and only one cube root – that root can be either positive or negative.

EZ RULE: A cube root of a number "n" is equal to a number which when cubed or multiplied by itself twice gives the number "n".
For any real number "a", there is a number "b" that satisfies the equation $b^3 = a$. That number is called the cube root of "a": $b = \sqrt[3]{a}$.

Every number has exactly one cube root – which is positive if the number is positive or negative if the number is negative.

5.3.1: CUBE ROOTS OF DIFFERENT TYPES OF NUMBERS:

(A) CUBE ROOT OF POSITIVE INTEGERS: Every positive number has only one cube root – which is a positive root. The cube roots of all positive numbers are always positive.
For Example: $\sqrt[3]{125}$ = 5 (since 5^3 = 5 × 5 × 5 = 125)

(B) CUBE ROOT OF NEGATIVE INTEGERS: Every negative number has only one cube root – which is a negative root. The cube roots of all negative numbers are always negative. Cube root of a negative number is defined as a real number. Unlike square roots, negative numbers do have real numbers as their cube roots.
For Example: $\sqrt[3]{-125}$ = –5 (since $(-5)^3$ = –5 × –5 × –5 = –125)
Note: Zero is the only number that has only one cube root, which is, 0 itself.

(C) CUBE ROOT OF FRACTIONS: To find the cube root of a fraction, consider the numerator and denominator as separate numbers, and find the cube root of each number separately.
For Example: $\sqrt[3]{\dfrac{125}{729}} = \dfrac{\sqrt[3]{125}}{\sqrt[3]{729}} = \dfrac{5}{9}$

(D) CUBE ROOT OF DECIMALS: To find the cube root of a decimal, consider the decimal number as a whole number, find out its cube root and place the decimal point at the appropriate place.
For Example: $\sqrt[3]{0.125} = \sqrt{0.25} = 0.5$

5.3.2: PERFECT & IMPERFECT CUBE ROOTS:
Every positive real number has a cube root, which can be a perfect cube root or an imperfect cube root.

5.3.2.1: PERFECT CUBE ROOTS:
Numbers whose cube roots are whole numbers are known as Perfect Cube Roots.

COMMON PERFECT CUBES ROOTS:
Although you can always figure out the cube roots by working out with paper and pencil, it is recommended that you memorize some of the most common cube roots so that you can recognize certain common numbers as cubes of some of the common numbers, and instantly apply it in a problem as and when needed. Knowing these common cube roots will also speed up your solution to some of the math problems.

5.3.2.2: IMPERFECT CUBE ROOTS:
Numbers whose cube roots are not whole numbers are known as Imperfect Cube Roots, in such cases approximation is used.
The following table shows some of the imperfect cube roots:

x	2	3	5	7	10	20	25	50	75	100
$\sqrt[3]{x}$	1.26	1.44	1.71	1.91	2.15	2.71	2.92	3.68	4.22	4.64

5.3.2.3: CUBE ROOTS OF BIG NUMBERS:
In some cases, we can find the cube root of a number by breaking it into its prime factors.

Example #1: $\sqrt[3]{216}$ $\Rightarrow 8 \times 27 = (2\times2\times2) \times (3\times3\times3) = 2^3 \times 3^3 = 2 \times 3 = 6$

Example #2: $\sqrt[3]{13824}$ $\Rightarrow (2\times2\times2) \times (3\times3\times3) \times (4\times4\times4) = 2^3 \times 3^3 \times 4^3 = 2 \times 3 \times 4 = 24$

Example #3: $\sqrt[3]{1728000}$ $\Rightarrow (2\times2\times2) \times (3\times3\times3) \times (4\times4\times4) \times (5\times5\times5) = 2^3\times3^3\times4^3\times5^3 = 2 \times 3 \times 4 \times 5= 120$

Example #4: $\sqrt[3]{5832}$ $\Rightarrow 8 \times 729 = (2\times2\times2) \times (9\times9\times9) = 2^3 \times 9^3 = 2 \times 9 = 18$

OTHER ROOTS: The following are some of the higher roots. They are outside the scope of this book or your test; however, it would be interesting for you to know them.

(A) Fourth Root: The fourth root of a number is the square root of its square root.

For Example: $16^{\frac{1}{4}} = \sqrt[4]{16} = \sqrt[4]{2 \times 2 \times 2 \times 2} = 2$

(B) Sixth Root: The sixth root of a number is the cube root of its square root.

For Example: $32^{\frac{1}{6}} = \sqrt[6]{64} = \sqrt[6]{2 \times 2 \times 2 \times 2 \times 2 \times 2} = 2$

(C) Eighth Root: The eighth root of a number is the square root of the square root of its square root.

(D) Ninth Root: The ninth root of a number is the cube root of its cube root.

Note: The most common root that appears on the test is probably square roots; cube roots tend to be rare. You can be assured that anything higher than cube root is extremely rare, unless the higher root can be broken into smaller roots.

5.4: ARITHMETIC OPERATIONS WITH RADICALS:

5.4.1: ADDITION OF RADICALS:

EZ STEP-BY-STEP METHOD: Apply the following step(s) to add two common or like radicals:

STEP 1: First, add the number outside the first radical and the number outside the second radical.

STEP 2: Then, place that number outside the common radicand.

STEP 3: Finally, simplify the result if possible.

ADDITION LAW OF RADICALS: $a\sqrt{n} + b\sqrt{n} = (a + b)\sqrt{n}$

EZ HINT: Only like radicals can be added: Radicals can be added only when the parts inside the radicals are identical: To add two or more radicals, the radicals must have the same radicand. We can't add two or more radicals with different radicands. $\Rightarrow \sqrt{a} + \sqrt{b} \neq \sqrt{a + b}$. For instance, we can't add: $\sqrt{7} + \sqrt{5}$

EZ NOTE: Only the number outside the radical/root is added, the radicand remains the same.

For Example: $2\sqrt{11} + 5\sqrt{11}$

$\Rightarrow (2 + 5)\sqrt{11}$

$\Rightarrow 7\sqrt{11}$

5.4.2: SUBTRACTION OF RADICALS:

EZ STEP-BY-STEP METHOD: Apply the following step(s) to subtract two common radicals/roots:

STEP 1: First, subtract the number outside the first radical from the number outside the second radical.

STEP 2: Then, place that number outside the common radicand.

STEP 3: Finally, simplify the result if possible.

SUBTRACTION LAW OF RADICALS: $a\sqrt{n} - b\sqrt{n} = (a - b)\sqrt{n}$

EZ HINT: Only like radicals can be subtracted: Radicals can be subtracted only when the parts inside the radicals are identical: To subtract two or more radicals, the radicals must have the same radicand. You can't subtract two or more radicals with different radicands. $\Rightarrow \sqrt{a} - \sqrt{b} \neq \sqrt{a - b}$. For instance, we can't subtract: $\sqrt{7} - \sqrt{5}$

EZ NOTE: Only the number outside the radical/root is subtracted, the radicand remains the same.

For Example: $9\sqrt{11} - 2\sqrt{11}$

$\Rightarrow (9 - 2)\sqrt{11}$

$\Rightarrow 7\sqrt{11}$

5.4.3: MULTIPLICATION OF RADICALS:

EZ STEP-BY-STEP METHOD: Apply the following step(s) to multiply two or more radicals/roots:

STEP 1: First, multiply the numbers outside the first radical with the number outside the second radical.

STEP 2: Then, multiply the number inside the first radical with the number inside the second radical and put that number under the radical sign.

STEP 3: Finally, simplify the product if possible.

MULTIPLICATION LAW OF RADICALS: $a\sqrt{n} \times b\sqrt{m} = (a \times b)\sqrt{n \times m}$

EZ HINT: To multiply radicals, deal with what's inside the radical sign and outside the radical sign separately, i.e., multiply both the numbers inside the radicals, and those outside separately.

For Example: $\sqrt{2} \times \sqrt{5}$

$\Rightarrow \sqrt{2 \times 5}$

$\Rightarrow \sqrt{10}$

5.4.4: DIVISION OF RADICALS:

EZ STEP-BY-STEP METHOD: Apply the following step(s) to divide two radicals/roots:

STEP 1: First, simplify both the numerator and the denominator.

STEP 2: Then multiply both the numerator and the denominator by the denominator so that denominator becomes a rational number. Note that by multiplying the numerator and the denominator by the same number does not change the value of that expression.

STEP 3: The numerators and denominators then should be factorized into smaller parts, to make the simplification process easier.

DIVISION LAW OF RADICALS: $\dfrac{\sqrt{a}}{\sqrt{b}} = \sqrt{\dfrac{a}{b}}$

EZ HINT: To divide radicals, deal with what's inside the radical sign and outside the radical sign separately, i.e., divide both the numbers inside the radicals, and those outside separately.

For Example: $\dfrac{\sqrt{10}}{\sqrt{2}}$

$\Rightarrow \dfrac{\sqrt{5} \times \sqrt{2}}{\sqrt{2}} = \sqrt{5}$

$\Rightarrow \sqrt{5}$

5.5: COMBINING AND SPLITTING RADICALS:

Sometimes there are two numbers inside the same radical sign, which you would like to simplify. In order to simplify this type of root, it is often helpful to split-up the numbers into two roots under two radical signs and then solve. Similarly, sometime there are two roots under different radical signs, which you would like to simplify. In order to simplify these types of roots, it is often helpful to combine the numbers into one root under one radical sign and then solve. Now, the question is when you can combine and when you can split.

WHEN YOU CAN COMBINE & SPLIT-UP RADICALS:
(A) You CAN split-up or combine radicals in multiplication and division.

(i) Multiplying Radicals: You can split-up or combine radicals in multiplication.
Split-Up $\Rightarrow$ When multiplying radicals, you can split-up a larger product into its smaller factors, which will result in two radicals. Solving each radical individually before multiplying can save you from complicated computations.
EZ RULE: $(a \times b)\sqrt{n \times m} = a\sqrt{n} \times b\sqrt{m}$
For instance: $\sqrt{25 \times 4} = \sqrt{25} \times \sqrt{4} = 5 \times 2 = 10$

Combine $\Rightarrow$ Similarly, when multiplying radicals, you can combine two smaller roots that are being multiplied together into a single larger root of its product. Solving the combined radical after multiplying can save you from complicated computations.
EZ RULE: $a\sqrt{n} \times b\sqrt{m} = (a \times b)\sqrt{n \times m}$
For instance: $\sqrt{25} \times \sqrt{4} = \sqrt{25 \times 4} = \sqrt{100} = 10$

(ii) Dividing Radical: You can split-up or combine radicals in division.
Split-Up $\Rightarrow$ When dividing radicals, you can split-up a quotient into the dividend and divisor, which will result in two radicals. Solving each radical individually before dividing can save you from complicated computations.
EZ RULE: $\sqrt{a \div b} = \sqrt{a} \div \sqrt{b}$
For instance: $\sqrt{100 \div 4} = \sqrt{100} \div \sqrt{4} = 10 \div 2 = 5$

Combine $\Rightarrow$ Similarly, when dividing radicals, you can combine two roots that are being divided into a single root of its quotient. Solving the combined radical after dividing can save you from complicated computations.
EZ RULE: $\sqrt{a} \div \sqrt{b} = \sqrt{a \div b}$
For instance: $\sqrt{100} \div \sqrt{4} = \sqrt{100 \div 4} = \sqrt{25} = 5$

	Multiplication	Division	
Split-Up	When multiplying radicals, you can split-up a larger product into its smaller factors, which will result in two radicals. **EZ Rule:** $(a \times b)\sqrt{n \times m} = a\sqrt{n} \times b\sqrt{m}$ **Ex**: $\sqrt{25 \times 4} = \sqrt{25} \times \sqrt{4} = 5 \times 2 = 10$	When dividing radicals, you can split-up a quotient into the dividend and divisor, which will result in two radicals. **EZ Rule:** $\sqrt{a \div b} = \sqrt{a} \div \sqrt{b}$ **Ex**: $\sqrt{100 \div 4} = \sqrt{100} \div \sqrt{4} = 10 \div 2 = 5$	**Split-Up**
Combine	When multiplying radicals, you can combine two smaller roots that are being multiplied together into a single larger root of its product. **EZ Rule:** $\sqrt{a} \times \sqrt{b} = \sqrt{a \times b}$ **Ex**: $\sqrt{25} \times \sqrt{4} = \sqrt{25 \times 4} = \sqrt{100} = 10$	When dividing radicals, you can combine two roots that are being divided into a single root of its quotient. **EZ Rule:** $\sqrt{a} \div \sqrt{b} = \sqrt{a \div b}$ **Ex**: $\sqrt{100} \div \sqrt{4} = \sqrt{100 \div 4} = \sqrt{25} = 5$	**Combine**
	Multiplication	Division	

(B) You CANNOT combine or split-up radicals in addition or subtraction.

(i) Adding Radicals: You cannot split-up or combine radicals in addition.
Split-Up $\Rightarrow$ When adding radicals, you cannot split-up a larger sum into smaller numbers, which will result in two radicals.
EZ Rule: $\sqrt{a+b} \neq \sqrt{a} + \sqrt{b}$

For instance: $\sqrt{16+9} = \sqrt{16} + \sqrt{9} = 4 + 3 = 7$ WRONG
$\sqrt{16+9} = \sqrt{25} = 5$ CORRECT

Combine $\Rightarrow$ Similarly, when adding radicals, you cannot combine two smaller roots that are being added together into a single larger root of its sum.
EZ Rule: $\sqrt{a} + \sqrt{b} \neq \sqrt{a+b}$

For instance: $\sqrt{16} + \sqrt{9} = \sqrt{16+9} = \sqrt{25} = 5$ WRONG
$\sqrt{16} + \sqrt{9} = 4 + 3 = 7$ CORRECT

(ii) Subtracting Radicals: You cannot split-up or combine radicals in subtraction.
Split-Up $\Rightarrow$ When subtracting radicals, you cannot split-up a difference into smaller numbers, which will result in two radicals.
EZ Rule: $\sqrt{a-b} \neq \sqrt{a} - \sqrt{b}$

For instance: $\sqrt{25-9} = \sqrt{25} - \sqrt{9} = 5 - 3 = 2$ WRONG
$\sqrt{25-9} = \sqrt{16} = 4$ CORRECT

Combine $\Rightarrow$ Similarly, when subtracting radicals, you cannot combine two roots that are being subtracted together into a single smaller root of its difference.
EZ Rule: $\sqrt{a} - \sqrt{b} \neq \sqrt{a-b}$

For instance: $\sqrt{25} - \sqrt{9} = \sqrt{25-9} = \sqrt{16} = 4$ WRONG
$\sqrt{25} - \sqrt{9} = 5 - 3 = 2$ CORRECT

	Addition	**Subtraction**	
Split-Up	When adding radicals, you cannot split-up a larger sum into smaller numbers, which will result in two radicals. **EZ Rule:** $\sqrt{a+b} \neq \sqrt{a} + \sqrt{b}$ **Ex**: $\sqrt{16+9} \neq \sqrt{16} + \sqrt{9} \neq 4+3 \neq 7$ $\sqrt{16+9} = \sqrt{25} = 5$	When subtracting radicals, you cannot split-up a difference into smaller numbers, which will result in two radicals. **EZ Rule:** $\sqrt{a-b} \neq \sqrt{a} - \sqrt{b}$ **Ex**: $\sqrt{25-9} \neq \sqrt{25} - \sqrt{9} \neq 5-3 \neq 2$ $\sqrt{25-9} = \sqrt{16} = 4$	**Split-Up**
Combine	When adding radicals, you cannot combine two smaller roots that are being added together into a single larger root of its sum **EZ Rule:** $\sqrt{a} + \sqrt{b} \neq \sqrt{a+b}$ **Ex**: $\sqrt{16} + \sqrt{9} \neq \sqrt{16+9} \neq \sqrt{25} \neq 5$ $\sqrt{16} + \sqrt{9} = 4+3 = 7$	When subtracting radicals, you cannot combine two roots that are being subtracted together into a single smaller root of its difference. **EZ Rule:** $\sqrt{a} - \sqrt{b} \neq \sqrt{a-b}$ **Ex**: $\sqrt{25} - \sqrt{9} \neq \sqrt{25-9} \neq \sqrt{16} \neq 4$ $\sqrt{25} - \sqrt{9} = 5-3 = 2$	**Combine**
	Addition	**Subtraction**	

EZ CAUTION: A problem may try to trick you into splitting the sum or difference of two numbers inside a radical into two individual roots, or combining the sum or difference of two roots inside one radical sign. Always remember that you may only split or combine the product or quotient of two roots, not the sum or difference. So, you can only combine roots in multiplication and division; you can never combine roots in addition or subtraction.

EVALUATING EXPRESSIONS WITH EXPONENTS AND ROOTS:

There may be some expressions that involve both – exponents and roots, and you should know how to evaluate such expressions.

FIRST TYPE: Evaluating exponential expressions by using radicals:

Example #1: If $x = 8$, what is $x^{\frac{2}{3}}$? $\Rightarrow 8^{\frac{2}{3}} = \sqrt[3]{8^2} = \sqrt[3]{64} = 4$

Example #2: If $x = 4$, what is $x^{\frac{3}{2}}$? $\Rightarrow 4^{\frac{3}{2}} = \sqrt[2]{4^3} = \sqrt[2]{64} = 8$

SECOND TYPE: This is the reverse of the first type given above:

Example #1: If $x^{\frac{3}{2}} = 64$, what is the value of x?

$\Rightarrow x^{\frac{3}{2}} = \left(x^3\right)^{\frac{1}{2}} = 64$ [Apply the rule of exponents]

$\Rightarrow x^3 = 64 \times 64$ [Square both sides]

$\Rightarrow x^3 = (16 \times 4)\,(16 \times 4)$ [Split the right side into two equal factor pairs]

$\Rightarrow x^3 = (16 \times 16 \times 16)$ [Rewrite the right side as three equal factors]

$\Rightarrow x = \sqrt[3]{16 \times 16 \times 16}$ [Cube root both sides]

$\Rightarrow x = 16$ [Simplify]

Example #2: If $x^{\frac{2}{3}} = 64$, what is the value of x?

$\Rightarrow x^{\frac{2}{3}} = \left(x^2\right)^{\frac{1}{3}} = 64$ [Apply the rule of exponents]

$\Rightarrow x^2 = 64 \times 64 \times 64$ [Cube both sides]

$\Rightarrow x = \sqrt[2]{64 \times 64 \times 64}$ [Square root both sides]

$\Rightarrow x = 8 \times 8 \times 8$ [Eliminate the square root sign]

$\Rightarrow x = 512$ [Simplify]

SUMMARY OF LAW OF RADICALS:
EZ RULE: EXAMPLE:

(A) $\sqrt{a} \times \sqrt{a} = a$ $\Rightarrow \sqrt{5} \times \sqrt{5} = \sqrt{25} = 5$

(B) $\sqrt{a} \times \sqrt{b} = \sqrt{a \times b}$ $\Rightarrow \sqrt{2} \times \sqrt{5} = \sqrt{10}$

(C) $\sqrt{a^2 \times b} = a\sqrt{b}$ $\Rightarrow \sqrt{5^2 \times 2} = 5\sqrt{2}$

(D) $\left(\sqrt{a} + \sqrt{b}\right)^2 = a + b + 2\sqrt{a \times b}$ $\Rightarrow \left(\sqrt{2} + \sqrt{5}\right)^2 = 2 + 5 + 2\sqrt{10}$

(E) $\left(\sqrt{a} - \sqrt{b}\right)^2 = a + b - 2\sqrt{a \times b}$ $\Rightarrow \left(\sqrt{2} - \sqrt{5}\right)^2 = 2 + 5 - 2\sqrt{10}$

(F) $\left(\sqrt{a} + \sqrt{b}\right)\left(\sqrt{a} - \sqrt{b}\right) = a - b$ $\Rightarrow \left(\sqrt{9} + \sqrt{2}\right)\left(\sqrt{9} - \sqrt{2}\right) = 9 - 2 = 7$

(G) $\sqrt{n}\left(\sqrt{a} + \sqrt{b}\right) = \sqrt{n}\sqrt{a} + \sqrt{n}\sqrt{b}$ $\Rightarrow \sqrt{2}\left(2\sqrt{5} + 9\sqrt{7}\right) = 2\sqrt{10} + 9\sqrt{14}$

PRACTICE EXERCISE – QUESTIONS AND ANSWERS WITH EXPLANATIONS: RADICALS:

ADDITION OF RADICALS: Add the following radicals and simplify:

Question #1: $2\sqrt{5} + 9\sqrt{5}$
Solution: $\Rightarrow (2+9)\sqrt{5}$ [Combine the numbers outside the radical with the same radicand]
  $\Rightarrow 11\sqrt{5}$ [Add the numbers in parentheses]

Question #2: $8\sqrt{9} + \sqrt{9}$
Solution: $\Rightarrow (8+1)\sqrt{9}$ [Combine the numbers outside the radical with the same radicand]
  $\Rightarrow 9\sqrt{9}$ [Add the numbers in parentheses]

Question #3: $7\sqrt{2} + \sqrt{50}$
Solution: $\Rightarrow 7\sqrt{2} + \left(\sqrt{25} \times \sqrt{2}\right)$ [Factor the radicands to get all possible perfect squares]
  $\Rightarrow 7\sqrt{2} + 5\sqrt{2}$ [Take the square root of the perfect squares]
  $\Rightarrow (7+5)\sqrt{2}$ [Combine the numbers outside the radical with the same radicand]
  $\Rightarrow 12\sqrt{2}$ [Add the numbers in parentheses]

Question #4: $\sqrt{98} + \sqrt{8}$
Solution: $\Rightarrow \left(\sqrt{2} \times \sqrt{49}\right) + \left(\sqrt{2} \times \sqrt{4}\right)$ [Factor the radicands to get all possible perfect squares]
  $\Rightarrow 7\sqrt{2} + 2\sqrt{2}$ [Take the square root of the perfect squares]
  $\Rightarrow (7+2)\sqrt{2}$ [Combine the numbers outside the radical with the same radicand]
  $\Rightarrow 9\sqrt{2}$ [Add the numbers in parentheses]

Question #5: $7\sqrt{5} + \sqrt{80}$
Solution: $\Rightarrow 7\sqrt{5} + \left(\sqrt{16} \times \sqrt{5}\right)$ [Factor the radicands to get all possible perfect squares]
  $\Rightarrow 7\sqrt{5} + 4\sqrt{5}$ [Take the square root of the perfect squares]
  $\Rightarrow (7+4)\sqrt{5}$ [Combine the numbers outside the radical with the same radicand]
  $\Rightarrow 11\sqrt{5}$ [Add the numbers in parentheses]

Question #6: $7\sqrt{17} + \sqrt{68}$
Solution: $\Rightarrow 7\sqrt{17} + \left(\sqrt{4} \times \sqrt{17}\right)$ [Factor the radicands to get all possible perfect squares]
  $\Rightarrow 7\sqrt{17} + 2\sqrt{17}$ [Take the square root of the perfect squares]
  $\Rightarrow (7+2)\sqrt{17}$ [Combine the numbers outside the radical with the same radicand]
  $\Rightarrow 9\sqrt{17}$ [Add the numbers in parentheses]

Question #7: $5\sqrt{11} + 8\sqrt{11} + 9\sqrt{11}$
Solution: $\Rightarrow (5+8+9)\sqrt{11}$ [Combine the numbers outside the radical with the same radicand]
  $\Rightarrow 22\sqrt{11}$ [Add the numbers in parentheses]

Question #8: $9\sqrt{5} + 7\sqrt{2} + 2\sqrt{5}$

Solution: $\Rightarrow (9+2)\sqrt{5} + 7\sqrt{2}$ [Combine the numbers outside the radical with the same radicand]

$\Rightarrow 11\sqrt{5} + 7\sqrt{2}$ [Add the numbers in parentheses]

Question #9: $2\sqrt{17} + 6\sqrt{17} + 8\sqrt{17} + 9\sqrt{17}$

Solution: $\Rightarrow (2+6+8+9)\sqrt{17}$ [Combine the numbers outside the radical with the same radicand]

$\Rightarrow 25\sqrt{17}$ [Add the numbers in parentheses]

Question #10: $2\sqrt{7} + 5\sqrt{11} + 7\sqrt{7} + 2\sqrt{11}$

Solution: $\Rightarrow (2+7)\sqrt{7} + (2+5)\sqrt{11}$ [Combine the numbers outside the radical with the same radicand]

$\Rightarrow 9\sqrt{7} + 7\sqrt{11}$ [Add the numbers in parentheses]

SUBTRACTION OF RADICALS: Subtract the following radicals and simplify:

Question #11: $9\sqrt{7} - 2\sqrt{7}$

Solution: $\Rightarrow (9-2)\sqrt{7}$ [Combine the numbers outside the radical with the same radicand]

$\Rightarrow 7\sqrt{7}$ [Subtract the numbers in parentheses]

Question #12: $7\sqrt{11} - \sqrt{11}$

Solution: $\Rightarrow (7-1)\sqrt{11}$ [Combine the numbers outside the radical with the same radicand]

$\Rightarrow 6\sqrt{11}$ [Subtract the numbers in parentheses]

Question #13: $7\sqrt{2} - \sqrt{50}$

Solution: $\Rightarrow 7\sqrt{2} - \left(\sqrt{25} \times \sqrt{2}\right)$ [Factor the radicands to get all possible perfect squares]

$\Rightarrow 7\sqrt{2} - 5\sqrt{2}$ [Take the square root of the perfect squares]

$\Rightarrow (7-5)\sqrt{2}$ [Combine the numbers outside the radical with the same radicand]

$\Rightarrow 2\sqrt{2}$ [Subtract the numbers in parentheses]

Question #14: $\sqrt{98} - \sqrt{8}$

Solution: $\Rightarrow \left(\sqrt{2} \times \sqrt{49}\right) - \left(\sqrt{2} \times \sqrt{4}\right)$ [Factor the radicands to get all possible perfect squares]

$\Rightarrow 7\sqrt{2} - 2\sqrt{2}$ [Take the square root of the perfect squares]

$\Rightarrow (7-2)\sqrt{2}$ [Combine the numbers outside the radical with the same radicand]

$\Rightarrow 5\sqrt{2}$ [Subtract the numbers in parentheses]

Question #15: $16\sqrt{5} - \sqrt{80}$

Solution: $\Rightarrow 16\sqrt{5} - \left(\sqrt{16} \times \sqrt{5}\right)$ [Factor the radicands to get all possible perfect squares]

$\Rightarrow 16\sqrt{5} - 4\sqrt{5}$ [Take the square root of the perfect squares]

$\Rightarrow (16-4)\sqrt{5}$ [Combine the numbers outside the radical with the same radicand]

$\Rightarrow 12\sqrt{5}$ [Subtract the numbers in parentheses]

Question #16: $11\sqrt{17} - \sqrt{68}$

Solution: $\Rightarrow 11\sqrt{17} - \left(\sqrt{4} \times \sqrt{17}\right)$ [Factor the radicands to get all possible perfect squares]

                     $\Rightarrow 11\sqrt{17} - 2\sqrt{17}$ [Take the square root of the perfect squares]

                     $\Rightarrow (11 - 2)\sqrt{17}$ [Combine the numbers outside the radical with the same radicand]

                     $\Rightarrow 9\sqrt{17}$ [Subtract the numbers in parentheses]

Question #17: $9\sqrt{5} + 7\sqrt{2} - 2\sqrt{5}$

Solution: $\Rightarrow (9 - 2)\sqrt{5} + 7\sqrt{2}$ [Combine the numbers outside the radical with the same radicand]

                     $\Rightarrow 7\sqrt{5} + 7\sqrt{2}$ [Subtract the numbers in parentheses]

Question #18: $15\sqrt{19} - 5\sqrt{19} - \sqrt{19}$

Solution: $\Rightarrow (15 - 5 - 1)\sqrt{19}$ [Combine the numbers outside the radical with the same radicand]

                     $\Rightarrow 9\sqrt{19}$ [Subtract the numbers in parentheses]

Question #19: $9\sqrt{22} - \sqrt{22} + 8\sqrt{22} - \sqrt{22}$

Solution: $\Rightarrow (9 - 1 + 8 - 1)\sqrt{22}$ [Combine the numbers outside the radical with the same radicand]

                     $\Rightarrow 15\sqrt{22}$ [Add/Subtract the numbers in parentheses]

Question #20: $7\sqrt{7} + 9\sqrt{5} - 2\sqrt{7} - 2\sqrt{5}$

Solution: $\Rightarrow (7 - 2)\sqrt{7} + (9 - 2)\sqrt{5}$ [Combine the numbers outside the radical with the same radicand]

                     $\Rightarrow 5\sqrt{7} + 7\sqrt{5}$ [Add/Subtract the numbers in parentheses]

MULTIPLICATION OF RADICALS: Multiply the following radicals and simplify:

Question #21: $\sqrt{2} \times \sqrt{11}$

Solution: $\Rightarrow \sqrt{(2 \times 11)}$ [Combine the numbers inside the radical sign]

                     $\Rightarrow \sqrt{22}$ [Multiply the numbers in parentheses]

Question #22: $\sqrt{5} \times \sqrt{19}$

Solution: $\Rightarrow \sqrt{(5 \times 19)}$ [Combine the numbers inside the radical sign]

                     $\Rightarrow \sqrt{95}$ [Multiply the numbers in parentheses]

Question #23: $5\sqrt{2} \times 2\sqrt{7}$

Solution: $\Rightarrow (5 \times 2)\sqrt{(2 \times 7)}$ [Combine the numbers inside and outside the radical sign]

                     $\Rightarrow 10\sqrt{14}$ [Multiply the numbers in parentheses]

Question #24: $11\sqrt{7} \times 7\sqrt{11}$

Solution: $\Rightarrow (11 \times 7)\sqrt{(7 \times 11)}$ [Combine the numbers inside and outside the radical sign]

                     $\Rightarrow 77\sqrt{77}$ [Multiply the numbers in parentheses]

Question #25: $\sqrt{7} \times \sqrt{7}$

Solution: $\Rightarrow \sqrt{(7 \times 7)}$ [Combine the numbers inside the radical sign]

                     $\Rightarrow \sqrt{49}$ [Multiply the numbers in parentheses]

                     $\Rightarrow 7$

Question #26: $\sqrt{9} \times \sqrt{9}$

Solution: $\Rightarrow \sqrt{(9 \times 9)}$ [Combine the numbers inside the radical sign]

$\Rightarrow \sqrt{81}$ [Multiply the numbers in parentheses]

$\Rightarrow 9$

Question #27: $5\sqrt{8} \times 2\sqrt{9}$

Solution: $\Rightarrow (5 \times 2)\sqrt{(8 \times 9)}$ [Combine the numbers inside and outside the radical sign]

$\Rightarrow 10\sqrt{72}$ [Multiply the numbers in parentheses]

$\Rightarrow 10\sqrt{36 \times 2}$ [Factor the radicands to get all possible perfect squares]

$\Rightarrow 10 \times 6\sqrt{2}$ [Take the square root of the perfect squares]

$\Rightarrow 60\sqrt{2}$ [Multiply the numbers outside the radical sign]

Question #28: $5\sqrt{10} \times 2\sqrt{5}$

Solution: $\Rightarrow (5 \times 2)\sqrt{(10 \times 5)}$ [Combine the numbers inside and outside the radical sign]

$\Rightarrow 10\sqrt{50}$ [Multiply the numbers in parentheses]

$\Rightarrow 10 \times \sqrt{25 \times 2}$ [Factor the radicands to get all possible perfect squares]

$\Rightarrow 10 \times 5\sqrt{2}$ [Take the square root of the perfect squares]

$\Rightarrow 50\sqrt{2}$ [Multiply the numbers outside the radical sign]

Question #29: $\sqrt{50} \times \sqrt{80}$

Solution: $\Rightarrow (\sqrt{25 \times 2}) \times (\sqrt{16 \times 5})$ [Factor the radicands to get all possible perfect squares]

$\Rightarrow 5\sqrt{2} \times 4\sqrt{5}$ [Take the square root of the perfect squares]

$\Rightarrow (5 \times 4)\sqrt{(2 \times 5)}$ [Combine the numbers inside and outside the radical sign]

$\Rightarrow 20\sqrt{10}$ [Multiply the numbers in parentheses]

Question #30: $\sqrt{56} \times \sqrt{72}$

Solution: $\Rightarrow (\sqrt{4 \times 14}) \times (\sqrt{36 \times 2})$ [Factor the radicands to get all possible perfect squares]

$\Rightarrow 2\sqrt{14} \times 6\sqrt{2}$ [Take the square root of the perfect squares]

$\Rightarrow (2 \times 6)\sqrt{(14 \times 2)}$ [Combine the numbers inside and outside the radical sign]

$\Rightarrow 12\sqrt{28}$ [Multiply the numbers in parentheses]

$\Rightarrow 12\sqrt{7 \times 4}$ [Again, factor the radicands to get all possible perfect squares]

$\Rightarrow 12 \times 2\sqrt{7}$ [Again, take the square root of the perfect squares]

$\Rightarrow 24\sqrt{7}$ [Multiply the numbers outside the radical sign]

DIVISION OF RADICALS: Divide the following radicals and simplify:

Question #31: $\sqrt{50} \div \sqrt{2}$

Solution: $\Rightarrow \dfrac{\sqrt{50}}{\sqrt{2}}$ [Divide the first radical by the second radical]

$\Rightarrow \dfrac{\sqrt{25} \times \sqrt{2}}{\sqrt{2}}$ [Factor the radicands]

$\Rightarrow \sqrt{25}$ [Cancel-out the common radicals from the numerator/denominator]

$\Rightarrow 5$ [Take the square root of the perfect squares]

Question #32: $\sqrt{128} \div \sqrt{2}$

Solution: $\Rightarrow \dfrac{\sqrt{128}}{\sqrt{2}}$ [Divide the first radical by the second radical]

$\Rightarrow \dfrac{\sqrt{64} \times \sqrt{2}}{\sqrt{2}}$ [Factor the radicands]

$\Rightarrow \sqrt{64}$ [Cancel-out the common radicals from the numerator/denominator]

$\Rightarrow 8$ [Take square root of 64]

Question #33: $\sqrt{49} \div \sqrt{7}$

Solution: $\Rightarrow \dfrac{\sqrt{49}}{\sqrt{7}}$ [Divide the first radical by the second radical]

$\Rightarrow \dfrac{\sqrt{7} \times \sqrt{7}}{\sqrt{7}}$ [Factor the radicands]

$\Rightarrow \sqrt{7}$ [Cancel-out the common radicals from the numerator/denominator]

Question #34: $\sqrt{121} \div \sqrt{11}$

Solution: $\Rightarrow \dfrac{\sqrt{121}}{\sqrt{11}}$ [Divide the first radical by the second radical]

$\Rightarrow \dfrac{\sqrt{11} \times \sqrt{11}}{\sqrt{11}}$ [Factor the radicands]

$\Rightarrow \sqrt{11}$ [Cancel-out the common radicals from the numerator/denominator]

Question #35: $\sqrt{10} \div \sqrt{2}$

Solution: $\Rightarrow \dfrac{\sqrt{10}}{\sqrt{2}}$ [Divide the first radical by the second radical]

$\Rightarrow \dfrac{\sqrt{5} \times \sqrt{2}}{\sqrt{2}}$ [Factor the radicands]

$\Rightarrow \sqrt{5}$ [Cancel-out the common radicals from the numerator/denominator]

Question #36: $\sqrt{250} \div \sqrt{5}$

Solution: $\Rightarrow \dfrac{\sqrt{250}}{\sqrt{5}}$ [Divide the first radical by the second radical]

$\Rightarrow \dfrac{\sqrt{50} \times \sqrt{5}}{\sqrt{5}}$ [Factor the radicands]

$\Rightarrow \sqrt{50}$ [Cancel-out the common radicals from the numerator/denominator]

$\Rightarrow \sqrt{25 \times 2}$ [Again, factor the radicands to get all possible perfect squares]

$\Rightarrow 5\sqrt{2}$ [Take the square root of the perfect squares]

Question #37: $\sqrt{98} \div \sqrt{7}$

Solution: $\Rightarrow \dfrac{\sqrt{98}}{\sqrt{7}}$ [Divide the first radical by the second radical]

$\Rightarrow \dfrac{\sqrt{14} \times \sqrt{7}}{\sqrt{7}}$ [Factor the radicands]

$\Rightarrow \sqrt{14}$ [Cancel-out the common radicals from the numerator/denominator]

Question #38: $\sqrt{11} \div \sqrt{5}$

Solution: $\Rightarrow \dfrac{\sqrt{11}}{\sqrt{5}}$ [Divide the first radical by the second radical]

$\Rightarrow \dfrac{\sqrt{11} \times \sqrt{5}}{\sqrt{5} \times \sqrt{5}}$ [Multiply the numerator & denominator by the original denominator]

$\Rightarrow \dfrac{\sqrt{55}}{\sqrt{25}}$ [Multiply the numerator & denominator straight across]

$\Rightarrow \dfrac{\sqrt{55}}{5}$ [Take the square root of the perfect squares]

Question #39: $\sqrt{56} \div \sqrt{8}$

Solution: $\Rightarrow \dfrac{\sqrt{56}}{\sqrt{8}}$ [Divide the first radical by the second radical]

$\Rightarrow \dfrac{\sqrt{7} \times \sqrt{8}}{\sqrt{8}}$ [Factor the radicands]

$\Rightarrow \sqrt{7}$ [Cancel-out the common radicals from the numerator/denominator]

Question #40: $\sqrt{200} \div \sqrt{25}$

Solution: $\Rightarrow \dfrac{\sqrt{200}}{\sqrt{25}}$ [Divide the first radical by the second radical]

$\Rightarrow \dfrac{\sqrt{8} \times \sqrt{25}}{\sqrt{25}}$ [Factor the radicands to get all possible perfect squares]

$\Rightarrow \sqrt{8}$ [Cancel-out the common radicals from the numerator/denominator]

$\Rightarrow \sqrt{2 \times 4}$ [Again, factor the radicands to get all possible perfect squares]

$\Rightarrow 2\sqrt{2}$ [Take the square root of the perfect squares]

SIMPLIFICATION OF RADICALS: Simplify the following radicals:

Question #41: $\sqrt{60}$

Solution: $\Rightarrow \sqrt{15 \times 4}$ [Factor the radicands to get all possible perfect squares]

$\Rightarrow 2\sqrt{15}$ [Take the square root of the perfect squares]

Question #42: $\sqrt{68}$

Solution: $\Rightarrow \sqrt{17 \times 4}$ [Factor the radicands to get all possible perfect squares]

$\Rightarrow 2\sqrt{17}$ [Take the square root of the perfect squares]

Question #43: $\sqrt{72}$

Solution: $\Rightarrow \sqrt{36 \times 2}$ [Factor the radicands to get all possible perfect squares]

$\Rightarrow 6\sqrt{2}$ [Take the square root of the perfect squares]

Question #44: $\sqrt{76}$

Solution: $\Rightarrow \sqrt{19 \times 4}$ [Factor the radicands to get all possible perfect squares]

      $\Rightarrow 2\sqrt{19}$ [Take the square root of the perfect squares]

Question #45: $\sqrt{80}$

Solution: $\Rightarrow \sqrt{16 \times 5}$ [Factor the radicands to get all possible perfect squares]

      $\Rightarrow 4\sqrt{5}$ [Take the square root of the perfect squares]

Question #46: $\sqrt{90}$

Solution: $\Rightarrow \sqrt{9 \times 10}$ [Factor the radicands to get all possible perfect squares]

      $\Rightarrow 3\sqrt{10}$ [Take the square root of the perfect squares]

Question #47: $\sqrt{75}$

Solution: $\Rightarrow \sqrt{25 \times 3}$ [Factor the radicands to get all possible perfect squares]

      $\Rightarrow 5\sqrt{3}$ [Take the square root of the perfect squares]

Question #48: $\sqrt{98}$

Solution: $\Rightarrow \sqrt{49 \times 2}$ [Factor the radicands to get all possible perfect squares]

      $\Rightarrow 7\sqrt{2}$ [Take the square root of the perfect squares]

Question #49: $\sqrt{125}$

Solution: $\Rightarrow \sqrt{25 \times 5}$ [Factor the radicands to get all possible perfect squares]

      $\Rightarrow 5\sqrt{5}$ [Take the square root of the perfect squares]

Question #50: $\sqrt{70}$

Solution: $\Rightarrow \sqrt{70}$ [This is the simplest form as there are no perfect square factors]

EZ SOLUTIONS ORDERS & SALES:

ORDERS & SALES INFORMATION: EZ Solutions products and services can be ordered via one of the following methods:

ON-LINE ORDERS:
On-line Orders can be placed 24/7 via internet by going to: www.EZmethods.com

E-MAIL ORDERS:
E-Mail Orders can be placed 24/7 via internet by emailing: orders@EZmethods.com

PHONE ORDERS:
Phone Orders can be placed via telephone by calling: (Please check our website for most updated information)

FAX ORDERS:
Fax Orders can be placed via fax by faxing: (Please check our website for most updated information)

MAIL ORDERS:
Mail Orders can be placed via regular mail by mailing to the address given below:
EZ Solutions
Orders Department
P.O. Box 10755
Silver Spring, MD 20914
USA

OTHER OPTIONS: EZ Solutions books are also available at most major bookstores.

Institutional Sales: For volume/bulk sales to bookstores, libraries, schools, colleges, universities, organization, and institutions, please contact us. Quantity discount and special pricing is available.

EZ SOLUTIONS PRODUCTS & SERVICES:

LIST OF EZ TEST PREP SERIES OF BOOKS:

EZ Solutions Test Prep Series Books are available for the following sections:
- EZ Solutions – Test Prep Series – General – Test Taker's Manual
- EZ Solutions – Test Prep Series – Math Review – Arithmetic
- EZ Solutions – Test Prep Series – Math Review – Algebra
- EZ Solutions – Test Prep Series – Math Review – Applications
- EZ Solutions – Test Prep Series – Math Review – Geometry
- EZ Solutions – Test Prep Series – Math Review – Word Problems
- EZ Solutions – Test Prep Series – Math Review – Logic & Stats
- EZ Solutions – Test Prep Series – Math Practice – Basic Workbook
- EZ Solutions – Test Prep Series – Math Practice – Advanced Workbook
- EZ Solutions – Test Prep Series – Math Strategies – Math Test Taking Strategies
- EZ Solutions – Test Prep Series – Math – Data Sufficiency
- EZ Solutions – Test Prep Series – Verbal Section – Reading Comprehension
- EZ Solutions – Test Prep Series – Verbal Section – Sentence Correction/Completion
- EZ Solutions – Test Prep Series – Verbal Section – Vocabulary
- EZ Solutions – Test Prep Series – Verbal Section – Grammar
- EZ Solutions – Test Prep Series – Verbal Section – Critical Reasoning
- EZ Solutions – Test Prep Series – Verbal Section – Writing Skills

Note: Most of these books have already been published and others will be released shortly.

EZ Solutions Test Prep Series Books are available for the following standardized tests:
- EZ Solutions GMAT Test Prep Series of Books
- EZ Solutions GRE Test Prep Series of Books
- EZ Solutions SAT Test Prep Series of Books
- EZ Solutions ACT Test Prep Series of Books
- EZ Solutions LSAT Test Prep Series of Books
- EZ Solutions PRAXIS Test Prep Series of Books
- EZ Solutions POWER MATH/ENGLISH Test Prep Series of Books